My Word!

My Word!

PLAGIARISM AND COLLEGE CULTURE

Susan D. Blum

Cornell University Press

Ithaca and London

First published 2009 by Cornell University Press
First printing, Cornell Paperbacks, 2010

Printed in the United States of America

Library of Congress Cataloging-in-Publication Data

Blum, Susan Debra.
   My word! : plagiarism and college culture / Susan D. Blum.
      p. cm.
   Includes bibliographical references and index.
   ISBN 978-0-8014-4763-1 (cloth : alk. paper)
   ISBN 978-0-8014-7661-7 (pbk. : alk. paper)
   1. Plagiarism.   2. Cheating (Education)   3. College students—
Attitudes.   I. Title.
   PN167.B48   2009
   808—dc22   2008038074

Cornell University Press strives to use environmentally responsible
suppliers and materials to the fullest extent possible in the publishing of its books. Such materials include vegetable-based, low-VOC
inks and acid-free papers that are recycled, totally chlorine-free, or
partly composed of nonwood fibers. For further information, visit
our website at www.cornellpress.cornell.edu.

Cloth printing   10 9 8 7 6 5 4 3 2
Paperback printing   10 9 8 7 6 5 4 3 2 1

For Lionel
Again, always

Contents

My Word!

Introduction

Plagiarism in College

State a moral case to a ploughman and a professor.
The former will decide it as well, and often better than the latter,
because he has not been led astray by artificial rules.
—THOMAS JEFFERSON, letter to Peter Carr, August 10, 1787

Nothing can be loved or hated
Unless it is first known.
—LEONARDO DA VINCI, *Notebooks*

"CLASSROOM Cheats Turn to Computers"; "Student Essays on Internet Offer Challenge to Teachers"; "Kids Use New Tools"; "Faking the Grade." Headlines such as these have been blaring the alarming news of an epidemic of plagiarism and cheating in American colleges: more than 75 percent of students admit to having cheated; 68 percent admit to cutting and pasting material from the Internet without citation. Web sites offer readymade term papers at a very low rate or custom-written papers at a higher rate.[1]

All these topics have been sensationalized in popular media such as the *New York Times* and the *Times Literary Supplement,* National Public Radio, and television's *20–20,* and dissected in technical publications for educators (*Chronicle of Higher Education, Journal of Higher Education, Inside Higher Education*). Publications from colleges all across the country discuss the rise in cheating and plagiarism, as well as what this means for their campuses.[2] Each article presents a new survey or theory explaining why cheating has reached epidemic proportions, why ours is a "cheating culture," why this generation does not have the integrity of previous generations. Honor codes have been implemented nationwide,[3] yet even schools like the University of Virginia, which has had an honor code since it was founded by Thomas Jefferson in 1825, have had their share of cheating scandals. One newsworthy violation occurred in 2001, when 122 students in an introductory physics class were found to have cheated.[4] Scandals have erupted because of the varying ways students worldwide understand the role of originality and credit, whether in plagiarizing or in downloading music.

Universities subscribe to on-line plagiarism-detection products such as Turnitin.com to check potentially suspect assignments. Ethics institutes and religious organizations express concern about the sudden flurry of cheating.[5] Scholarly and journalistic inquiries into causes and potential cures reveal, for instance, that there is no less cheating in religious than in secular high schools; that students in fraternities are more likely than others to cheat; and that teachers who are willing to probe into apparent violations are less likely to encounter cheating in their classes.[6] The likelihood of cheating is increased, psychological studies show, by individual factors including age, grade point average (GPA), self-esteem, gender, personality type, and sense of alienation.[7] To these six factors others add four more: intrinsic versus extrinsic motivation, perceived social norms, attitudes toward cheating, and knowledge of institutional policy.[8]

Serious cheating on tests, according to data from Donald McCabe, Linda Klebe Treviño, and Kenneth Butterfield, increased from 39 percent in 1963 to 64 percent in 1993.[9] It has increased again since then. Serious cheating on written work remained stable, however, at 65 percent in 1963 and 66 percent in 1993.[10] McCabe, Treviño, and Butterfield acknowledge that the lack of increase

> may be due to a changing definition among students of what constitutes plagiarism. In general, student understanding of appropriate citation techniques seems to have changed, and selected behaviors that students may have classified as plagiarism in Bowers's [1964] study do not appear to be considered plagiarism by many students today. For example, although most students understand that quoting someone's work word for word demands a citation, they seem to be less clear on the need to cite the presentation of someone else's ideas when the students present them in their own words.[11]

So here's the question: Are the majority of today's students immoral? Do most of them cheat and plagiarize? If not, why do we think they do? If so, why do they do it? Is plagiarism the same thing as cheating? How *do* students understand plagiarism?

I spent three years conducting research on these questions, doing ethnographic research at my own university and reading widely about plagiarism. The topic of plagiarism in college sits like a big spider in a web of other factors having to do with the nature of higher education (which is in turn connected to the nature of childhood and adulthood), the nature of texts and authorship, and the nature and motives of the person doing the work turned in for credit. The Internet is part of the story, but not in the way people usually think about it. Morality is also part of the problem, but not because most students are immoral.

What I learned from my research was not entirely what I expected. I thought I would learn that students did not pay as much attention to the academic side of their college experience as I had when I was a student, or as much as I hoped they would. This *is* borne out by the interviews. I thought I would learn about the rampant drinking that is typical of almost half of all contemporary college students, and I found this as well. What I did not expect, but what is crystal clear, is how thoughtful, articulate, and earnest these young people are about very important matters of purpose, morality, and activity.

It became clear that most students—and here I am generalizing with some trepidation about the nation's 15 million or so undergraduates, but mostly about those in traditional, selective residential colleges—are desperately trying to figure out their paths in life. They agonize about how to deal with dishonest friends, how to juggle too many activities, how to do chemistry homework, how to tell their parents that they are not, after all, going to medical school, how to save money on books, how to get a job after college, and how to break up with their girlfriend or boyfriend.

Here are some thoughts about what else I learned:

Their social conditioning prior to college has shaped students' lives *in* college. Most come from families that have nurtured, praised, and encouraged them, from communities in which they were shining stars. Students at selective schools have been focused on getting into college as long as they can remember. They have been evaluated by grades and test scores, which they and their parents have scrutinized for their tea leaf prognostications about which colleges they might be allowed to enter. And for the most part, they have been very busy.

When they are lucky enough to arrive at college, they bring with them this busy-ness, this focus on evaluation as the goal of education. It is not just that they jam their day full of the kinds of activities that got them there: classes, clubs, sports, social gatherings, work. They know this is a short, precious, expensive period in their lives. Few families can shrug off the cost of their children's college education, and students are aware of their parents' sacrifices, both before they came to college and while they are there. Nearly half of all *full-time* students also work to support their own education. They have to make sure that their families' support and their own efforts are justified by success.

They are in a hurry—because of technology, because their parents encouraged them to pile on more and more activities so they could get into a good school, because our society in general is concerned with the fruits of our labors. They may dash off a paper, seeking mainly to satisfy requirements regarding number of pages, references, quotations. Students have a lot on their minds, which they share with the adults who raised them. Everyone wants to know about their performance. *Was the paper high quality? What grade did you get on it?*

Contemporary students are swimming in a sea of texts. (Here I'm using "text" as a technical term, meaning anything written or spoken that involves language, or even images, anything that can be "read" or analyzed.) They e-mail, blog, and text message day and night. In some ways this is the *wordiest* and most *writerly* generation in a long while. These students are writing all the time, reading all the time. Some of what they are writing and reading does not measure up to serious academic standards, but they are writing and reading all the same, busily immersed in a world of words.

The Internet and electronic communication have affected much about their lives—and not just because the Internet makes copying easy and tempting. It has *changed* how they think of texts.

They are engaged with media constantly. They spend hours watching TV, maybe whole series on DVD, or watching movies. And they quote them to one another. This kind of quotation—one form of what academics call, so multisyllabically, *intertextuality*—shows verbal sophistication, memory, and sensitivity to context and appropriateness. This is very much what we ask them to do with academic texts, except that when they quote in an academic context, they have to slow way down, set up boundaries around each little piece of text, trace its origin, and document its source. This slowness and deliberateness is at odds with their customary focus on speed and efficiency, on completing one task as fast as possible so they can get on with the next one that is inevitably hanging over their head, whether it is another paper, a meeting for a group project, or a dorm party.

Student engagement in intertextual activity is of a different nature and different purpose from the intertextuality demanded by academia. The reason for this difference, in the end, lies in profoundly different values concerning boundaries and originality and individuality. Academic standards, which vary across disciplines and even more so across cultures, tend to be guided by notions of creativity that are essentially individual. Authors, according to the dominant understanding of the term, receive inspiration alone, write alone, and can identify their written work with themselves alone. Thus anyone using a writer's words must trace them back to the person of the writer, because he or she was their lone creator. This concept of intellectual property, which I develop in detail in chapter 2, characterizes what I call the "authentic self."

In addition to busy-ness, there is another relevant aspect of contemporary college life: students have been raised to be sociable, and they like to work together, to be in groups. One of the greatest forms of praise, which I heard over and over, is that someone is "really outgoing." When young people spend time together living, studying, preparing, eating, partying, they are less concerned about tracing influence from one person to another. After all, haven't we told them since early childhood that one of the primary virtues is sharing? That's what Robert Fulghum said in his book *All I Really Need to Know I Learned in Kindergarten*, a 1988 classic.

These students have absorbed their elders' lessons about communalism. They accept their society's emphasis on productivity, on performance, on speed. They want to be successful, not only financially but also in terms of making a meaningful contribution to the world.

Higher education itself is in crisis, and not only because of costs, insanely selective admissions (for a relatively small number of highly visible colleges), and affirmative action. Higher education is a behemoth that attempts to achieve so many goals that it has no single focus. It aims to prepare students for work. It attempts to "level the playing field" and provide economic opportunities for a large proportion of American society.

It attempts to inculcate "values," "general knowledge," and "character," as well as information that all citizens should know. (Needless to say, huge battles are fought about which specific facts and values should be included.) It provides skills. It offers contacts for future career opportunities. It provokes young people to look at the world in a new, more complex way. It can be a precious opportunity or just the expected next step in their long series of educational roads. It gives late adolescents time and space to become young adults. It is about having fun, like year-round summer camp. It is a business. It is the responsibility of the state, or the taxpayers, or donors and alumni, or the church, or the students themselves. Some people worry that affluent adolescents are receiving a broad liberal arts education while their less affluent counterparts receive only vocational training.

This institutional and national confusion of aims is jumbled together with students' own motives for being in college. They are trying to fulfill so many different purposes, believing many more than six impossible things before breakfast. (That's an allusion to Lewis Carroll's *Through the Looking Glass*—assumed to be common knowledge, and therefore not in need of citation. So my quoting it is not plagiarism, even though I did take it directly from Carroll without crediting my source.)

Students who plagiarize, who improperly incorporate someone else's text into their own without giving credit, may be committing a grave academic misdeed. Some really don't know how to avoid it, because the rules are terribly subtle and take many years to master. Some deliberately do so to get the job done. There are many motives, many reasons, many biographical details.

The term "plagiarism" itself covers a vast amount of territory, to be sure, from outright submission of a paper written by someone else, which is fraud, to omitting quotation marks around a passage from another text, which is often a matter of skill and care (see chapter 1).

The bottom line is that we cannot treat all student plagiarism solely as a matter of individual morality, independent of all the supporting messages from the educational and social contexts in which they find themselves. If more than half of all students plagiarize, then there is clearly some cultural influence urging them to do so.

Today's students stand at the crossroads of a new way of conceiving texts and the people who create them and who quote them. As in all cross-cultural conversation, the first step is recognizing that there are two systems at work here. It has become obvious that the difference between the views of twenty-first-century students and their twentieth-century elders is profound and in need of examination. Only after we recognize this can we begin to seek translators, people who can tell us where those differences lie. Only then can we speak meaningfully across our years and positions in order to understand one another.

AFTER TEACHING for twenty years, I had come to suspect that my own training as an academic had made me a member of what is almost an entirely foreign culture in contrast to that in which our students live. As Clifford Geertz has said, "Foreignness does not start at the water's edge but at the skin's."[12]

As an anthropologist, I believe that to understand another culture—even one we encounter every day—we must go into the field and investigate often unarticulated beliefs, patterns, expectations, and practices. So that's what I did. This book is a report back from the field, with interpretations of what I found all around me, once I had the correct lens through which to see.

Although I could observe students' behavior, I wanted to get at their thoughts about plagiarism and to understand the context of those thoughts and actions. To this end I enlisted the help of four gifted undergraduates—Theresa Davey, Katherine Kennedy Johnson, Rupa Jose, and Jacob Weiler—endowed with the ability to get fellow students to talk without leading them to particular conclusions. For twenty-six months (six semesters), from February 2005 through March 2007, these four students set up interviews with their peers to talk about college. These student researchers, three women and one man, were remarkable in their commitment to the project, willing to follow my meandering interests, and able to provide insightful comments and analysis along the way.

Sometimes when I hear an exchange or read a portion of a transcript, I gasp in awe at these four young adults, of whom I am so fond. They were able to think about their goals while listening carefully to their fellow students, setting them at ease, and remaining nonjudgmental and welcoming, eliciting a wide range of responses to a loose set of focal questions. There is no doubt that this project owes everything to them.

Our questions touched on the following topics: students' views of and goals for college in general (as an intellectual endeavor, as a required step on the way to financial success, and so on); their conduct in work and play; their daily activities; their understanding of how to write papers; their attitudes toward rules; their common practice of quoting songs, TV shows, and films in ordinary conversation and the values and meanings of such quotation (intertextuality); the downloading and sharing of music; their knowledge of student cheating and plagiarism and the circumstances surrounding these cases; their notions of integrity, individuality, and conformity; their ideas of success; and their views of their appearance and self-concept.

We did not ask directly whether the students had engaged in cheating or plagiarism themselves, though about half the interviews did pose the question whether the interviewee knew of others who did. Sometimes the topic was volunteered by the student being interviewed, either because the interviewees had plagiarized or cheated themselves or knew students who had, or because it followed from other topics. (As in all interviews, we can understand the students to be not exactly "telling the truth" but rather performing a virtuous—or daring—self in front of a peer interviewer.)[13]

The four students began by interviewing their friends and friends of their friends, but they also tracked down strangers. Given the random assignment of roommates at the university where I teach, students' base of acquaintances is not limited to those who are similar to themselves.

I also had the interviewers set up conversations among other students, asking them to record just ordinary informal exchanges among friends. The interviewers had the option of being present at the conversations or not. There was no agenda for them, no hidden topic. Anthropologists and others who study language know that a lot of important cultural information is passed along in exchanges like these.

All participants were guaranteed confidentiality and anonymity. They were invited to choose their own pseudonyms, and many did. Their selections ranged from the grandiose (actor "John Stamos") to the pedestrian (Karen), and from descriptive (Monkey Friend) to blasphemous ("JH Christ"). In cases in which students chose not to select a pseudonym for themselves, I chose one for them. Thus none of the names by which students are identified is real.

The interviewers are similarly anonymous. When the work began we were not sure what would happen, so I assured them that their words would not be traced.

In all, a total of 234 people participated in 154 interviews (a few involving more than one student) and 32 conversations. The transcripts take up more than five thousand single-spaced pages.

In a survey with the goal of statistical significance and representative samples, 234 would be an inadequate number of respondents; but the goal here is different.[14] The goal is not to predict which particular students—of what gender, class, ethnicity, major, or residence—are most likely to cheat or plagiarize. It is not to explain statistics. It is to explain *patterns,* by using the notion of cultural context, or waves. The students' words filled in the background of what I was learning from the vast literature on the various contexts I have identified as relevant to the questions of plagiarism and cheating.

Although I make no claims that my university is "representative," I do believe that much of what I found is applicable across institutions, especially other private, selective colleges. Of the approximately 1,400 accredited four-year colleges in the United States, only 146 are considered "most" or "highly selective"; about 170,000 students attend these colleges (fewer than 10 percent of all students at both four-year and two-year colleges).[15] But we should care about this tiny sliver of the population pie, not because these schools are necessarily better than others—in fact some research shows that how selective a college is has *no* bearing on its educational effectiveness[16]—but because so much cultural energy goes into thinking about them. Their students are considered the elite, and these schools are where we may find the most successful adolescents adding to their cultural capital through higher education.

To avoid readers' focus on any particular university, I use the textual device of referring to this school as "Saint U." Anthropology has a long tradition of using pseudonyms for field locations, both to protect the identity of villages and to emphasize that the choice of a particular research setting does not mean that that place should be evaluated or judged or taken as inherently the target of attention. Though the identity of Saint U. would not be likely to remain unknown, I prefer to direct attention away from its particularity. There are three prominent examples of anthropological studies of colleges: Dorothy Holland and Margaret Eisenhart's *Educated in Romance: Women, Achievement, and College Culture,* in which they referred to the locations of their research—universities, not villages, of course—as "Bradford" and "SU"; Michael Moffatt's *Coming of Age in New Jersey: College and American Culture,* where he identified the setting as Rutgers University;

and Cathy Small's *My Freshman Year: What a Professor Learned by Becoming a Student,* where she published under the pseudonym Rebekah Nathan and called Northern Arizona University "AnyU" but was "outed" and both the author and the school identified. Each anthropologist had different circumstances suggesting the wisdom of either revealing or concealing the location of their study. Here I readily admit where my research took place but insist that this not be the object of readers' attention.

Readers should regard this as a case study of the culture of higher education. Case studies are relevant to the extent that they reveal deep patterns in thought and behavior. They have the advantage of researchers' profound familiarity and commitment. In my case, having taught at Saint U. for eight years, I have both an insider's perspective (as a professor) and an outsider's perspective (as a researcher deriving information from students). When appropriate, I draw on information about other colleges that demonstrates shared tendencies.

You might wonder how different Saint U., an explicitly religious institution, is from other colleges and universities. The Josephson Institute of Ethics has shown no significant difference in reported cheating behavior between students from public and private religious high schools, and I assume that is true of colleges as well.[17] There may be different emphases on what I identify as the performance self (see chapter 3) in religious versus nonreligious colleges. There may be, for instance, increased emphasis on solidarity. I sought to discover explanatory cultural patterns rather than the statistical incidence of plagiarism, and since students at Saint U. are fully immersed in the culture of the United States, the webs within which plagiarism is entangled are fully evident here. I am not trying to "bust" a religious institution. I have great admiration for these students' eloquence and thoughtfulness, and I believe that, like much else they say and do, these qualities are common to their generation.

The concept of plagiarism—"improperly" taking someone else's words—is changing because higher education, the meaning of a "text," and notions of the self are changing around it. Although the term "plagiarism" itself, like "cheating," includes a range of behaviors from the innocuous to the criminal, any understanding of the forces that lead students to choose to engage in it requires an understanding of these three changing contexts. We start by unpacking the concept of plagiarism itself and then move on to see how it interweaves with these areas of cultural change. Students are often the avant-garde of social transformation. Let us look at what that means.

1

A Question of Judgment

*Plagiarism Is Not One Thing,
Once and for All*

> When I worked at a newspaper, we were routinely dispatched to
> "match" a story from the *Times*: to do a new version of someone else's
> idea. But had we "matched" any of the *Times'* words—even the most
> banal of phrases—it could have been a firing offense. The ethics of pla-
> giarism have turned into the narcissism of small differences: because
> journalism cannot own up to its heavily derivative nature, it must
> enforce the originality on the level of the sentence....
>   The final dishonesty of the plagiarism fundamentalists is to encour-
> age us to pretend that...chains of influence and evolution do not exist,
> and that a writer's words have a virgin birth and an eternal life.
> —MALCOLM GLADWELL, "Something Borrowed"

WANT to hear a funny story? I heard it thirdhand. It could be an
urban legend, but whether true or not it still shows us how we
think about it.

A teaching assistant encountered an instance of plagiarism in her class.
She returned all the papers and said to the students: "Someone has committed plagiarism. If you confess, I will work with you to teach you how to
improve and won't file charges." Nearly all the students in the class, maybe
seventeen out of twenty, confessed to varying types of plagiarism.[1]

What do students understand when they hear the term "plagiarism"?
Is it the same thing that is understood by faculty? By writers in general?
How firm are the standards? What is the relationship between plagiarism
and cheating? Is plagiarism bad? What should we do about it? It will take
most of this book to answer these questions. This chapter addresses them
by showing how wobbly are the guidelines for citation, the remedy to

the threat of plagiarism, and the penalties for plagiarism. It demonstrates that plagiarism is not one thing, once and for all, but that there is profound disagreement about what it is and how it should be regarded.

What Is Plagiarism?

According to the *Oxford English Dictionary, plagiarism* means (1) "the action or practice of plagiarizing; the wrongful appropriation or purloining, and publication as one's own, of the ideas, or the expression of the ideas (literary, artistic, musical, mechanical, etc.) of another" or (2) "a purloined idea, design, passage, or work." The *OED* traces the first appearance of the word in English to 1621, when Bishop R. Montague wrote, "Were you afraid to bee challenged for plagiarisme?" The term has Latin roots (*plagiarius* meaning "plunderer," from *plagium,* "hunting net," from *plaga,* "net"); according to *Webster's,* the English word was originally "plagiary."

Even within the dictionary definition—wrongfully using another's words or ideas and publishing them as one's own—plagiarism includes several not necessarily related actions. One definition suggests a moral, ethical, or technical violation. The other ("purloined") points, essentially, to a crime. But dictionary definitions can take us only so far. Words are used in a variety of ways; natural language as used in society is always fuzzy. The first point to make, then, in understanding plagiarism is that it involves a range of behavior. How "bad" each instance is depends on what kind of plagiarism we are talking about.

The term at its core means to copy someone else's work; even paraphrasing without attribution counts as plagiarism. Although the meaning sounds clear, however, it is murky in reality. Furthermore, different constituencies have different meanings for and histories with plagiarism. We might helpfully regard it as a triple entity, a triangle. At one point of the triangle, plagiarism is a kind of cheating involving written works. At the *cheating* corner, a student knowingly, willfully, unambiguously engages in forbidden behavior such as buying a term paper, an act that enters the realm of conscious criminality, or fraud. (Presumably the seller agrees to the exchange, so there is no theft involved.) It is an academic crime: academic credit is received without the work being done (see chapter 4).

At a second, *inadvertent* corner, plagiarism results from a failure to master conventions. Proper citation practices are difficult skills to acquire; they can be learned only through slow, careful teaching. Students regularly make mistakes about how to cite without any intention of breaking rules, let alone laws.

At the third corner are professionals who steal another writer's work without permission and for their own benefit. At this *professional* corner, copyright infringement and other matters of law come into play.

But even beyond the threefold nature of plagiarism, in many cases the guidelines are unclear. Although writers are told to be guided by the short and sweet rule "Cite your sources," this rule can be—and is—followed only in some contexts.

The Wobbliness of Guidelines

I came across the following two sentences one day on a single page of the *New York Times:*

> It is a truth universally acknowledged, at least among humans, that a giant tortoise in the possession of the last sperm of his species must be in want of a wife.[2]

> Conquistadors from Spain came, they saw and they were astonished.[3]

Both sentences allude to well-known lines from well-known literary sources—a practice often considered "homage." The first is a variant of the opening sentence of *Pride and Prejudice* ("It is a truth universally acknowledged, that a single man in possession of a good fortune, must be in want of a wife"). The second refers to the words uttered by Julius Caesar, *veni, vidi, vici,* "I came, I saw, I conquered," frequently quoted with the third verb varied for effect. Allusions need not be cited, especially allusions to well-known works. These are a nod to members of the club who recognize them. (It is a matter of judgment to determine how well known a source is.) But journalists in general do not provide publication information for material they cite; it is verified behind the scenes by fact checkers. Sources are simply not credited.

Most people encounter journalistic writing far more commonly than they do scholarly writing. I noticed the lack of citation only because I was engrossed in writing this book. To find the kind of documentation in which sources *are* clearly cited, we have to look to academic writing. Here is a good example of proper citation from a scholarly journal, one writer quoting another academic writer:

> Ortner encourages researchers to explore *all* the intricacies of a subculture as a means to avoid romanticized conceptions: "It is the absence of analysis of these forms of internal conflict in many resistance studies that gives them an air of romanticism, of which they are often accused" (1996: 285). We acknowledge that multiple subcultures likely exist within the SSC [Students Serving Christ] subculture, but we focus on what we perceive to be its dominant and shared understandings.[4]

This is a typical scholarly use of quotation—not elegant or playful, as in the *New York Times,* but functional. Here the authors acknowledge a potential criticism of their work, from a position similar to that expressed by Sherry Ortner, though she did not specifically address their writing. Ortner is well known, so having her words stand for a prevailing scholarly position is effective.

A different usage arises when concepts are borrowed from an authority; that person's work—at least a representative one—is also cited:

> The metaphor of script has been used in the social and cognitive sciences for the last thirty years to explain the interplay between cultural models and social action (D'Andrade 1995). In this context, concepts with a similar meaning have been borrowed from other fields, mainly those of literature and drama, such as frame, scene, scenario, script, schema, and folk model.[5]

Proper academic citation provides a way for authors to trace their influences, to situate themselves intellectually, to prove that they have done their background theoretical reading, to demonstrate engagement in an ongoing community of inquiry, and to provide sources for readers who want to consult earlier thinkers or data (see chapter 2). In the social sciences and humanities this is what we wish our students to learn how to do. But even this model is not so simple, even for academics. Standard practices vary considerably.

To determine how much of a consensus exists about what constitutes plagiarism, Kell Julliard conducted a study among professors of medicine, medical students, English professors, and journal editors.[6] Respondents were presented with an original passage, two rewordings with verbatim quotations, and one rewording that was slightly paraphrased. Participants were asked which were acceptable and which constituted plagiarism. Most medical school faculty—who themselves publish articles—saw all as acceptable, in contrast to the other three groups. Julliard's study reveals that a different standard exists for quotation and paraphrase in medical journals than in other academic fields.[7] But it is not just medical journals that differ from all other areas.

Other studies have similarly revealed a range of practices, from very strict—in which even tiny amounts of verbatim quoting are considered plagiarism—to fairly lax acceptance of uncredited verbatim quotation.[8] Writers in different disciplines expect and accept varying amounts of quotation and citation, with some embracing it and others shunning it. Furthermore, professionals and academics disagree with editors, those ultimate arbiters of correct practice. (Instability of judgment, as you will see in chapter 2, stems from the historical development of the notion of literary property and authorship but also from the very nature of language.) So if even professors lack a shared clear-cut judgment about what constitutes plagiarism, it should not be difficult to see why students have even less certainty. As I will show later, even the most subtle legal thinkers, in developing the concepts of copyright and intellectual property, struggled with the same fuzzy issues.

I think we do an injustice to students by overlooking the genuinely contentious nature of citation. By pretending that the standards are firm and fixed—despite students' experience of often getting very different instructions from different professors, sometimes within the same department—we reject an educational opportunity and force students to conclude, on their own, that the rules don't make any sense. That makes it easier for them to disregard them entirely.

Plagiarism outside the Walls of Academe

Mention plagiarism, and certain writers' names are bound to come up. The public appears fascinated by plagiarism, a sin for which only some of the prominent are likely to be singled out and even fewer punished. Let's recall a few of the most notorious cases.

Doris Kearns Goodwin, Pulitzer Prize–winning historian (Harvard Ph.D. in government), former frequent commentator on PBS, was accused in 2002 of plagiarizing large amounts—passages on ninety-one pages—of material from Lynne McTaggart, an expert on Kathleen Kennedy, for her book *The Fitzgeralds and the Kennedys*.[9] Goodwin admitted that she had been sloppy in identifying her sources, settled with McTaggart for an unrevealed amount of money, acknowledged having failed to credit other authors as well, promised to withdraw all copies of the book, and published a corrected version of it. People argued about whether Goodwin's plagiarism was "intentional" or "inadvertent." Some critics lambasted her for failing to live up to the standards set even for *undergraduates* at Harvard (where she served on the board of overseers), who could be punished for lifting a single phrase without attribution. In her defense, a list of noteworthy public intellectuals commended Goodwin's generally excellent character and excused her "slight" misdeed. Goodwin kept a somewhat lower profile for a time, though she has continued to publish and has returned to her role as commentator. She continues to be represented by the exclusive Washington Speakers Bureau, earning $25,000 to $40,000 per engagement.[10]

Dr. Martin Luther King Jr. not only was a minister and a civil rights activist but also had earned a doctorate in theology at Boston University. In 1988, while working on annotating his papers, researchers were disheartened to realize that substantial amounts of his writing revealed pervasive plagiarism.[11] Since King was not alive to answer the charges, the question was essentially one of how history should regard his legacy. In general, it seems to have been agreed that he had gone on to lead a life of great importance despite his significant and lifelong tendency to use others' words without crediting them.

Some people responded with anger at King's professors at Crozer Theological Seminary and Boston University, where his dissertation included significant verbatim copying from Paul Tillich and other prominent theologians and philosophers. They claimed that the professors were racist for not having held a capable young black man to a higher standard. Some excused his plagiarism as a common practice in African American discourse. Others condemned his plagiarism but retained a high regard for his character, focusing on the effects of his activism (that is, they judged him by historical standards as an activist rather than by publication standards as a scholar). Still others excoriated his defenders as soft-headed liberal affirmative action apologists.

Whether exculpated or vilified, King was either a uniquely gifted employer of an African American tendency toward intertextuality or a fraud who deserved neither his fame nor even his doctoral degree. *Racism! Oversimplification! Literal-minded legalism!* Whatever the accusation, the case remains highly charged.

Jayson Blair was a brilliant, "hungry" young reporter at the *New York Times*. He wrote passionate stories about Lee Malvo, the youth who had been accused of sniper killings in the Washington, D.C., area in 2002, and about wounded soldiers recovering from amputations and other combat trauma. But he violated all professional ethics: he lied, he fabricated stories, he lifted other reporters' descriptions of places he had never actually visited, and he faked interviews with people he had never met. The fabrications relied on his clever manipulation of information and mining of others' reports or photographs.[12] It was an article he quoted nearly verbatim in spring 2003 from the *San Antonio Express-News* that finally led to the unraveling of his journalism career. His resignation led in turn to the resignation of the executive editor of the *Times*, Howell Raines, and to a torrent of journalistic criticism and soul-searching.[13] Was the debacle entirely Blair's fault? Was the editorial staff at least partly to blame? Were obvious signs ignored? In pages and pages of analysis, some journalists deplored the profession's state of ethics, standards, and so forth, while others charged the *Times* with arrogance.[14]

Kaavya Viswanathan, a Harvard sophomore, was on the verge of publishing a novel for teenage girls called *How Opal Mehta Got Kissed, Got Wild, and Got a Life*. Having availed herself of a pricey college advising service, IvyWise, whose founder happened to have connections with publishers, she had been admitted to Harvard partially on the basis of her standing out from other applicants as a published writer. Then someone noticed that a number of passages in her novel were quite similar to passages in teen novels by Megan McCafferty. Viswanathan's book was not published, the film to be based on it was not made, and Viswanathan was both attacked and defended. The *Harvard Crimson* reported the story;[15] the *Harvard Independent* blamed the plagiarism, perhaps, on the ghostwriting team that the publisher uses to churn out formula books for teenage girls;[16] Malcolm Gladwell excused it as part of the genre's attraction;[17] and *New York* magazine explained it as stemming from her youth.[18]

There is no shortage of other equally relevant and edifying cases. The late Stephen Ambrose, a popular and prolific writer of history, whose many books (*Undaunted Courage, Band of Brothers*) often served as the basis for television series, admitted that he had copied from Thomas Childers in his book *The Wild Blue*. Ian McEwan, highly regarded British novelist, was accused in 2006 of having copied portions of *Atonement* from a work by Lucilla Andrews.[19] In McEwan's defense, Thomas Pynchon, John Updike, Margaret Atwood, and other prominent writers protested the narrow accusation of plagiarism.[20]

The reactions to these cases run the gamut from fury to relativism, with a lot of interesting nuances in between. Some of them (using my own words, as best I can...) may be characterized as follows:

Off with their heads! We must not tolerate any amount of plagiarism. I don't care how inadvertent it was, it doesn't matter how brilliant the new uses of others' purloined material, we must cast the first stone; plagiarism equals hubris and must be punished!

This is just highbrow posturing. Writers have always borrowed, and the niceties of quotation marks would destroy what most readers like, which is a good story.

How dare these successful people steal material from generally more obscure writers and profit from it!

An editorial on plagiarism in the *Economist* points out triumphantly that the comeuppance of these celebrities proves the wisdom of the market![21]

David Plotz observes that good writers often improve the writing they plagiarize. The practice "is confusing because we don't know whom it hurts." Readers may even benefit from the plagiarists' selection of wonderful prose. Nevertheless, Plotz ultimately concludes that plagiarism hurts the writer whose work is lifted: "The plagiarist violates the essential rule of his trade. He steals the lifeblood of a colleague. A few paragraphs have made Stephen Ambrose a vampire."[22] Ambrose, however, had a less highbrow audience, and his readers appeared, essentially, to shrug off the incident as a technical error.

Judge Richard Posner suggests that we begin to tease out three sets of contrasts: between "creativity" and "originality," between deliberate and negligent plagiarism, and between fraud and plagiarism on the one hand and copyright infringement on the other.[23] As a jurist, he does not wish to see cases of crude copying brought into the courts, nor does he believe that we would benefit if all novelists were held to a strict standard forbidding the incorporation of any kind of influence.

Plagiarism within the Walls

Though not as sensationalized or broadcast as professional or student plagiarism, there are many cases of plagiarism by college faculty. Academics are punished even less frequently than students are. Faculty plagiarism can take many forms. The most common are self-plagiarism (that is, copying from one's own work or repackaging articles in a second or third journal); copying from others' published work; and unrightfully copying graduate students' research.

A forum in the *Chronicle of Higher Education* in 2004–5 turned up a long list of bitter complaints, including reports of outright copying of other scholars' dissertations or articles. The victims' greatest sense of demoralization and betrayal stemmed from the fact that even when these misdeeds were revealed to university administrators, in almost every case there was no consequence or punishment.

In 2003 the American Historical Association made a decision to stop ruling about plagiarism in its journals. Even when plagiarism had been clearly demonstrated, there had generally been little follow-up to the accusations, and almost no contributors were punished in any way. At the 2008 American Historical Association meetings a group of journal editors concluded that this position was correct. Still, a study published in *Nature* described a search program for abstracts in biomedical journals, called eTBLAST, which turned up 70,000 suspicious cases of plagiarism and double publication. A manual check of 2,600 of those revealed that about one-fourth of the items were legitimate.[24] That means, of course, that more than 50,000 articles contained improperly published materials—usually repeat publication. This essentially means getting "double credit" for work. It is not, technically, copying from another person, but it is against professional ethics, which could be seen as somewhat arbitrary. Why not get "the truth" out into the public more frequently?

Although I am primarily concerned with plagiarism by students on college campuses, not in the worlds of journalism, literary publishing, or musical composition, and not among faculty, the broader context of social norms regarding intellectual property is relevant. Universities aim to socialize students toward those broader norms. To the extent that the norms are unclear or unevenly enforced, the students' burden in learning them—or teachers' charge in teaching them—becomes that much harder.

Enforcement

Penalties for students caught plagiarizing are much more severe, then, than those for professional writers or academics. At most colleges and universities, students are threatened with expulsion—what Rebecca Moore Howard calls the "academic death penalty"—if they are caught deliberately plagiarizing (or cheating more generally).[25] *Intention* is often at the core of the investigation; those found to have plagiarized through ignorance are usually given a lighter penalty (say, a failing grade for the assignment). But students who deliberately plagiarize—the "cheating" corner of the plagiarism triangle—are failed in the course, suspended for up to a year, presented with a letter in their file, or dismissed entirely. All universities have detailed procedures for dealing with suspected violations.

At Saint U., where I have been on the Honesty Committee for my department, students accused of plagiarism formerly had to be brought to a hearing before two professors and three students. Since very few cases were brought, while surveys suggested high rates of violations, the policy was changed to permit faculty and students to come to a private agreement, which is forwarded to the associate provost. This way, if there is a pattern of violations, it will be discovered. Repeat offenders are treated more harshly—usually with expulsion. Only in cases where the student disputes the charges or the penalty is the matter taken to a hearing.

Literature on the punishment of plagiarism and cheating shows that at most U.S. universities faculty do not bring official charges against students, for a variety of reasons: because they don't think it's worth their time, because they do so privately rather than through institutional channels, or because they share students' views that such behavior is understandable.[26] Canadian faculty similarly decline to impose severe sanctions on students.[27]

If the rates of cheating and plagiarism are sky-high, with three-quarters of all students surveyed, on average, reporting having cheated at least once in the previous year, yet at most universities a maximum of a few dozen cases are brought forward, then how seriously *is* plagiarism taken by universities? Do faculty implicitly recognize the wobbly nature of the standards? Is it too much trouble, in a job filled with many demands, to pursue every case?

Plagiarism is a confusing issue. Although there are clear-cut instances, even these provoke a range of responses. In part this is because plagiarism is not a crime in the legal system but rather a breach of social norms among writers and scholars.

However widespread plagiarism is inside the academy and outside its walls, it is clear that, like a sudden discovery that we are breathing oxygen, plagiarism is a topic that has found a ready reception in the public sphere. The Lexis-Nexis database counted 410 articles about plagiarism in 1994 and 1,373 in 2006. Articles available through the scholarly database EBSCO Host include two published about plagiarism in 1994 and 283 in 2006. Many see this increase as evidence of a crisis; others see it as evidence of moral panic.

A New Crisis? Cats and Mice in Imperial China

Although writing about "our cheating culture,"[28] and pointing to sudden alarming statistics in support, is an effective strategy for selling books and raising excitement, the truth of the matter is that all cultures experience some degree of cheating, lying, deception, corruption, and plagiarism. In fact, my interest in this topic initially stemmed in part from a book I wrote on deception and truth in human life, beginning with an analysis of deception and truth in China. If you think contemporary American cheating and plagiarism are bad, consider what the Chinese empire contended with for much of its history.

For nearly fourteen hundred years, the Chinese empire was run by bureaucrats selected, in principle, through an impartial and open examination system (the civil service examination, or *keju,* on which the

U.S. system, and those of several other countries, is modeled).[29] Young men would study the classical texts of the tradition and sit for a series of entrance exams at ever-increasing stakes, followed by three levels of civil service examinations. The school entrance examinations too had several phases: district tests administered by magistrates, prefectural tests administered by prefects, and qualifying examinations overseen by the provincial director of studies. In later centuries a preliminary examination was given, sorting students who could sit for the civil service exams. Passing these tests then qualified them for the provincial, metropolitan, and palace exams.

Only by passing the tests could they become administrators; the higher their score, the more prestigious the position they attained. Along with their position came titles, wealth, power, and opportunities for their families to advance; successful candidates were also exempt from taxes and from military conscription. At the same time, there were quotas restricting the numbers of successful candidates, especially at the uppermost levels. One estimate is that with only two to three hundred men eligible to attain the highest level (*jin shi*), the chance of achieving it was between one and four in a million.[30] Talk about high-stakes testing!

The young men who took the examinations were educated by tutors or in academies where they studied the classics and practiced writing the kinds of essays that would be called for in the test. The examinations were originally given to youth. Over time, though, the tests were taken by older and older men, so that by the final years of imperial China, men of fifty shaved their beards and claimed to be teenagers, sometimes aided by the complicity of examiners.[31]

The civil service tests, which lasted three days in the provincial and metropolitan forms, were administered and supervised very carefully to ensure transparency and to deter cheating. Candidates were searched prior to entering the little booths within which they would write, and in a kind of panopticon (an allusion to Foucault's use of Jeremy Bentham's notion of surveillance, but not usually cited because the assumption is that people educated in the human sciences will recognize it) were scrutinized periodically; there were many watchtowers. A person who had already passed the exam attested to each new candidate's identity. Doors were sealed several times over. Test booklets were checked to ensure that they were blank and that no cheat sheets had been smuggled in. Scores were awarded only by seat number, not the candidate's name. Prior to grading, tests were recopied to prevent examiners' recognizing a candidate's handwriting (and thus favoritism or bribery), and the copyists' work was checked by proofreaders. The examiners, graders, copyists, and so on were locked into the compound, along with the candidates; the officials might stay as long as a month.

But despite the severe penalties for cheating—culminating in execution—the evidence suggests that it was rampant. Benjamin Elman notes that "cheating dated back to the inception of the civil examinations. . . . [I]rregularities such as plagiarism were noted in the 1230s and 1240s."[32] The methods were ingenious.

Candidates would copy classics on their underwear in invisible ink. They bought essays: model compositions became increasingly available for memorization with the development of printing, despite decrees outlawing them.[33] Some people—up to 30 or 40 percent—hired substitutes to take the test.[34] Bribery of officials was common. Some very wealthy families bought ultra-thin gold leaf versions of the nine classics that could be rolled up and placed in the hollow shaft of a pen. Other candidates put notes inside bread, clothing, shoe linings. Or they had a system of confederates who waited outside the compound and responded to signals.

The security measures were astoundingly thorough, but candidates often outdid the authorities.

> Rampant cheating was not caused by insufficient security measures. With its specially built[,] secured[,] and guarded examination compounds, its body search procedures, its sequestered examiners, and many other preventive measures, coupled with severe physical punishments upon being caught cheating, the Keju system was perhaps one of the examination systems with the most elaborate security measures. Despite this security, creative examinees found new ways to cheat. Exam officials, examinees, and people who provided supplies to examinees were engaged in a continuous 1300-year cat-and-mouse game.[35]

Hoi K. Suen and Lan Yu conclude that this cheating was a consequence of the high-stakes nature of the test, not of any particular method of administration or content.

Ichisada Miyazaki, whose classic *China's Examination Hell* describes the ordeal in great detail, affirms the value of the test at certain points in its long history as an attempt to challenge aristocratic control over government, but concludes that by the end of its use, it was not the fair and equitable process originally intended. "To the very end the government, or at least the emperor, wanted to maintain the integrity of the examinations." But the scandals came in waves. "All too often fairness was compromised by corrupt candidates and examiners. When the competition became too stiff, some candidates felt that they must pass at any cost and, in the end, turned to dishonest methods. Once such a dishonest act succeeded, other candidates felt that they would be hurt unless they acted in the same way, so gradually the evil spread." Examiners too often colluded in the dishonesty, but public opinion weighed against them, citizens even going so far as writing "street posters charging [officials with] favoritism."[36] Following such events, standards would be enforced and reexaminations administered for several years, until the next similar occurrence.

There are some interesting continuities into the present, involving different forms of high-stakes tests. In 2001 and 2002 in China, several cases of widespread cheating on the Graduate Record Exam (GRE) and the Test of English as a Foreign Language (TOEFL) were uncovered, resulting in changes in how the tests were administered.[37] Some students had hired surrogates to take the test for them; others had memorized tests transmitted electronically by earlier test takers.[38] One Saint U. science professor told me that he has to go to China every year to interview candidates for graduate school. There had been too many past cases of students with perfect TOEFL scores or with brilliant telephone interviews who walked off the plane completely unable to communicate in English. The department decided that the ease of impersonating a candidate was too tempting without face-to-face checks. In Beijing cases were reported of writers writing essays for students applying to school abroad. Asked about this, one such writer did not see it as a moral issue but only as a practical problem that she had the skills to solve.[39]

A charge of plagiarism occurred in 2002 at Beijing University, the most prestigious in China. Wang Mingming, an anthropologist, had been the authorized translator of William Haviland's *Anthropology*, but then wrote his own book. A student accused Wang of copying chunks of Haviland's book into his own, creating a scandal met by a series of loud protestations that many other people in China do a lot of copying verbatim: Why single out Wang?[40]

It is not only China and the United States that struggle with these issues. Even Sweden, considered one of the least corrupt nations in the world, ranking sixth for "transparency," has had plagiarism scandals.[41] A reporter apparently copied four articles from the *New York Times*.[42] Student plagiarism must also be a concern, since a plagiarism-prevention system (Urkund) is advertised, which issues reports in either Swedish or English.

In *Campus Life: Undergraduate Cultures from the End of the Eighteenth Century to the Present* the historian Helen Lefkowitz Horowitz provides details of the history of student life in both the United States and Europe which put current practices into historical perspective. The dominant mood was far from the decorous reverence for knowledge that we might imagine. In the twelfth century, for example, faculty in Paris and Bologna had to form guilds in order to use their collective strength to gain the right to examine students, who did not want professors to interfere with their comfortable existence.[43] In the early nineteenth century at Princeton there was prodigious student misbehavior—scraping of chairs during religious services, nailing doors shut—resulting in mass tattling and expulsions.

Horowitz notes an early and enduring division between affluent students attending college essentially for "finishing," who spent their time in hedonistic pursuits (drinking, sport), and those strivers, usually sons of ministers, hoping to rise above their class origins, who diligently studied and aimed to please the faculty. Cheating scandals involved half the student body at Yale in the 1860s. Since grades had no import, and since privileged students had no aim beyond simply being there, the details of what occurred within the walls were irrelevant. Some of the striving poor students were willing to sit for examinations in place of the wealthy. According to the diaries of Yale student Lyman Bagg from the late 1860s,

> fingernails, cuffs, and boots served as obvious slates for formulae and outlines. The daring hid texts in holes dug in the floor or on the other side of windows, and devised ingenious mechanical devices to keep rolls of notes up their sleeves. Whole classes cheated on examinations. The use of ponies (translations of texts) was almost universal. At Yale in the 1860s, perhaps less than half of the compositions were actually written by the supposed author for the occasion.[44]

This makes the sudden "plague" of plagiarism and cheating today appear to be much ado about something enduring rather than the sign of a new phenomenon. If the "cheating" corner of the plagiarism triangle is perennial and ubiquitous, found in China in the fourteenth century and at Yale in the nineteenth, the "inadvertent" corner of incorporation is even more common and, at least some would argue, *essential.*

Encouraging ~~Plagiarism~~ "Patchwriting"

Many novices struggle to figure out exactly how to incorporate others' work into their own, whether in quoting, paraphrasing, summarizing, echoing, or engaging in other forms of conscious and unconscious incorporation. Coming from the background of composition studies, where she is involved daily in teaching students how to write, Rebecca Moore Howard has wrestled, as do we all, with the meaning of plagiarism. She acknowledges the universally banned practices of "copying from a source text and then deleting some words, altering grammatical structures, or plugging in one synonym for another," which she names *patchwriting.*[45] And she comes to a startling conclusion:

> Students' patchwriting is often a move toward membership in a discourse community, a means of learning unfamiliar language and ideas. Far from indicating a lack of respect for a source text, their patchwriting is a gesture of reverence. The patchwriter recognizes the profundity of the source and strives to join the conversation in which the source participates. To join this conversation, the patchwriter employs the language of the target community.[46]

In her pathbreaking book *Standing in the Shadows of Giants: Plagiarists, Authors, Collaborators,* Howard argues that patchwriting is a *necessary* stage in student learning. In trying to teach writing, Howard was certainly familiar with the strict enforcement of rules against plagiarism and with norms of academic integrity. In the end, though, she came to see her students' plagiarism as part of the educational process: "My zeal to socialize them into the avowed conventions of academic writing," she found, "was actually preventing their learning. Patchwriting was for them—as it is for us all—a primary means of understanding difficult texts, of expanding one's lexical, stylistic, and conceptual repertoires, of finding and trying out new voices in which to speak."[47] Howard does not condone outright fraud, such as buying a term paper, but she does suggest a different policy with regard to earnest students who commit the more common sort of "plagiarism" by copying bits and pieces of challenging material. She urges a permissive rather than a punitive stance with regard to student learning. Many in composition studies have now been persuaded of the rightness of her position.

I propose that we keep in mind a typology of plagiarism. Many authors have proposed the same thing, and enforcement of academic integrity requires it.[48] Penalties for each type would vary along a continuum from the kind of plagiarism that is clearly fraudulent, and deserving of severe penalties, to the kind of plagiarism that is uninformed, and deserving of education. In fact, as you will see in the conclusion, many instances of student plagiarism involve a combination of types.

So when an entire class of students essentially throws up its hands and confesses to plagiarism, as the opening anecdote recounted, we should see this not as an admission of moral turpitude on a vast scale but as evidence that plagiarism is a fundamental and correctable stage of learning how to write.

Students are actually very sophisticated in their use of quotation and other textual references, but their norms differ from those enforcing originality in academe. In later chapters we will explore a prevailing sense of self among contemporary youth that might promote plagiarism, a self

Table 1. Types of Plagiarism

Professional Plagiarism	Copyright Infringement	Student Plagiarism		
		Deceptive	*Nonce*	*Uninformed*
Incorporation	Unauthorized republication	Buying a paper	Using components from elsewhere Patchwriting	Imperfect mastery of citation conventions
Double publication		Using someone's freely given paper		
Theft		Importing a paper		

concerned with performance, collaboration, and multiplicity. We will examine what campus life is like today and how that too contributes to students' choosing to plagiarize. And we will see how, rather than treating plagiarism as an individual moral problem, we might regard it as a far from unitary collective cultural matter. But first of all, we need to investigate further the meaning of plagiarism as it depends on a particular view of the author, of texts, and of the relationship between the two, a matter that students tend to see differently from faculty.

2

Intertextuality, Authorship, and Plagiarism

*My Word, Your Word,
Their Word→Our Word*

> Any text is constructed as a mosaic of quotations;
> any text is the absorption and transformation of another.
> —JULIA KRISTEVA, "Word, Dialogue, and Novel"
>
> The word in language is half someone else's.
> —MIKHAIL BAKHTIN, "Discourse in the Novel"

IF plagiarism involves *improperly* taking another person's words and claiming them as one's own, it follows that (1) there are proper ways to take others' words, (2) people can "own" words, and (3) others' words (ideas as well as texts) can be distinguished from one's own. All these assumptions intersect with conventions of quotation and citation, and with notions of originality and authorship. In this chapter we'll see how the practice of citation—the antidote to plagiarism—arose and how the norms (connected to what anthropologists and linguists call the "language ideology") on which it is based are being challenged.[1] It seems that rather than being entirely ignorant of the principles of citation, students are often aware of them but do not entirely accept them.

Intertextuality and Quotation

> The footnote is bound up, in modern life, with the ideology and the technical practices of a profession. One becomes a historian, as one becomes a dentist, by undergoing specialized training.... Learning to make footnotes forms part of this modern version of apprenticeship.
> —ANTHONY GRAFTON, *The Footnote*

What exactly is the relation between authorship and writing? This relationship is not identical everywhere and at all times. It has to do with how a particular society regards ideas such as originality, individuality, and influence, as well as the goals of speech. Economic and technological factors also play a part.

As we have seen, despite the clarity of college and publishing guidelines about the need for citation of influence—"*Whenever you use someone's words or ideas, you must give their originator credit*"[2]—the procedure for following the rules is quite murky, for professional writers as much as for student novices, because the rules unrealistically assume an ability to trace the origins of all our thoughts and utterances (including written texts). Originality may be prized, but all speech—including writing—draws in some way from other texts and speakers. This interdependence of words and ideas on prior sources is what we call "intertextuality."[3] Any detailed look at real-life speech or writing shows that people frequently utter or write words that were first spoken or written by others, "interanimating"—that is, enlivening and entwining—them with a selection of other voices.[4]

Decades' worth of research on conversation by linguists and linguistic anthropologists shows, further, the significant contribution made by participants in conversation, which is technically termed "collusion"[5] or "interaction."[6] Songs quote other songs; poems allude to other poems; fiction weaves in themes from other works; films parody or visually refer to other films; music plays with themes from other composers.[7] Jazz and fiddling improvise on familiar chord progressions, demonstrating the performer's musical education and creating a sophisticated dialogue with the development of the medium.

Outside the arts, people reiterate their parents' admonitions when they become parents themselves, and preachers mix lines of scripture with their own improvisations and interpretations. Indeed, quotation is a great source of pleasure and a recognized practice. In the English-speaking world we have *Bartlett's* and other compendia of quotations to refer to; in China there are *chengyu* (four-character fixed-phrase) dictionaries. Including others' words invites other experience into the discourse. In only some contexts are they set apart from the speaker's words.

Quotation is a form of direct reported speech.[8] It is used to tell stories, to evade responsibility for or to distance the speaker from what is said, to create ambiguity about a source or the intended use of that source.[9] A simple explanation is that quotation relies on a distinction between *use* and *mention*, but in fact many instances of quotation straddle that distinction.[10] If I quote Gottlob Frege writing about quotation, am I agreeing with those words or merely reporting his having said them? Am I decorating my text with another's well-stated and impressive ideas? Academic quotation is used for all these purposes, but also to disagree:

> If words are used in the ordinary way, what one intends to speak of is what they mean. It can also happen, however, that one wishes to talk about the words themselves or their sense. This happens, for instance, when the words of another are quoted. One's own words then first designate words of the other speaker, and only the latter have their usual meaning. We then have signs of signs. In writing, the words are in this case enclosed in quotation marks. Accordingly, a word standing between quotation marks must not be taken as having its ordinary meaning.[11]

Frege points out the ambiguity of quoted words. In writing, the distinction between the author's words and words from another source is made clear through the use of quotation marks. Because of the work of researchers on speech, we know that quotation occurs orally as well, often through "quotative" verbs ("she said," "he goes," "I was like"),[12] or through prosodic cues such as pitch, amplitude, or vocal quality.[13] Quotation may invoke authority or bring in objects of ridicule. It provides material to consider "metalinguistically."[14] It entertains. It expands the interaction to include others not physically present. As a very common form of intertextuality, it reminds us of the multiple voices that are present in every interaction.

But in a real sense, everything we say or write incorporates previous texts; we include others' words and ideas as a matter of course. In some cases we signal their origin—syntactically, or with explicit quotative terms, or by shared understanding. We inherit our language, its sounds and words and rules. When we say, "I left it up to her," we are relying on a combination of words, a directional metaphor, that we have heard many times before. If we quote Shakespeare, saying, "Parting is such sweet sorrow," we rely on our listener's recognition that we are borrowing, and we use the well-known words to varying effect: to convey emotion, to show off our erudition, to mock those who use Shakespeare to show off their erudition. When we say, "Gerald said, 'I ain't messin' with you,' but I know he was," we convey Gerald's voice and words, set off from our own by a change in vocal quality or by a pause, as in writing we use quotation marks and commas. Sometimes we want to borrow the words, and sometimes we want people to know that we are borrowing them. Often we don't know where phrases originate, and often we and our listeners don't care. Sometimes, though, as in gossip or legal testimony, the source of words must be very carefully traced. In short, different genres have different conventions for attribution and intertextuality.[15] These variations are a source of richness in our expression, but they can become a source of confusion when that expression turns formal.

Originality, Authorship, and Ownership

In sorting out what is being quoted from what is original, we rely on a specific understanding of what an *author* is. According to *Merriam-Webster,* an author is generally regarded as "one that originates or creates" or "the writer of a literary work." Originality—a quality thought to spring from a unique essence, soul, or "genius"—is a concept that has long dominated Western thought but has not always been associated with authorship.[16] Many works that are treasured in the Western canon—the *Canterbury Tales,* the plays of Shakespeare, the works of Homer, the Bible—are collective, collaborative, mutable works passed down in part orally.[17] One genre, the cento, was made up entirely of lines from other poets' work. Mark Rose, writing about the history of copyright, authorship, and ownership, acknowledges Shakespeare the author of sonnets and poetry as an individual, identifiable author, but says, "It would not be wholly inappropriate...to characterize Shakespeare the playwright...in a quasi-medieval manner as a reteller of tales."[18] In fact, "in the seventeenth century...not only was the modern notion of the author as an autonomous creator, the producer and first proprietor of original works, not yet formed, but even the Renaissance notion of the author as an individuated authority was often problematic."[19] Modern authors, who do see themselves as "individuated authorities," seek to emphasize their originality by minimizing the extent to which they have absorbed other writers' style, words, or images.[20]

The "anxiety of influence," as Harold Bloom terms it, arose with the notion of the author, a concept that is in turn connected to the legal concept of copyright. Copyright is a commercial privilege that developed in the seventeenth and eighteenth centuries in England and Germany.[21] It came into being as printing became widespread and consumers began to pay for printed works. As patronage declined, writers had to earn a living. But the mere production of literary or scholarly works was no longer adequate to qualify someone as a writer; originality and creativity were required.

In the Middle Ages the "right to copy"—the literal meaning of "copyright"—rested with the *owners* of manuscripts, which were copied by hand. Each copy was rare and precious. Over several centuries, with painstaking reasoning, rights of ownership became attached to the text, and from there to its author, rather than to the physical copy, to the spirit of the work rather than to the commodity.[22] Issues of "propriety" and inalienability, or "ownness," were explicitly contrasted with issues of property, or ownership.[23] Propriety, according to Rose, referred to "the author's control over the form and content of his writings," as opposed to property, which was meaningful only "in an economic sense."[24]

Authors' rights were also pitted against those of the printing guilds, such as the Stationer's Company, which profited from the publication of works. In England booksellers had a monopoly over some works. The right to print resided with the crown, along with the power of censorship and regulation. In 1710 a law known as the Statute of Anne separated the matter of censorship from copyright, which was thereafter held to be a personal right, like the right to property.

Booksellers worried about pirates; authors worried about unauthorized publication of their books. Sometimes authors sought to control the circulation of controversial material. Many fascinating, and still unsettled, issues were debated during this formative period: Was a translation a new work, or did the original copyright apply? Did the copyright laws protect authors or booksellers? Were authors' rights to their work like claims to physical property or more like claims to real estate? Did the right to the "copy" apply only to the author's creative labor or to the material manuscript as well?[25]

From the 1740s to the 1770s a distinction arose between the material embodiment of the literary property and products of the mind or spirit. Johann Gottlieb Fichte, for instance, argued that only the form (or style, or expression) of the book was the author's property, not the content or ideas (or sentiment). Ideas could not enjoy copyright protection; expression could.[26] Prominent lawmakers, writers, and publishers engaged in debates over whether copyright should be perpetual or limited.[27] Their disputes revolved around the relative weight of the rights of authors to profit from their literary property as opposed to the right of the public to benefit from their contributions. It was decided that copyright protection should be valid for a period of fourteen years, renewable for another fourteen. Usually those seeking to extend the copyright were booksellers rather than authors.

Eventually the author became paramount. In a definitive and influential legal decision, *Millar v. Taylor,* Justice Aston in 1769 expressed his views—which have endured—about the importance of the author's originality. As Rose summarizes: "A work of literature belonged to an individual because it was...an embodiment of that individual. And the product of this imprinting of the author's personality on the common stock of the world was a 'work of original authorship.' The basis of literary property...was not just labor but 'personality,' and this revealed itself in 'originality.'"[28]

Finally, the question of originality versus imitation was debated. What Carl Pletsch calls "the cult of genius" was in the ascendant.[29] A genius was precisely a person who did not need to imitate but was born with singular insights and style.[30] "The genius became the demigod of the nineteenth century," writes Pletsch, "and the belief arose that 'a genius is born, not made.'"[31] A recognized genius like Schopenhauer could teach others by example to create "whole and unique selves," with innovation stemming entirely from within the individual.[32] Geniuses could be found in philosophy, music, art, and literature. Edward Young celebrated the "genius" of the unique individual Shakespeare, a mind untainted by imitation.[33] This view of the author, in short, had to do with "ownness" rather than "ownership."[34]

In recent decades the role of "author" has been deconstructed by Roland Barthes, Michel Foucault, Erving Goffman, Judith Irvine, and others from a variety of perspectives.[35] The "author" may be regarded as dead, or irrelevant, or impossible to fix or retrieve, or not unitary. Barthes reminds us that "the author is a modern figure, a product of our society insofar as, emerging from the Middle Ages with English empiricism, French rationalism and the personal faith of the Reformation, it discovered the prestige of the individual."[36] Some writers, such as Mallarmé, have attempted to struggle against "the sway of the Author." For him "it is language which speaks, not the author; to write is, through a prerequisite impersonality[,]...to reach that point where only language acts, 'performs,' and not 'me.'"[37]

It is the author, then, and his or her utterly independent individual creativity, that lies at the heart of the contemporary notion of copyright and of the requirement to cite. In summarizing his study of the history of copyright, Rose emphasizes the ideological and contingent nature of the concept:

> Copyright is not a transcendent moral idea, but a specifically modern formation produced by printing technology, marketplace economics, and the classical liberal culture of possessive individualism. It is also an institution built on intellectual quicksand: the essentially religious concept of originality, the notion that certain extraordinary beings called authors conjure works out of thin air.[38]

He notes that with new technology, copies have become easy to make, yet few regard the rights of authorship as something that should be abolished entirely:

> The institution of copyright is of course deeply rooted in our economic system, and much of our economy does in turn depend on intellectual property. But, no less important, copyright is deeply rooted in our conception of ourselves as individuals with at least a modest grade of singularity, some degree of personality. And it is associated with our sense of privacy and our conviction, at least in theory, that it is essential to limit the power of the state. We are not ready, I think, to give up the sense of who we are.[39]

Rose was writing in the early 1990s. Today there *are* those who are willing to give up some ownership of ideas. But before we see what they have to say, we need to take a look at how the law deals with the notion of intellectual property.

Plagiarism and the Law

"Intellectual property" is a metaphor; it takes something intangible and applies to it the concept of property, something that is by its nature visible.[40] Property implies ownership, but that raises more questions: What can be owned? What can be stolen? From where do property rights derive? How should we regard violations of intellectual property? Is plagiarism a criminal breach, a form of theft, or is it an ethical breach, not a crime but a socially stigmatized act, a violation of community norms?

The legal scholar Stuart P. Green argues against treating plagiarism as theft, suggesting that "a thing should be regarded as 'property' for purposes of theft law if and only if it is commodifiable—i.e., if and only if it is capable of being bought or sold."[41] With plagiarism, by contrast, he believes that what is "stolen" is not a commodity but *credit:*

> An author offers her work to the world by publishing it in a book or magazine. Under...widely accepted academic, literary, and journalistic norms and practices..., the author's presentation of her ideas constitutes a conditional offer to the effect that anyone may read the work and quote it or take ideas from it, *provided that such a person makes attribution to their originator.* Under this model, *A* pays for the privilege of copying *B*'s words or ideas by giving *B* credit for having been their author. Plagiarism, of course, occurs when *A* uses words or ideas originated by *B* but fails to pay *B* proper credit.
>
> So what, if anything, has *A* stolen?...[W]hat is stolen is not the author's words or ideas (since they are essentially there for the taking), but rather the "credit" to which the author is entitled.[42]

If our society were to decide to make plagiarism illegal, what existing law would the law against plagiarism most resemble? As Green notes, plagiarism may be seen as akin to theft, if what is stolen is words or ideas and what is gained is credit or honor. Others might see plagiarism as more akin to fraud, as when a student buys a term paper from a Web site; although the actual "author" has abdicated all rights to authorship, the student submitting the paper is not entitled to claim it as her own.[43] Still others may consider plagiarism a form of copyright infringement, but ultimately it is not the same thing, for as Green explains, "even plagiarism involving copyrighted work will entail an 'extra element' not present in copyright law—namely, passing off someone else's work as one's own."[44] Furthermore, copyright expires, while the sanctions against plagiarism do not.

Another, even more basic question to consider is whether the harm caused by plagiarism rises to the level of what we generally consider a crime. As Green puts it: "Is plagiarism really so harmful that we should want to use the criminal law to deter it? ... The answer is probably not." After all, most laws aim to protect society as a whole, while plagiarism affects only the small population of people who write. Says Green, "While rampant plagiarism would certainly tend to destabilize the narrow world of the intelligentsia, it would likely have only an indirect impact on the larger community."[45]

As for whether plagiarism represents an offense that requires retribution, here too Green considers it to be meaningful primarily within a narrow community of academics and writers:

> To those who are within the relevant community..., the act of plagiarism conveys extreme disrespect. The reactive emotions plagiarism elicits are much like the emotions elicited by other forms of theft—a feeling of having been invaded, ripped off, exploited, even brutalized. The fact that so many writers on plagiarism have used the language of theft is revealing; it is more than just a metaphor. To its victims, plagiarism is no less harmful than fraud or embezzlement.
>
> To those who are outside the relevant community, however, the moral content of plagiarism is less clear. Some may think of attribution, footnotes, and quotation marks as something they heard about in the ninth grade and haven't thought much about since....
>
> We seem to be headed towards the conclusion that plagiarism may best be dealt with internally by academic and professional institutions that should be capable of policing themselves.[46]

The Digital Revolution

Yet how well do our existing institutions guard against plagiarism and other violations of intellectual property rights? Intellectual property laws are violated with astonishing frequency. Up to about one-quarter of all software used in the United States is pirated.[47] Many young people download music illegally. There is clearly more at work here than an occasional disregard for social norms.

Just as the notion of authorship and intellectual property rights originated in the economic and technological innovations of past centuries, current transformations in our views of these same issues arise from new economic and technological changes. And among the most noteworthy technological changes in recent years—as revolutionary, some argue, as the invention of printing—is the digital revolution.

Sharing and transmitting materials of all sorts—music, video, text, images—has become routine with the development of computers and the Internet. And as with the development of printing and the market for printed works, huge legal battles are now being fought over control of electronically disseminated material and the right to profit from it.

Since the late 1990s a movement has arisen known as "Open Source," "Creative Commons," "Open Access," and the like, prominently given voice by Lawrence Lessig in his book *Free Culture*.[48] Lessig advocates generous circulation of creative works, with "some rights reserved," in order to encourage innovation in the arts, sciences, technology, and media. Inspired by Lessig, the "Free Culture" movement, begun by students at Swarthmore College in 2004, aims to promote sharing on the "digital commons."

In conscious contrast to Harold Bloom's *Anxiety of Influence*, Jonathan Lethem wrote an essay titled "The Ecstasy of Influence."[49] Lethem is especially interested in promoting "art that comes from other art." Through his "Promiscuous Materials Project," he offers stories on the Web for adaptation by filmmakers or dramatists for a dollar each.[50] Users sign an agreement and in turn receive certain rights. Similarly, the Creative Commons Web site offers licenses for circulation of creative material with six levels of control, ranging from utterly unrestricted invitation to use and alter material to the mandate to attribute and not alter ("no derivatives")—but still an invitation to share.

Thanks to the Web and the way it is changing the thinking of those who use it, the traditional understanding of ownership of a text—body and soul, expression and ideas—as the moral equivalent of the unique author, to be borrowed only through the prescribed exchange of credit, is under assault. It is today's college students, the first generation of the Internet era, who are storming the barricades. No wonder the faculty members whose job it is to initiate them into the ways of the academy are feeling increasingly embattled and bewildered.

The Footnote and Scholarly Norms

It is on the foundational principle that one person's words and ideas can be differentiated from another's and must be traced that scholarly norms are built, and these are the norms that students are supposed to master. Central to the norms governing scholarly production is the footnote. Anthony Grafton's book *The Footnote: A Curious History* traces the development of the idea of providing credit in writing at particular locations in a text.[51] For historians in eighteenth-century Germany, footnotes embodied the historiographic evidence on which arguments were based. They were not merely used to demonstrate erudition; entire satires and arguments could be carried out in the footnotes.

Whether the specific format for providing reference material is a footnote, an endnote, in-text citation, or something else, they all share the same purpose: to provide the reader with information sufficient to seek the origin of the material, to demonstrate gratitude to the originator of that material, to acknowledge influence and the writer's membership within an academic field, and sometimes to disparage those with whom the writer disagrees. On occasion the data to support an argument are provided in a footnote. Often a path back to inspiration may be traced there. But even the footnote cannot carry the entire burden of proving scholarly worth. As Grafton puts it:

> The footnote cannot carry out all the tasks that the manuals claim it does: no accumulation of footnotes can prove that every statement in the text rests on an unassailable mountain of attested facts. Footnotes exist, rather, to perform two other functions. First, they persuade: they convince the reader that the historian has done an acceptable amount of work, enough to lie within the tolerances of the field.... Second, they indicate the chief sources that the historian has actually used. Though footnotes usually do not explain the precise course that the historian's interpretation of these texts has taken, they often give the reader who is both critical and open-minded enough hints to make it possible to

work this out—in part. No apparatus can give more information—or more assurance—than this.[52]

The period of entering a scholarly profession involves building one's credentials, establishing one's authority, declaring membership, and even learning how to entertain. In many disciplines this apprenticeship is completed in part through mastering the use of footnotes. But the specifics have varied considerably over time. Grafton goes into great detail about national variations in the meanings and uses of footnotes, differences within the same nation, and differences in practice in various academic fields. For instance, in engineering, quotations are seen as unnecessary and frivolous. In cultural studies they are de rigueur. In law they consume the labors of students and clerks.

Graduate students are socialized into their fields through many years of reading and writing technical works. But undergraduates are expected to master the conventions of citation and attribution in each field they encounter, often with no explicit introduction to the field's practices—which have become second nature to its professionalized instructors—and despite all the self-contradictory foibles present even in a single field. Obviously this is extremely challenging, and it is no surprise that most students do not actually achieve this mastery. Writing instructors pour heroic efforts into attempting to teach this hodgepodge of rules, usually in the single-semester composition course required of the often resentful students who did not place out of it.

Quotation, paraphrase, incorporation, argumentation, influence, and provision of support and authority: all of this is supposed to occur in citations, even while students acknowledge the point of the class for which the assignment is due, indicate that they have done class readings and more, and demonstrate that they have their own original perspective, different from everyone else's, including the experts. References are where the academic action is, and quotation with proper citation is the proof that a student has joined the club.

When students fail at some aspect of this daunting task—when they consult outside works but neglect to cite them correctly—they are accused of committing plagiarism. Even in the best of situations, this is a skill that cannot be learned without meticulous attention—and most students, as we will see, are not paying that kind of attention to the details of their class work. But they are quoting a lot, without references, simply because that is how they behave in "real life."

Shared Bits: How Students Quote

> I am trying to imagine a Bob Dylan album with footnotes, asterisks, ibid.'s and nifty little anecdotes about the origins of each song. It's not going to happen. He's never pretended to be an academic, or even a nice guy. He is more likely to present himself as, well, a thief. Renegade, outlaw, artist. That's why we are passionate about him.
> —SUZANNE VEGA, "The Ballad of Henry Timrod"

For over ten years students in my introductory classes in linguistic anthropology have recorded, transcribed, and analyzed conversations. Gradually, in good inductive fashion, I began to notice that a substantial proportion of the transcripts included what I call "quoted shared bits" from popular culture. These might be lines from a TV show, changing over time from *The Simpsons* to *The O.C.*, from *Family Guy* to *Friends* to *Desperate Housewives*. They might be lyrics from the music that is popular on campus, which varies among different ethnic, regional, and class groups. They might be lines from favorite movies, from *Austin Powers* to *Old School* to *Caddyshack* to *Napoleon Dynamite* to *Juno*. Impressive overlap and conversational harmony occur with the sharing of quoted bits. They happen fast and are gone in a flash.

I began to wonder about the connections and contrasts between the way students behave in their daily lives—incorporating elements of other people's Web sites in their own, sharing music, watching shows together—and the rigid norms of individualistic composition and tracing of influence that faculty were requiring from them in their academic work. I wondered about the rules of citation and proscriptions against plagiarizing, and whether students' ideology of quotation might have anything to do with a perceived increase in plagiarism.

All language users draw on multiple genres, but the proliferation of the genre of quotation seemed to me to hold the potential for shaping the way students think about intertextuality in academic writing. While the classic eighteenth-century idea of the author as a solitary genius still dominates mainstream models of authorship and citation, twenty-first-century college students—and some writers and scholars—increasingly point out the pastiche-like quality of all language, especially in the arts.[53] Furthermore, growing numbers of students and some faculty, in particular those who teach writing, support the notion of collaborative work and question the assumption of individual creation.[54]

In sharp contrast to the explicit ideology stated in honor codes and apparent in administrative efforts to curtail plagiarism, which prohibit incorporating or expressing the ideas of others unless they are duly attributed, students *celebrate* quotation in ordinary conversation, as it fosters, and indeed constitutes, their ideas of successful and pleasing relationships.

Student norms contrast with official norms not just because of this proliferation of quoting without attribution, but because students question the very possibility of originality. They often reveal profound insights into the nature of creation and demonstrate a considered acceptance of sharing and collaboration.

Today's college students tend to be fully aware of their intertextual activities, "quoting" being an active, named genre for them. Web sites offering "movie quotes" teach their users how to be more accurate in their film references and to employ them more often.[55]

TV, iconic college movies, and songs are the most popular sources of quotation. Students generally say they do it for fun. One reported, "Even if people don't know where it's from, I explain and then they find it funny and laugh." Another student, Chas MacGonagal, had a different view. Generally he quotes a movie or TV program with friends who "have had the shared experience of...watching it together or we talked about it before so we know we both like it.... I'm not gonna quote [*Upright Citizens' Brigade*] around regular people because I'll have to explain it and it wouldn't be as funny." When asked what the point is of so much quoting, Chas likened it to a form of comedy; it works best because of reiteration and familiarity: "If you liked it the first time and it made you laugh a lot and then...thinking of it again makes you laugh again, why not bring it up[?]...Something happens in real life that will remind you of a line from a movie and then you throw it out there and everyone laughs 'cause you sort of have the double effect of what just happened plus the movie."

An engineering student from Ohio, "Turd Ferguson," spoke of common catchphrases around campus, lines from popular movies like *Old*

School which embody the college lifestyle or other experiences young people can relate to: "People tend to take those catchphrases and make them parts of their own lives.... It's easy to relate to a quote about drinking in a movie to when you're drinking at a party, so people tend to do things like that." It gets them talking and laughing. What he terms "college-y music" is another form of common knowledge shared even by students with different musical tastes.

Some people quote long stretches of text. To pass the time one summer, a student with an excellent memory for movies and TV programs, along with his brother, tried to recreate verbatim the entire text of several favorite shows, including *Family Guy*. During high school—when he had had virtually no homework—he had watched two hours of sports before school, one hour after school, and two to three hours of other shows in the evening. Thus he had quite a stock of material to draw on.[56]

The importance of shared prior experience is clear in this statement by Brittany, a science and art major from Wisconsin:

We quote *Friends* a lot.... [T]hey have such crazy situations on there, and...their responses are...equally crazy,...so I think it works...in a serious situation best whenever you just say something off-the-wall. All my friends would [recognize a *Friends* quote]. I don't do it as much around people that I don't know as well or that...don't like the show as much, 'cause then they just have no idea. It kind of brings [people] together, like they're...common bonds, they both like the same show or movie or whatever.

Similarly Margaret Ann, an accounting and psychology major from the Midwest, said:

Friends is the only thing that I quote, because I have a hard time remembering quotes.... As it's going on or something like that, or we're telling a story about something that happened that was kind of like *Friends*, and...it...triggers a random quote.... They're usually things that when [she and a friend are] watching it together, that we both laugh at, and we just think it's hilarious.... And...when I say it,...it just makes us laugh.... Usually we both know it's [from] *Friends*.... Sometimes we say[,]... "You remember that from *Friends*?" and the other one's like, "Yeah I do.".... But a lot of times you can just say [the line and] she'll know what I'm talking about.

Again, the social connection here is crucial, with the audience participating and sharing the same background. Shared unspoken recognition of the source is assumed.

One student, "Johny Chimpo" (spelled thus on his consent form when he chose his pseudonym), specified that quoting from movies and old TV shows is a source of shared levity, not suitable for profound discussions. He too assumes that the source is known to all participants.

> *Johny:* When [*Old School*] came [out],...people quoted that a lot....
>
> *Interviewer:* and it seems like people quote comedies more often....
>
> *Johny:* Yeah 'cause [they] think they're trying to be funny. I don't think you quote a movie to be deep and profound usually....Because when you wanna be profound, I think you kinda wanna express your own...I don't think...you're making all that intelligent of a comment when you're just trying to recite a movie quote....With a movie quote...it can just be a lot funnier if you use a phrase. To know the reference, where it's from, apply it to your life....I think you usually assume your listeners know [where it's from]. That's usually why it has the effect you want.

As Lauren, a freshman biology major from Las Vegas, summed it up, she and her friends "[quote *Family Guy*] all the time....When we're together we'll just say stuff, and then everyone will just laugh. We quote all the time, movies and stuff....Everybody does it."

We asked students if they quoted from books as well as TV, movies, common experience, and songs. Nobody quoted from books because, as one said, "you can't assume people would know what books others have read." Ashley, an engineering major from Indiana, echoed Lauren's point about the importance of sharing a laugh. She was adamant that quoting from books would not be as successful as quoting from movies or TV because they are not shared experiences, in contrast to the communal nature of watching TV shows.

> *Ashley:* Right now...*Napoleon Dynamite* is the big one that...everybody quotes....From my group of friends...we quote *Friends* all the time. There will be a situation that happens, we'll be like, "Don't you remember that was just like in this episode when...Joey blah, blah, blah," or whatever....We all laugh. A couple [of] people

might not get it, and we're like, "Don't you remember?" Like, you should know.

Interviewer: Do you guys ever quote books?

Ashley: Not really, because for books it's hard...to get something everyone would know....It's not like you generally read a book with your friends, whereas you're gonna watch a show with your friends.

Supporting Ashley's claims about how people "don't get it" if students quote unfamiliar material is a conversation about a student's "gold-digging" aunt. The student, Ava, cited and referred to Pierre Bourdieu; her interlocutor had not heard of him. In an eighteen-turn segment of the conversation, her friend, "Penny Lane," contributed nothing except "oh yeah" or "mm-hmm," while Ava expounded on the social differentiation of taste in the United States and France. Her reference does not yield a rousing symphony of sharing but rather falls flat as Ava dominates the floor:

Ava: [Did you ever] hear of Pierre Bourdieu?

Penny: No.

Ava: He's really cool....He was a French sociologist...and anthro-pologist and...everything-ologist...

Penny: Mm-hmm.

Ava: ...and...he talked about the embodiment of taste,

Penny: Mm-'kay.

Ava: ...It works especially well...in France because...there is such a hierarchy, y'know?

Penny: Mm-hmm....

Ava: It really...doesn't work here as much, but...in France it really...

Penny: No, it makes sense.

Clearly this was different from the enthusiastic sharing that is idealized as occurring among like-minded students. There are surely exceptions, but one norm appears to be: if you are having a fun conversation, allusion has to be about shared knowledge. And that is unlikely to come from books.

In their ordinary conversational lives, in fact, students aim *not* to have to specify the source of their quotations. After all, if the goal is sharing, the need to explain would mark some kind of missed connection, since it could arise only from a lack of shared knowledge and background. Danny said this explicitly: "The goal is to not have to say [where a quotation came from] 'cause hopefully [people] just know. But every now and then...if you don't feel like giving up the joke or the quote or whatever and they don't know the movie, you say, 'Oh that was from blah, blah, blah.' And so you do give up the credit then." "Give up the credit" suggests reluctantly making the source explicit.

Between Talking and Writing

Assessing the degree of shared knowledge is the determining factor for attributing a source in another favorite medium: instant messaging. Instant messaging (IM) is a form of communication halfway between talking and writing. People refer to it as "talking," but of course the medium for the talk is written text. One intriguing and relevant aspect of AIM (AOL Instant Messenger) is the "away" message, a posted message conveying something about the poster's whereabouts, activities, or personality. Almost all away messages end with quotations, some attributed to specific authors or composers.[57]

Curious about quotations on away messages, I spoke with a teenager, Sophia, about her reasons for providing sources (or not). If she provides a source for something obscure, she worries that one of her friends may decide to use it on her own away message, essentially stealing Sophia's originality—which lies in her selection and consumption rather than production. She might, though, provide a source when she wants to make sure that something she uses is not mistakenly taken for her own words.

Among away messages there is a mix of attribution and non-attribution. A good percentage of quoted material comes from songs. One goal is to be original and unique in one's selection of a quotation; the ideal is to present obscure but meaningful and mysterious quotes. Sophia scoffed at the ones that "everyone" knew.

Like AIM, social networking sites like MySpace and Facebook allow users to present a "face" to the world made of continually manicured snippets of material designed, as a whole, to convey one's selectivity and depth, and often an ironic stance. The "Favorite Quotes" option in Facebook "profiles" demonstrates a wide mastery of popular and even high culture. I found intellectual extracts, with quotation marks and the author specified, included among references to John Stuart Mill, James Baldwin, Karl Barth, the Dalai Lama, Einstein, Ziggy Marley, Stephen King, Tom Petty, The Replacements, Homer Simpson, and "my mother" (this last for an adage for which the student wished to renounce responsibility). One college student included a quote—attributed to Rollo May—along with a discussion of the Myers-Briggs test, which the poster had just completed. Some students quote their friends in the same format they use for quoting famous people, playfully giving their pals the role of well-known author.

In a collection of fifty quotes, however, only one gave a reasonably formal citation. (It was from a history textbook, complete with page numbers and publisher's name but not place of publication.) Many appeared without any attribution at all. Again, sources are provided only when students assume that others will not know where the quote comes from. It is common to presume that others will recognize the source when it is a song. Attributions are more commonly provided for quotations from books, as viewers are assumed to "need" the information in this case. Although there are unspoken guidelines for this practice, they are far from identical to scholarly norms of citation.

It is not surprising that students' views of oral quotation and electronic incorporation only sometimes echo the official line regarding citation in written work. It is common to regard students as uninformed about or even resistant to academic rules, but in their discussions one can find a fair amount of well-reasoned concern about those rules. The question of originality often arises, too, usually to be dismissed.

Questioning Originality (and Credit, and Property . . .)

Charlie, an earnest freshman from Pennsylvania, spoke at length about writing papers—he loves writing history papers but not philosophy papers—puzzling over the mandate against copying.

There's not a lotta ways to say, ..."The Germans invaded France on this date."...I read a while back about a historian who got in a lotta trouble because he was accused of plagiarizing...another author, and there's...two ways to say this phrase [chuckles], and he happened to choose the one that this other guy had chosen....For example, for philosophy we had to...analyze an argument of Thomas Aquinas using the structure of another author. At times it seems like you're just...taking out this word and putting in...another.

He expresses anxiety about the ever-present possibility of committing plagiarism, wondering what happens if "it's your argument but it's...framed by another person, so...it's almost...their argument with your words." In that case "it doesn't seem like...it's purely your own work, but I guess it's not supposed to be." Asked if anything can be one's own work, he suggests as an example Shakespeare's poetry. He does think that his own language or tone could be considered his own, even if he is using writings from, say, Aristotle.

Charlie alludes more than once to what he calls "the cloud of plagiarism," meaning "accidentally tak[ing] the argument of another author without realizing it, and then getting kicked out of school." When pressed about the severity of such a punishment for a minor transgression, he explains that "the formal definition of plagiarism is [copying] three...or more words...in a row," which shocks the interviewer. But Charlie remains adamant: "And...sometimes there's only...two or three ways to say something,...and if you think too much about plagiarism, then you're gonna get into awkward sentence structure just to make sure you're not plagiarizing." But when the interviewer asks about how strictly faculty treat plagiarism, Charlie admits, "I think you'd...have to go pretty far off the edge to encounter a problem."

The interviewer then asks about Turnitin.com, the plagiarism-detection Web site. Charlie's high school had used this service. In one of his classes every paper had to be run though it. Charlie explains how it works:

I'm pretty sure the site gives you a percent of what is...used in another source....Some people would come back with 15 percent plagiarized, but it's..."in the case of,"... "the name of," that comes back as plagiarized....It might be longer...than three words....But...you'll get other papers with, y'know [chuckles], whole paragraphs [flagged]..., and I think that's important to figure out. [chuckles]...[If students are] taking another person's source, er, work and just making it their own, I mean, they have to learn a lesson one time or another....I thought [the checking] was a good thing,...'cause people who didn't do the work weren't able to get away with it...by plagiarizing a source or...copy-pasting so much stuff.

When asked why it is "such a big deal that we cite authors and we cite scholars," another student, Kristen, a political science and philosophy major, instinctively equated "words and ideas" with "property," unaware that she was echoing eighteenth-century discussions:

Well, I mean I guess in a way...when you work really hard or if you have something...innovative to say, you can consider that your property in a sense because it's being used for a purpose, and for those people, a lot of times,...those theories are more important than their possessions, and if we're going to have laws against taking people's things, it should [extend to taking] their words and their ideas.

Kristin has clearly absorbed the dominant notion of intellectual property and uses this to explain the mandate to cite.

"John Stamos," a junior economics major from New York, distinguishes the borrowing of direct quotes from the borrowing of ideas. He doubts that much originality is possible, especially in the domain of ideas, yet attributes most apparent borrowing to unconscious influence:

Interviewer: Define plagiarism.

John: ...I think it's just taking somebody else's work. I mean in the most primary state....I wouldn't really know how to define past that.

Interviewer: Okay. Do you think it happens much?

John: Oh yeah....I don't think people take direct quotes and that happens much....But I think in terms of taking other people's ideas or taking other people's thoughts, that happens all the time....I don't think people even realize they're doing it. I think people look at something and say, "Oh, that's a great idea." And then they throw it in their paper, as if it was their own and it's not...[chuckle]. I mean, it's somebody else's, and they're not taking a direct quote, but they still are taking somebody else's idea, and in that sense, they're kinda innocent. I don't think they realize what they're doing,... but it still is plagiarism. I think most papers are not people's own ideas.

John continues to elaborate on his claim that original ideas are rare, giving examples of a paper topic on the proof of God's existence.

> *John:* The difference is this: If I in writing that paper looked up Descartes, saw his proof, and that gave me all these ideas for mine and I used them, to me that's kind of plagiarism. But if I sat down with a pen and a pad and happened to come up with the same things he came up with, then that's what we're talking about here. That ideas are gonna get recycled. There's no way that a hundred kids in a class could write papers with all fresh ideas. That'd be a hell of a class if you could. In fact, I'd be willing to say that no one—not even one student—will come up with something that's never been come up with before. And that's not an indictment of them, it's just these ideas are all over the place. But I feel like a lot of people, instead of thinking of it themselves, use somebody else's thought instead.

What John touches on here is the unsettled issue of borrowing or sharing ideas and the necessity of attribution.

"JH Christ" (students typically test limits, including the line between blasphemy and humor) was a senior majoring in marketing. He admitted having cheated by typing equations into his calculator prior to taking a test. Asked what kind of student he was, he said he was lazy but aimed to be "slightly above average." Most days he slept until just before lunch; he had no classes before noon. He made a lot of choices on the basis of their being "easy," including using in his papers ideas he found on the Internet without attributing them. JH claimed to have a clear understanding of owning ideas and gaining financially from them, but when presented with murky cases, he stumbled to articulate a policy. Yet JH could express well the importance of separating his and others' words. Mulling over ownership of the idea for a coffeemaker, explanations of Custer's loss in battle, rights to the song "Happy Birthday," JH distinguished between patents, copyrights, and casual quotation:

> *JH:* I don't think... anytime someone quotes a... movie or something [in conversation] it doesn't necessarily need to be cited.
>
> *Interviewer:* Why not?

JH: ...I don't know... either because it's something that everyone might assume everyone has seen, knows about or, ...I'm not sure....

Interviewer: And would you say... it happens a lot that they'll refer to the source when they make the quote?

JH: Yeah, a lot of times they will... say, ... "Yeah, that was in that movie."

Interviewer: Do you think... that's in the same spirit as when they write a paper?

JH: Yeah, I think it is. I think in that sense... with friends, maybe with people who have seen the movie, [they would] kind of think less of that person if they tried to play it off as their own kinda joke or something.

JH suggests a moral obligation to distinguish quotations from the speaker's own words. Callista, by contrast, volunteers that the quoting people do in conversation differs from that in writing:

Interviewer: Okay. So...is it just because someone's already said [something] before that we have to give them credit, or is it...

Callista: Yeah. But it's so different in...the written word and papers versus what we say....I mean, how funny would it be if every time you said something from a movie, you had to be like, "And that's from this," like—"From 1980."...That'd be insane, but [laughter]...conversations would get nowhere....People wouldn't probably be as inclined to quote things if they had to do all that stuff. But...I think there's something about publishing something...that in the act of writing it down, it just becomes so much more important to give people credit.

Callista is very clear that in conversation it is not possible or necessary to slow down and give sources for every quote, but that academic writing is a different matter.

It is not only that norms of spoken quotation differ from the norms of academic citation. Despite years of academic socialization, even thoughtful students may reject the whole premise underlying the need to trace influence, with views approaching that of the "Free Culture" movement mentioned earlier. Fiona didn't accept the importance of citation at all, arguing against the need for recognition as well as the value of tracing influence:

> *Interviewer:* Why do you think that it's important for us to cite works that we used in papers?
>
> *Fiona:* ... Just as a recognition that you're getting ... ideas or ... your ideas have been influenced by other people, and ... I think that for a lot of people, it's very important for them that they get that recognition.
>
> *Interviewer:* Why do you think it's so important for them to be recognized?
>
> *Fiona:* ... I don't know. ... To be honest, I don't really understand it; it's not important to me. ... I think that it's something that is unfortunate in our society. I mean, you do some good, academically, athletically, whatever, you get a trophy, ... and it's like recognition that you've done something, ... and ... I think [citation is] more of the same thing, ... just more of, "Look at what I've done ... I'm influencing these people," ... or as the person who's citing it, "This person influenced me and I want to show everyone else that they influenced me, ... because I respect them and they had such an impact in what I'm thinking."
>
> *Interviewer:* Do you think that, when we have an idea, ... do we own that idea? ... Is it safe to say that ... this was my idea. ... I had this idea to, I don't know, go out to lunch today or something?
>
> *Fiona:* [chuckles]
>
> *Interviewer:* ... Is that [idea] mine?
>
> *Fiona:* Um, it's yours, but I don't think that that negates the fact that other people can have the same one.

Fiona articulates principled reasons for rejecting the insistence on recognition ("a trophy") and on citing ("I want to show everyone else that they influenced me"), since she is quite aware of the possibility of one person's having the same ideas as others.

The official requirement to give credit to authors whose words or ideas are used is apparently contradicted by the instruction to list only "works cited," as in many professional publications. Authors—whether student or professional—who consult other authors but do not use their works directly may not include them in their bibliographies. Yet if *influence* is to be traced, in order to give credit even to authors whose ideas are merely formative, these works would have to be cited—a list that, in reality, would be endless.

Callista, an English major who wishes to trace influence dutifully, disagrees with her teachers' guidelines but follows them, though reluctantly:

> *Interviewer:* Do you think it's necessary...to...cite every author you look at?
>
> *Callista:* Mm-hmm. Yeah....And this is something that's disputed among English professors;...they want you to just cite the people whose stuff you quote. But I think...it's very important to...cite the people, or at least in theory,...people who you don't quote but whose ideas...still influenced your...argument....Like if I read a book and I'm like, "Huh. That's interesting. Doesn't quite fit with what I'm saying, but this'll...be interesting to think of things." And I'd still put [books like that] in the bibliography, 'cause they still shape the way I'm gonna write.

Callista has identified a contradiction in the official norms. She acknowledges Bloom's "anxiety of influence," although the actual rules for citation do not go that far.

For students, quotation is an often obligatory component of papers written in school. In some sense they accept this only because quotations satisfy requirements and fill up pages. Callista expresses ambivalence about quoting; she deplores the lack of originality that is inevitable with too much quotation. Although she had written a lot of papers, incorporating enough quotations to satisfy professors' precise demands about the number of sources and references, she sees originality as especially desirable and feels that it is threatened by the need to cite from the work of others:

> *Callista:* I was thinking about...this two days ago because I just wrote a thirty-page English seminar paper, and you have to have twenty sources, and...two of them can be from the Internet but everything else had to be a book, and so you spend so much of your time reading these critical essays;...every page has...four quotes on it, and your

footnotes are *this* big, but...I feel like I'm...just tying together what
other people have said....My argument is only in how I shape these
other people's arguments to fit what I think....I don't like having
that many sources required because I think that that doesn't make
as much room for my original thought....The critical essay that I'm
looking at has these bibliographies, so everyone is just pulling ideas
from other people and putting them in a different package—

Interviewer: Right—

Callista: ...That's just what we're doing today....You could publish
any of our essays and it'd be the same exact thing....

Interviewer: Hmm. So if it's the same exact thing, why is it important
to do it? Why is it important to include all these people that you've
looked at and all this stuff?

Callista: It's a good question. Well...it's not the same exact thing....
What's unique is that...through plagiarism, anti-plagiarism, you can't
copy a person's argument exactly. You have to be unique in...some-
thing you say—at least the way you tie everyone else's stuff together.
So I'm assuming that kind of is a universal code, so everyone has
to be unique in how they group stuff together,...but...you're still
using other people's words. You still have to...give them credit for
their ideas....But...yeah, I guess the uniqueness is in how you order
what other people think.

Callista understands the conventions of citation fairly well and contrasts
them with the implicit value of originality and uniqueness, but she
also questions the demands of some of her instructors that she cite only
works mentioned, not all those that influenced her thought. In the end
she decides that "uniqueness" resides in "how you order what other people
think."

Pastiche, Collaboration, and Other Techniques

To students like Callista, there is creativity and self-expression—
uniqueness—in pastiche, a concept quite different from the traditional
academic value of originality in thought and expression. A Facebook "Favorite Quotations" section, consisting entirely of other people's words,
supposedly displays the uniqueness and creativity of the compiler. And

although an instructor might disagree, so would a composition made up of nothing but a string of quotations.

When we asked students about tracing the origins of amusing quotes in conversation and whether the quoter has ownership of the lines, one insightful person (Chas MacGonagal) responded, "You don't own it, you just...own the quickness of mind to associate" the lines with the situation. The prevalence of this attitude toward pastiche or collage is evident in the collections of songs that students compile on their iPods. Evan, from Texas, went so far as to claim that his playlist essentially defined him. Like wearing clothing emblazoned with corporate logos as an expression of personal taste, the selection of songs, none of which Evan had composed, defined his identity: "When it comes to the iPod,...I think your personal little soundtrack is almost representative of who you are and...where you come from and what you're doing and where you're gonna go."

Similarly, many students accept that intellectual concepts can be simultaneously their own and someone else's. Much of their time outside class is spent in the company of friends, who might offer help with a difficult paper or assignment. In considering whether it is acceptable to use a friend's ideas or even "the exact phrasing for an idea," Colin tried to distinguish accepting a gift of "an original way of arranging the words" from borrowing someone else's original idea.[58] When the interviewer asked Colin what he would do if his roommate offered an excellent opening sentence or two for a paper, Colin saw that the issue was larger than just the question of how the roommate "worded a sentence or two":

> *Colin:* I think it would be fine to take the premise,...a big idea, because you're not going to get a big idea necessarily from doing the readings; you're going to get a big idea from class discussion, a more comprehensive view of the course. Whereas...the real issue would come in if...you got the big idea from him and then [asked him],..."Hey, what pages did you see stuff for that idea [on]?"...and he just wrote down a list of page numbers for you to look at—...that would be questionable....I don't think that using the exact idea or the exact phrasing for an idea would be appropriate. But...I think to allow other people's thoughts to enhance yours, regardless of your level of preparation, is fine, as long as it's not the primary drive....

> *Interviewer:* ...What if he had this great sentence and he just said, "Yeah, man, go for it. It's all for you,...I don't have a problem if you use that sentence exactly. You don't even have to cite it"?
>
> *Colin:* I...well, I don't know. I guess it depends....If it's a sentence that's...a thesis,...if he words the thesis really well as compared to...just a nice way of arranging the language,...it sounds poetic or whatever,...the sentence structure is eloquent, or whatever,... I think the second scenario is different than the first. If he has the idea that's original, his own, and worded particularly well, if you use that as the core of a paper, [it] would be unethical. But...if your roommate just has a way with words that is particularly impressive and he's open and shares that and says, "Absolutely, go ahead," and it's not something that's...essential or original,...not an original thought, just an original way of arranging the words, then...I don't really see a problem with it.

Colin struggled with the notion of borrowing ideas as opposed to the expression of ideas, again pointing to originality as the fundamental value, yet ended by endorsing the idea of accepting a freely offered suggestion ("[if] he's open and shares that and says, 'Absolutely, go ahead'").

"Bean Pole" contrasts receiving ordinary help from classmates with taking something he considers "set in stone." Receiving ordinary help involves what Bean Pole regards as the "communal," synthetic nature of writing. A writing tutor, he has been trained to work with students to help develop their own ideas and voices. He distinguishes between ideas, which are always circulating, in flux, and expression of them, which may be "set in stone." To the same question put to Colin about borrowing a roommate's idea, Bean Pole gave a slightly different answer:

> *Bean Pole:* Did [the idea] arise out of discussion with your roommate?...I think, okay, the balance is this: I think writing is ultimately, in a lot of ways, a communal activity....You're going after ideas, and in order to get those ideas, you're talking to other people, and you're...puttin' 'em forth, and people are giving their responses, and ideas themselves are not...bound to particular people....The balance is,...it should be your own work, but it can be the result of talking to other people and synthesizing their ideas.

Elaborating on what he means when he calls writing "a communal activity," he explains that in his work at the writing center he has learned that writing "is something that you should be able to talk to other people about; it's not just you alone at your computer." The interviewer persists in asking about quoting a few sentences from the Internet:

> *Bean Pole:* Well, taking from the Internet is taking words that are set in stone, have already been... arranged... and sticking them into your paper. Now, talking about ideas with someone else is... not taking words... which have been used,... it's taking another person's ideas; but then it's synthesizing when it's putting them into your own words, so... in a certain sense,... if you're gonna say that taking ideas is plagiarism,... then every paper... is chock-full of plagiarism, 'cause you have to learn ideas to get to these ideas, and you can't cite every single sentence that you write, so I think you draw the line at the level... of taking words that are already set down,... but taking ideas which are from dialogue or... even... reading a book [is all right,]... I suppose, if you're putting [them] into... your own words.

Once again, Bean Pole differentiates ideas, which are inevitably shared, from "words that... have already been... arranged," that is, "set in stone." If we couldn't incorporate other people's ideas into our own thinking, then "every single sentence that you write" would have to be cited—and this clearly makes a mockery of academic norms, not to mention common sense.

When I work with students on independent projects, one challenge is to teach them the value of multiple drafts and editing; they are often accustomed to throwing together a decent draft in one sitting and turning it in for a decent grade. With a year-long honor's thesis, this strategy doesn't work. I showed one student the draft of an article I'd written, along with the editor's changes. I thought I was teaching a lesson about the value of editing, but the student had a different question: If the editor made so many changes, how can the work be credited to me alone? There's only one answer to her question, and perhaps not a very satisfying one. The credit is mine thanks to an unwritten rule, a convention of the contemporary writers' guild.

Conventions, unwritten rules: these are another way of saying "norms." And as we have seen, student citation norms differ considerably from academic citation norms. Students accept that in everyday conversation, quotation is fun and playful, though certainly not obligatory; they provide citation only when necessary to direct their peers to rare or unfamiliar sources; they regard the cutting and pasting of pastiche as evidence of originality and creativity; they embrace the notion of collaboration in writing; and they question the possibility of originality in ideas.

IN HER WONDERFUL essay "Repetition in Conversation," Deborah Tannen describes the convergence of words among people in conversation as akin to an aesthetic experience.[59] We want to be like the people we like, and we want to enjoy the same things. Those who recognize the same references are most alike; such references require no introduction, no citation, no explanation. As we say to demonstrate how close two people can be, "We finish each other's sentences." Adolescents' enjoyment in quoting small bits, of picking up references, is thoroughly at odds with the hypervigilance demanded by academic norms of citation. Whenever norms differ so drastically, practices and behaviors are likely to be contested. In part, these differing ideologies of intertextuality explain the discomfort currently evident on college campuses with regard to plagiarism.

The official rules governing citation, stemming from Enlightenment notions of authorship, ownership, and originality, and the distinction between ideas and expression of ideas, are simply not accepted by today's college students. They quote constantly in their ordinary lives and rarely have to cite their sources. They are more in tune with Lethem's "ecstasy of influence" than with Bloom's "anxiety of influence." The ecstasy is magnified when influence is shared. And when it is shared, there is no need to cite explicitly. The unstated but commonly known, through shared experience, bonds peers. The academic premium placed on citation merely emphasizes the distance between academic practice and students' values as expressed in their daily lives.

The kind of inadvertent or careless plagiarism that results from uncertainty about the norms of citation in part reveals the ongoing change in the way intellectual property is regarded. And in fact, evidence from linguistics and linguistic anthropology supports students' sense of the instability of origins and the convergence of invention. While quoting lines from popular culture offers a chance to celebrate shared identity, the painstaking tracing demanded in academic writing reinforces the distance between student and teacher. We cannot improve student practice without acknowledging that at least two different ideologies of quotation are in effect. We faculty ignore this fact at our peril. (Did I invent that phrase? Plagiarize it? Would I be found guilty of copying? Is it a cliché? Did someone own it once but now it has slipped into the public domain? Oh, the anxiety of influence.)

The ideal—or myth—of originality does not drive this generation of students. They are more interested in sharing, belonging, resembling, converging. Thus plagiarism—the violation of originality—does not horrify them, does not cause revulsion or despair. They can be taught to understand that it is a breach of academic practice, but without their feeling it intensely, the fear of plagiarism is not likely to retain its grip.

Ideas of the author and intellectual property rights point to another, even more profound mismatch between faculty and students in how they view the role of the self in all its words and actions. This aspect of contemporary life is shaped by technology, as well as by the waves of social and psychological change sweeping over twenty-first-century American youth. I call it a shift from the ideal of the authentic self to that of the performance self, and see in it yet another reason why today's students may engage so unapologetically in a variety of behaviors that the academy lumps together as "plagiarism."

3

Observing the Performance Self

Multiplicity versus Authenticity

> The work of art is…authentic by reason of its entire self-definition:
> it is understood to exist wholly by the laws of its own being, which
> include the right to embody painful, ignoble, or socially inacceptable
> subject-matters. Similarly, the artist seeks his personal authenticity in
> his entire autonomousness.
> —LIONEL TRILLING, *Sincerity and Authenticity*

> We live in a "cut and paste" culture enabled by technology.
> —LAWRENCE LESSIG, *Free Culture*

PLAGIARISM, to repeat the mantra from the previous chapter, involves improperly presenting someone else's words or ideas as one's own. We saw how difficult it is to separate out other people's ideas and words from our own, and how particular (or perhaps peculiar) is the genre of academic citation. In this chapter we look more closely at the differing valuations placed on being the unique originator of words, which traditionally attach firmly to their originator's essence, although this is only one of a variety of relationships possible between self and words. The concept of "academic integrity" presupposes wholeness, oneness, "ownness," an identity between the writer and what she or he has written, but this value is not dominant among today's youth. Moral judgments of plagiarism, as we shall see, depend on even more fundamental views of personhood and the relations among selves.

Those motivated by the ethic of "authenticity" insist that their words are theirs alone and that all utterances derive from their own, their singular, their individual, integral truth. Nothing could make them pronounce what is not intended as an expression of their own thoughts and feelings. These authentic selves would never plagiarize because they believe to their core that all they say should be theirs and theirs alone. Their key concepts are *own, genuine, essence, integral, means, undivided.*

By contrast, those motivated by the ethic of what I call "performance" accept that their behavior is mutable, depending on circumstances. All that matters is the effect of their actions, including their speech and writing. Thus they are not wedded to the notion of a singular relationship between their inner feelings and thoughts and their outer expression. They will say what is expected, whatever suits the occasion, whether it is their personal truth or not. Performance selves say and write whatever works for their practical purposes; it need not belong to them alone. They don't feel a tight connection between their words and their inner being, so they don't sweat it if others use their words or if they use the words of others. For them the notion of "self" is multiple rather than singular and unified. Their key concepts are *efficacy, nimbleness, comfort, circumstance, ends, goals.*

Technology plays a role in the generational transformation that has occurred between the emphasis on authenticity and the emphasis on performance, but it is not an entirely causal one. The shift from authenticity to performance—with all the accompanying desires for play and so on—has in turn led to the development of certain technological innovations.

The authentic self celebrates uniqueness, individual contribution, essence, fixity, and authorship. It is inner-directed. Its words are its own, and are always meant and sincerely believed. The performance self celebrates collaboration, incorporation, fluidity, appearance. It is goal-oriented. Its words are derived from many different sources and may be spoken or written in earnest or in jest, with conviction or just to get along.

It is clear that the principles of the academy—including practices of citation—accord with the authentic self, and to the extent that students share this model, they too adhere to the academy's guidelines. The performance self, however, is more likely to regard boundaries between its own and others' contributions as permeable, to focus on accomplishing goals by any means necessary, and to regard the origins of textual material as unimportant. To the extent that students share the values of the performance self, they are more likely to regard both cheating and intertextual plagiarism as valid strategies, to juggle outward appearances and behavior to fit others' expectations, and to incorporate texts casually in all aspects of their self-expression.

Authenticity, or Saying What You Mean

> To the successful American, the sense of his own greatness is quite unre-
> lated to the people surrounding him, and certainly he does not feel that it
> depends at all upon the community of his origin. The dream of the ambi-
> tious person is to have the world at his feet, not at his side.
> —FRANCIS L. K. HSU, *Americans and Chinese*

Authenticity is a matter of genuineness, a hallmark of the unalienated original self. In his brilliant book *Sincerity and Authenticity,* literary critic Lionel Trilling identifies the ethos of authenticity, of individual impulses that are expressed freely and spontaneously without concern for pro-priety or others' reception. This value is associated with the 1960s—the generation to which many of today's college faculty belong—and the re-jection of convention. It abounds in such mid-twentieth-century literary classics as *The Catcher in the Rye,* with its disparagement of "phoni-ness"; *Zen and the Art of Motorcycle Maintenance,* with its search for "quality"; or *On the Road,* with its rejection of conformity and its cel-ebration of spontaneity. (Interestingly, the central characters in all these books hover just above the line of mental illness.)[1] A logic of authenticity seeks a singular self, a unique individuality that does not change or yield according to circumstances. The roots of this ethos can be traced through eighteenth- and nineteenth-century art and thought, from Emerson's no-tion of self-reliance back to the roots of Protestant Christianity, in which a person's history and family become irrelevant to the notion of the soul, and all that matters is individual faith, not ritual action.[2]

The authentic self is often characterized by solitude. Groups are anathema to the authentic self, because participating in a group requires compromise, while authenticity requires consistent loyalty to one's own principles. As Freud pointed out in *Civilization and Its Discontents,* be-cause we are members of society, individuals can never attain complete happiness, for we must always compromise our desires.[3] The authentic self therefore celebrates separation of the person from society. It is dis-trustful of convention and even of success, since achieving worldly suc-cess means meeting the expectations and desires of the populace at large. Vincent van Gogh was the perfect authentic self: he had his own distinct, original style, suffered during his lifetime for his singularity, and was never commercially successful.

For authentic selves, the concepts of originality and authorship are critical. Since each self is unique, so are its words. In the celebration of authenticity that began in earnest in the eighteenth century, each text had to have a singular author. Authorship might have to be "authenticated" in order to ascertain precisely the identity of the originating individual.[4]

Authentic individuals are especially prominent among the literary and musical geniuses whose oeuvre is perceived to have bubbled up spontaneously from their souls.[5] Unlike in earlier times, their inspiration was not thought to derive from a muse or from God; their creativity came from the internal inspiration of the writer or artist herself or himself.[6] As these moments of inspiration "are increasingly credited to the writer's own genius," writes Martha Woodmansee, "they transform the writer into a unique individual uniquely responsible for a unique product."[7] Wordsworth was the quintessential author, forever emphasizing his originality and creativity. And because authors are originators, they own rights to their work.[8] Johann Gottfried von Herder's view, which guided this idea of authenticity, was that "one ought to be able to regard each book as the imprint of a living human soul."[9] Thus it is not just possible but essential to trace the book back to its originating soul.

Not only is the self uniquely connected to its products, but it must be whole and undivided in all things. In psychology and psychoanalysis, a "divided self" has been regarded as unhealthy, even dangerous. Relying on philosophers' ideas of bad faith (Sartre) and alienation (Marx), in the 1960s R. D. Laing explained schizophrenia as stemming from the social compulsion to divide the self and create a false self.[10] According to his views (prevalent several decades ago, though currently marginal in the psychiatric community, which is now more interested in locating a biological cause of and pharmaceutical cure for mental disorders), a healthy person is one with a firm sense of ontological security, "a sense of his integral selfhood and personal identity, of the permanency of things,... of the substantiality of others."[11]

Performance, or Doing the Done Thing

Since the 1980s a new ethos has been arising, associated with a concern for achieving set goals and constant consideration of observers' reactions.

It is this ethos, which I call the "performance self," that I find operating in many contemporary students.[12] By examining it we can more easily understand student behavior, including plagiarism.

"Performance" refers to young people's emphasis on goals and outward behavior, a meaning I draw from ordinary usage, industry and business, and anthropology and other human sciences.[13] In literary, cultural, and queer studies a kindred term, "performativity," points out that social categories are enacted in behavior rather than following from preexisting, abstract realities. "Performance selves" focus on knowing what the expectations are in particular contexts and are adept at meeting those expectations. It is insufficient to learn a single role, or even a sequence of different roles along one's lifespan, because contexts may vary from moment to moment. This ethos is often an anxious one, for the performance self must constantly worry about the judgments of others, must constantly wonder if a given set of actions is the most effective, or is even appreciated, and what the consequences will be of her or his actions.

In terms akin to postmodern understandings of literature and science, the performance self does not regard itself as possessing the sole truth but rather sees itself existing in and with multiple truths, multiple roles, multiple purposes. The performance self is exemplified by an artist such as Madonna, who changes her style and appearance with great frequency. When asked whether they would dye their gray hair when they got older, many students said they hoped they would not but probably would. Whereas an authentic self might regard aging as the natural condition of life and accept the accompanying changes in appearance as inevitable and genuine, a performance self seeks to improve her appearance, no matter what the biological reality. Performance emphasizes change, embracing methods such as plastic surgery. Performance selves, male and female, are often sleek, toned, tucked, decked out in synthetic materials with no concern for practicality. What matters is the result, if only an image.

My young students find the shedding and donning of new names as comfortable as the shedding and donning of clothing and the changing of hair color. Screen names may provide practice for this sense of ease. The portability of so much technology—cell phones, Web addresses, e-mail providers—may serve as an analogue for the desirability of personal flexibility and movement. If the authentic self wishes to find *the* place in which to feel at home, the performance self wishes to feel at home in *all* places, as long as there is a way to connect to everyone else. Performance selves enjoy success; it certifies their ability to assess circumstances and to adapt accordingly. The performance self considers material success the measure of worth, unlike the authentic self, whose worth is measured only by internal criteria.

These two selves—authentic and performance—are models, ideal types. Both may exist in the same society or may alternate within the same individual. But understanding the surge in celebration of performance, especially in popular culture, helps explain the disparate views of academic integrity between faculty and their students. Authentic selves must speak for themselves; performance selves can allow others to speak for or through them. Of course, not all students are defined by the performance self, any more than all faculty are defined by the authentic self. One pre-med student, Sawyer Jackson, who had a very strong work ethic, dismissed "pop culture…[because it] pushes people away from [integrity],…not so much conformity, but more…putting up a fake exterior…just so that you can be more socially acceptable." Nevertheless, the performance self is prevalent and widespread among today's college students, and it explains among other things the casual donning of words that is the essence of plagiarism.

Being Connected in the Twenty-first Century

> I am my own experiment. I am my own work of art.
> —MADONNA

Performance selves are not solitary or unitary. Their values lie in changing and sharing. Integrity may be important, but it is the integrity that is gained from the respect of others in society rather than from a sense of wholeness.

According to specialists in human development, adolescents crave belonging. One of their major tasks in this view (for instance, that of Arthur Chickering) is to move through autonomy toward interdependence.[14] This is accomplished in part through a good deal of interaction with their peers, while at the same time paying close attention to increasing their self-understanding.

The tendency toward joining that is typical of the performance self is very evident among college students, though whether this is a new phenomenon or not is an open question. Helen Lefkowitz Horowitz's history of college life shows that fitting into one group or another has been a concern on college campuses for decades, even centuries. The virtues of joining and belonging, however, are much more emphasized now than in the 1960s and 1970s, when there was at least a prominent discourse of individuality and individualism.[15]

Although some people claim that students have become isolated and lonely, especially as a result of new technologies, I believe that there is greater interaction today than in the past, though some of this interaction is mediated by technology. The collective dimension of the performance self is evident in the ways students listen to music (often sharing songs with two ear buds from a single iPod) or watch movies (in groups while talking) or use instant messaging and social networking technology.[16] These sociotechnological innovations provide links that mirror and reinforce the focus on sharing and fitting in and socializing that has been bred into contemporary students since childhood.

At Saint U. the collective instinct is sustained and supported in a number of ways. All first-year students live on campus, with rare exceptions, and are randomly assigned to residence halls. Athletes live among fellow students, with no special residence facilities. There are no fraternities or sororities, though several of the dorms have taken on some of the behavior of fraternities, with certain risky hazing activities and so forth. First-year students receive their orientation in an intensive three-day session, during which they play group games and are brought into the Saint U. culture. Most courses for first-year students are designed to fulfill the school's extensive requirements.

Football, which is notorious for creating rituals of sociality (Durkheimian "effervescence"), fostering ties to the collective, and embodying the organizational structure of society, has the function of cementing students' loyalty to the institution.[17] Virtually all students attend every home game, at least their first year; pep rallies and other celebrations preceding the games are very well attended. A number of what the students call "traditions" are incorporated into the games, such as standing for the duration of the game, performing a number of "pushups" in the air corresponding to the score of the game, throwing marshmallows at the crowd (an activity now not only deemed "illegal" but actually prosecuted), and the tailgating and drinking that accompany games.[18]

Since college students of the new millennium have been extolled for their involvement and activity in school, sports, and organized religion, it is understood that alongside celebrations of individuality and independence there is powerful pressure to participate in groups.[19] Bill Wasik wrote in *Harper's* magazine about "deindividuation," or the pressure to lose one's individuality and become part of a group.[20] Wasik originated "flash mobs" in 2003, sudden but fleeting appearances of large numbers of people, organized through e-mail or cell phone notification and instructed to perform a gratuitous or absurd action. A group of hundreds or even thousands of people, mostly in their twenties and thirties, would gather briefly, perform as directed, then disperse. Although this phenomenon had only a brief faddish moment of popularity, Wasik explains its success as stemming from the "joining urge" and claims that it especially characterizes modern-day New York hipsters. He connects the phenomenon with the notorious studies of social psychologist Stanley Milgram, who demonstrated in the 1950s that, to please authority figures, subjects were willing to administer apparently fatal shocks to an unseen victim. (This study appeared just after revelations about the Holocaust, when people were asking how it was possible that ordinary Germans and Poles could have done such terrible things.) From this perspective, humans tend to seek groups within which to submerge their individual identity. Wasik especially enjoys pointing out the irony of the hipsters' conventionality and unanimity as they advertised their supposedly independent avant-garde tastes.

When we asked students to describe themselves, many volunteered that they were extroverts, though some—a smaller number—called themselves introverts. When we asked how they spend their time—alone or with others—a majority said that they are often with people but also enjoy solitude. (The typical assessment of Americans is that 60 to 70 percent of us consider ourselves extroverts.)[21]

The experience of sharing—whether while doing homework, or listening to music on their iPods with one ear bud connected to a friend, or talking on a cell phone, or engaging in multiple instant messaging conversations at once—has become the norm, at least in many contexts in which contemporary students find themselves. Even on AIM, one person has access to her buddies' buddies. Boundaries are porous, and pleasurably so. Nobody wants to be seen as a loner. "Loners" are dangerous people, like Seung-hui Cho, who killed thirty-two students and faculty at Virginia Tech in 2007: friendless, bitter, angry, and violent, plotting destruction against others. A relationship with anyone guarantees at least some resonance with other humans.

Diana explained about the pressures at Saint U. to remain socially connected at all times:

> It's always "Who are you going out with, do you wanna go out tonight, where are you going, what's going on?" So I think that puts a lot of pressure on you if you want to say, "Oh, I'm just gonna go to [the] mall by myself" or "I'm just gonna go to dinner," kind of have an alone night. But at the same time,...if you do decide to do that, people aren't necessarily judging you, so it's not a problem. But I would say [Saint U.] is a very social place, and people here tend to be very people-oriented, and by that very nature there is some sort of pressure to interact with other people.

The Collaboration Ethic

Given the pressure to be with others, it is not surprising that many students work near other people. Group studying is popular; libraries have group study rooms. Students often study in noisy settings, such as the student center, where huge TV screens blare programs (often sports) continually. Some students did tell us that they preferred silence, or classical music, but their apologetic explanations reinforce the impression that working around others is the norm. At some colleges—for instance, Carleton and Macalester—different floors of the library are designated by degrees of silence; the floors farthest from the entrance are entirely tomblike. One tour guide shuddered at the thought of having to sit in silence and study.

The preference for working with and around others, so natural a part of campus life today, is a fairly recent phenomenon. Not until the 1980s did students commonly begin to do group projects and presentations. One impetus behind the change was research on learning which showed that the kind of active mastery gained in group work was more lasting than knowledge gained passively. Another was the democratization and anti-elitism of post-1960s American education, including a backlash against the lecture system, which had been introduced in the late nineteenth century as colleges became universities.[22]

Numerous studies have demonstrated the benefits of teamwork, cooperative learning, and problem-based education.[23] Among the virtues of group learning is that it better mimics "real life" than does individually based learning: it is more effective in conveying knowledge; it enhances both written and oral communication skills; it increases students' "metacognitive awareness" (that is, students think about what they are doing rather than just doing it); it enhances motivation; and it teaches the principle that knowledge is jointly shared and constructed rather than the property of authorities.[24] Although group work originated in business and engineering classes, it has become widespread throughout higher education.[25]

From the students' perspective, group projects may be livelier than independent projects, though they also present the challenge of scheduling meetings: some groups in my classes haven't been able to meet until 10:00 P.M., or even midnight. Team projects also carry the risk of a student's receiving a lower grade than she might earn working alone, as the average for the group is awarded to everyone. Another typical problem is that some members slack off and fail to do their share.

Ward is an electrical engineering major. During his first year of college he participated in group projects. "I like to work in groups," he said, "but I like to do the pre-work on my own, to try to learn it by myself and then figure out what questions I have, try to go through the problems on my own and find out what I stumble over, and then find a group to see if they found it any different." He claimed that he generally found it beneficial, despite the occasional slacker on the team: "I've met people that I don't even know [if] they're up for going over homework problems and stuff."

By contrast, Sawyer Jackson, a Vietnamese Canadian pre-med and psychology student, was not convinced of the value of working in groups:

Interviewer: What are your thoughts on collaborative learning?

Sawyer: …I think it's inefficient to an extent, and eventually it could create problems because you learn [the material] as a group

> but...you're not tested as a group,...so everyone's gonna learn at [a] different level, at a different pace, so,...people can only get so much out of [a] group.

Sawyer got the most out of big projects, such as "huge lab reports," because they require examining data, but didn't get as much out of writing papers, which involve interpretation. His purpose in learning was primarily to do well on tests. And since testing remains individual, he did not see the point in learning as a group.

Studying with others may promote self-consciousness. The awareness of others' gaze is a prominent aspect of contemporary life in a voluntary panopticon. Students feel the need to perform before others at all times, which accounts in part for the burst of blogs and social networking applications, in which people present a constantly groomed version of themselves to the entire world.[26] The proliferation of electronic communication also makes other people continually available, only a button and a screen away.

Collaboration without a Trace: Wikipedia and the Lack of Author(ity)

One of the new visions of self and text that are being worked out in the global village is the collective authorship made possible by the interactive Web sites known as wikis. Wikipedia is one technological innovation that takes to its logical conclusion the general unconcern among the young about tracing individual contributions to a written product. This is regarded with great consternation by educational authorities, guided by their model of the authentic self.

Wikipedia, the collectively written on-line encyclopedia, is now the primary source for students and others on a huge number of informational topics. Begun by Jimmie Wales in 2001 using as its foundation encyclopedias no longer governed by copyright,[27] Wikipedia quickly caught fire; as of April 11, 2007, Wikipedia contained 1,746,944 articles in English and over 5,300,000 articles in more than one hundred languages. (Within a month, on May 9, there were 1,776,078 articles in English—an increase of almost 30,000.) It aims to contribute to the building of the "creative commons," much as open source software has.

Despite some claims about the impressive accuracy of Wikipedia (the preeminent scientific journal *Nature* did an investigation into Wikipedia, comparing entries on it with similar entries in *Encyclopedia Britannica* and found Wikipedia's record more error-free, at least for scientific topics), it provokes panic.[28] Articles have been written protesting it, lamenting it, deploring it, ridiculing it, celebrating it.[29] Middlebury College has banned its use in student papers.[30] Wikipedia has produced imitators and political competitors: Conservapedia is a conservative Christian alternative to what it claims is the liberal bias of Wikipedia.[31] Students consult it as a matter of course. Linguist Geoffrey Nunberg admits that he and other scholars do as well, but with reservations and ironic casualness, distancing themselves from genuine involvement, the way they read popular magazines in doctors' offices, "for research."[32]

One of the preeminent features of Wikipedia is its acceptance of all emendations (pending further emendations by others), further denoting that individual authorship is not critical; it is a collective, anonymous product, and it is never finished. It is evaluated over time by more eyes and changed by more hands, only some of whom are authorities or experts.

If faculty are attempting to force students to attend to individual authorship while a non-authorized work is at the top of most Google searches, this constitutes another mismatch between authentic and performance selves, between the generation of teachers and administrators and that of today's college students. The prohibition on plagiarism—the unacknowledged use of material by a named author—makes no sense in a context in which unnamed series of people offer their work free of credit, free of charge, free of attribution.

Adapting to Circumstances

It is not only the constant sharing and interconnectivity that characterize the performance self. The performance self is also not unitary in the sense of having a single appearance and personal style. Whereas the authentic self, preeminently the "genius" model of the artist/author, is consistent and singular, the performance self is variable and multiple. This multiplicity may be a means to accomplish results, according to each situation, or it may be used for fun and experimentation.

With parents, teachers, strangers, and others in positions of authority, students report that they have to alter their behavior to fit expectations— not swearing, appearing responsible, seeming friendly and cheerful—to such an extent that some students said they feel completely themselves only with their closest friends. Many appear troubled by the sense that they must always be on their game, alert to different circumstances. None seem to resist, though, to declare, "I will just be myself, no matter what." All are quite aware of and articulate about the kinds of changes they are expected to make, whether in speech or body language or clothing. Tattoos, for instance, are seen as something that has to be concealed in certain contexts but as problematic if visible at all times. A premium seems to be placed on the need for malleability. It is very common for students to acknowledge their own mutability, as did Monica:

> Well...I'm so different around different people and in different situations. I guess that's normal, but...sometimes I'm just really quiet. I guess, in class, usually, I'm quiet,...and in...big groups of people, but...one-on-one with someone, I'm really chatty, 'cause I just like to talk, and it's pretty much my favorite thing to do ever, is talk.

Like Monica, Edward differentiated between his outgoing nature with people he knew well and his shyness around new people. He described his widely varying groups of friends, from people he lived with to people he knew from his summer job to classmates. Confident and with a clear sense of his identity, he nonetheless felt it important to portray different versions of himself in different contexts. As a mature college student, a senior, he said that he was usually free to be his "own person," though he spoke of acting "a lot more crazy" when he was with his close friends in the dorm, with "our own sense of humor,...inside jokes and different things we talk about." When the interviewer asked if either of these personas was an act, Edward answered:

> An act? Not particularly,...not really....Part of it too is just...the comfortability level....When I first meet people I'm more shy and I'm more reserved, but...I'm still very nice and confident and everything like that, but...only through...being really comfortable will I...really start to open up, or...joke around...and be really candid with people....Not that...that's an act, it's just kind of me; that's just how I am in certain

situations, I guess. But...with my friends in the dorms...I've lived with them for three years now, and...we all have the same type of humor, and we all...can joke around with each other a lot.

Asked if he ever has to act differently from the way he normally acts in order to be accepted, Edward assented readily. He gave the example of a trip with students he knew only from class:

Edward: You don't wanna portray...yourself being...more of a nerd,...but you don't wanna be...too cool and...really careless about...the class or whatever, you know what I mean?...

Interviewer: You can't be too nerdy, but you can't be—

Edward: Yeah,...too cool....For me...there's a good balance for...just being able to...get along with all the kids...and not trying to...really offend anybody or say anything too outrageous or anything like that, and...again there'd be...comfortability factors.... I think just as human beings you always want to fit into...whatever group you're in,...but...personally...I would rather care less what people thought of me....I will be...my own person,...most of the time,...unless I'm in...a really uncomfortable situation and I really...wanna get along with somebody because,...if I'm not, then maybe it'll be...a huge disadvantage for me.

Although Edward couldn't think of a situation in which he would act completely differently, for a graduate school interview he would certainly consider how he comes across:

Well,...I would definitely be more...upbeat and try to...portray...an image that I'm very confident, that I'm very...well-spoken and things like that....But I also feel...that I am that way most of the time....I'm never really nervous about going into an interview, I'm not...worrying about...what are they gonna ask me....I feel...I'll be ready for whatever they're gonna...ask me or whatever they demand of me, I guess,...but...it's in the back of your mind that you wanna look good, you wanna say...the right things, you don't wanna screw up or anything like that.

Edward would not alter himself for the sake of a grade, though he would do it to "fit in." He regards this as a natural and inevitable choice. He prefers to be "his own person" unless he is especially uncomfortable and has to get along with people. He believes that everybody wants to fit in.

Diana wished that she were more like her mother and younger brother, but admitted that she was not strong enough to assert a consistent personality:

Interviewer: Do you feel like you change depending on the situation?

Diana: Umm, yes.... If I'm surrounded by certain people, I'd say I change in that effect that I may say things different than if I'm surrounded by a different group of people.... Because... I don't want to be judged, so I would say that has a huge impact on the way I act and, that's not always how I want to be, but there's room for improvements, I hope.

Interviewer: Do you think it's okay to act differently in different contexts? Like, say, in class versus... with your friends or with your family?

Diana: I would say generally, no, I would say it's important to keep whoever you are. You shouldn't be afraid to be that person in whatever context you're in, or... if you're in a class that's one-sided and you happen to be that way, but then you go outside of class and tell people something different, that's a falsity in your character, and you obviously haven't figured out the person you want to be if you can't stick to that, so I would say that's a thing that needs to be worked on. But when you finally reach that success, it will matter who you've figured out who you want to be, and it shouldn't be something that changes from group to group.

Interviewer: Do you find that you talk differently when you're talking to a teacher versus a priest versus a friend?

Diana: I would say yes,... because... a teacher has an education background, whereas a priest has a religious background, and your friends tend to be, will stick with you through thick and thin,... no matter what you say, or what you've been through, whereas if you try to tell a priest something you're struggling with,... not that they ever have made me feel this way, but I would worry more about a priest judging me. And then a teacher, well, you just don't want them learning anything about your personal life. Because they're the person educating you. [As for] friends..., I feel that they're the group that I can tell them whatever, and no matter what, I don't feel like they'll judge me or make me feel that I made a wrong... decision even if they don't agree with it.

Diana believes it is best to remain constant, but like Edward, she accepts that people change their behavior in different settings for the sake of comfort. "I just don't feel that comfortable in a classroom," she says, "whereas in a [dorm] room—and just the atmosphere around you—you can feel much more comfortable. Or...in a restaurant that even isn't very comfortable because you have people sitting behind you or to your side." Diana is clearly self-conscious around people she knows only slightly and feels obliged to change to suit their expectations.

Julia similarly acknowledges that she molds her behavior depending on the situation, despite regarding consistency as the essence of integrity. Like Edward and Diana, she explains this choice as a matter of comfort and of "what works best," acknowledging that there are automatic advantages to certain kinds of behavior. Above all, "awkwardness" is to be avoided:

> *Interviewer:* Do you find that you...act the same way in different contexts? Or do you act differently?
>
> *Julia:* Oh, definitely don't act the same. Definitely act different. I would say I probably act a little differently with each person that I encounter. I sort of take cues from the way people are acting, and I guess sort of try and adjust to what I feel would make them most comfortable. So, yeah. Definitely in class versus other situations, I think I would feel like I act differently.
>
> *Interviewer:* Is that...okay with you? Do you think that that's a good thing?...
>
> *Julia:* Well, sometimes I think about it, and it bothers me [laughs]. Because I think, why would I do this in [one] situation but I just can't do it in another situation? It kind of bothers me. But overall I think it's what works best. Because that's what is the most comfortable, overall....
>
> *Interviewer:* What about it bothers you?
>
> *Julia:* I don't know. I guess that everyone likes to think of themselves as being consistent,...being the same person across situations. And then if in one situation you don't do something...you might've done another time, I feel like...[you] start to question that self....Whether it's a healthy or good thing for you, personally, is a different thing, but definitely a good social thing....It makes interactions very smooth and...more comfortable.

When the interviewer asks if this lack of consistency shows a lack of integrity, Julia rejects this suggestion:

> *Julia:* I don't honestly think about it in terms of integrity that much. Because if a teacher asks me how I do on something, I feel like I'm automatically going to put a more positive spin on it [laughs]. Because...there are just advantages to presenting yourself in a certain way to a teacher versus your friends. And, maybe...in that situation it would show a kind of a lack of integrity, but almost a necessary one....
>
> *Interviewer:* That's a really interesting idea. A necessary lack of integrity....What do you mean exactly by that?
>
> *Julia:* [sighs]...All the time, I'll say things that...aren't quite true, you know? [sighs]...It's hard to explain. But I think everyone would know that feeling...[sighs]. If my professor...asked me how an interview went, heh, for example, and I say, "Oh, I think it went really well, I think I was really prepared,"...that's kind of what I want to present to that person. And...maybe I was really prepared,...but maybe I wasn't quite as confident as I came across, but maybe I just want my professor to see me in the most positive way possible. Whereas if a friend asked me how it went,...I may say, "Oh gosh, I stayed up all night, and I was obsessing about it, and I thought I was going to fail, but then, you know, it turned out okay."...In both senses the result is okay, but it's definitely more positive to the professor. But I feel like it would make things way too uncomfortable....My professor might not put in a good word for me if I seem like I'm not together. But I think it would just be very uncomfortable if...in a professional relationship I would say, "Oh, well, you know, Professor So-and-so, hah, I was really freaked out, and I stayed up all night and blah, blah." I think the professor would be like, "Oh, okay," and it would be really awkward [laughs]. So, it seems like in order for things not to be awkward, and...move smoothly, you kind of have to...fudge on the truth sometimes.

Julia articulates the authentic self's notion of consistency as part of her goals yet acknowledges that she is different with each person she encounters. She is also aware that she chooses to portray herself in ways that confer benefits, such as demonstrating her confidence to professors who may be in a position to write letters of recommendation in the future. She proffers "what works" and "advantages" as explanations for her varying presentation of self and of the truth.

While many students celebrate, or at least accept, the common trait of changing the self, some, including Rachel, are put off by it—especially in others:

> I have a friend who acts very differently in...different situations....She lived with us freshman year, so [with] the group of people...that she met freshman year like me and...my close group of friends, she's...pretty open and stuff. But when she goes out to, say, a bar or something, or is around guys especially, she's very different and...very flirtatious, or even [with] another group of friends who are...older than we are, like a year older, she kind of...becomes almost a different person....She becomes who she thinks they want to hang out with....It's very interesting....She tries to be...really cool and will say things that are the exact opposite of what she said to us. I was actually out at a bar with her the other night [laughter]....It was...awkward because she...became this completely different person, and it's frustrating to see that....It's frustrating because...it's like she becomes a person I don't really like to hang out with, and if she were that person, I don't think I would have necessarily been friends with her.

Typically, Rachel's criticisms of her friend's malleability are mild. It is extremely rare for students to condemn other students or faculty as "wrong" or "bad." Instead they use psychological jargon, describing behavior as "awkward" or "frustrating," "confusing" or "uncomfortable." Perhaps this is a holdover from their growing up at a time when the prevailing child-rearing practice was to teach them to use "I-messages" rather than "you-messages" in a confrontation: "I felt scared when you threatened me" instead of "Don't threaten me!" or "I'm confused about the assignment" instead of "You didn't explain the assignment clearly."[33] Edward and Julia, too, spoke of "comfort" as a desirable—even explanatory—goal.

Of course, different situations call for differences in behavior and demeanor, for professors as much as for students. But the multiplicity of the performance self is something larger and more fundamental than a response to ordinary social cues, and it is occurring on an unprecedented diversity of stages.

A Collection of Selves On- and Off-Line

Confirming Erik Erikson's observation that one of the tasks of adolescence is to determine one's individual identity,[34] in the 1960s many adolescents believed that their goal was to "find themselves," meaning the one true nature of their self. This self was to be known, acted upon, and fixed once and for all. Now there is much broader acceptance of the notion of self as multiple rather than singular. Young people may have a whole set of selves, which they "find" and lose at will.

The epitome of performing different versions of the self is visible in the on-line world of fantasy gaming, such as Dungeons and Dragons, a pseudo-Renaissance fantasy world. Here the player invents a persona and attempts to portray, to perform, a self through self-description (*I am a twenty-four-year-old black woman, a physician,* and so on), and through utterances and actions plausible for such a character.

Sherry Turkle writes of such "multi-user domains" (MUDs) and the "second self" that users create.[35] She believes that "'our lives on the screen' facilitate an increased fluidity of identity play." Selves and identities are both fluid and multiple: "On the Internet. . . . one can be many and usually is. If traditionally, identity implied oneness, life on today's computer screens implies multiplicity, heterogeneity, and fragmentation."[36] Since 1989 SimCity and other simulations create virtual worlds. Beginning in 2003 a game called Second Life set up a virtual world with virtual money and points. According to Turkle, players explicitly revel in contrasts between these "second" selves and lives and "RL," Real Life.[37] In April 2007 more than 5.6 million people were participating in Second Life.

All such activities employ "avatars," a term borrowed from Hinduism, in which it refers to gods who appear in multiple forms. In selecting the appropriate avatar, usually represented by an icon, a computer user must decide which aspect of the self to reveal, or which aspect of a self to simulate.[38]

Turkle describes how "on [the Internet], people are able to build a self by cycling through many selves."[39] She shows how unusual this is in human history; in the past, as recently as the twentieth century, the commonly invoked metaphor for identity was "forged," as if by a blacksmith.[40] People whose personalities were "split," like Dr. Jekyll and Mr. Hyde, were considered monstrous.

Now, in postmodern times, multiple identities are no longer so much at the margins of things. Many more people experience identity as a set of roles that can be mixed and matched, whose diverse demands need to be negotiated.... The Internet has become a significant social laboratory for experimenting with the constructions and reconstructions of self that characterize postmodern life. In its virtual reality we self-fashion and self-create. What kinds of personae do we make? What relation do these have to what we have traditionally thought of as the "whole" person? Are they experienced as an expanded self or as separate from the self? Do our real-life selves learn lessons from our virtual personae? Are these virtual personae fragments of a coherent real-life personality?[41]

In her exploration of role-playing games like Dungeons and Dragons and social MUDs like Sim games, Turkle wonders about the distinction between a constructed persona and a real self and notes periodic slippage between them. People try on different characters in order to figure out how best to behave in the real world. For many, as one player told Turkle, "you are what you pretend to be... you are what you play."[42]

Selves and identities are now created from a collage of other people, places, and images. If in the past a stable and integrated identity was regarded as the basis of mental health, in recent years a fluid, flexible self is seen as more responsive and more socially desirable. The game-playing aspect of the contemporary world, at least as it has become available to educated middle-class Americans with access to computers, is just the most striking example of the performance self, with its malleability and changeableness.

This self, made out of various readily available components, is as unconcerned about strict attribution of authorship as it is about strictly tracing an unchanging identity. The value of citation stems from the authentic self's focus on an individual's singularity: you give credit to the author, the unique person, because the book is "the imprint of a living human soul." But how can the performance self see the point of tracing the products of a unique self when it doesn't believe in the unique self?

Getting Results: Writing for Whom?

If many students feel compelled to modify their self-presentation in social contexts, do they feel the same way when expressing themselves in writing? Specifically, we asked students if they would be willing to write something they didn't believe in or agree with just because their professor expected it. An authentic self would insist on writing what she or he believed, no matter what the consequences. We found that the students' decision, however, would depend on the stakes: if it meant the difference between a grade of A or B, they might not do it, but if it meant the difference between an A and an F, then there was no question. Failure for these students is not an option; any means necessary to avoid it is acceptable. Fiona was very explicit about this:

Fiona: There have been times where I have taken classes where the professor is just not interested in what you believe about the...subject and would really just like you to regurgitate what they believe and what they have been teaching you, and I think that that's unfortunate....I don't think that's a great way to teach,...I don't think people remember as much, I don't think they get as much out of it, and I don't think they grow as much.

Interviewer: What do you do in that circumstance?

Fiona: Um [chuckles], well, it was my...philosophy class, sophomore year....I didn't really care too much about philosophy, and didn't really like my professor, so I basically just wrote essays that weren't necessarily what I believed and told him...what he wanted to hear 'cause it got the grade [chuckles], and I thought that was unfortunate because there were a few times where...I wish I had gotten to say what I really thought, or, like the first essay....I wrote it from what I thought, and he just completely ripped it apart, and...I thought it was obnoxious, actually, because it's philosophy. There's a lot where you can just debate till the end of time, and people have [laughs],...and so there is no right answer, and...whether or not my argument was sound or not, he just rejected it because...it wasn't the one he had presented in class.

Interviewer: ...Do you think that it's okay to write something you don't believe just because you know...that you'll get a better grade?

Fiona: ...[chuckles] I don't know whether I can say it's right or not....The only word that I can use for it is that it's *unfortunate,* because I think it stifles the learning of concepts and thinking in...[the] development of thought....

Interviewer: ...What do you think about the idea of going along to get along?

Fiona: ...I think that in...limited...interactions, I guess that's acceptable....If you don't really care...and it's probably gonna be a limited interaction, I don't see any harm in it. I also don't see that type of interaction—say it's between two people—blossoming into friendship, because if the only reason you're saying things is to appease the person, and...you don't believe it,...it's eventually gonna come out, and...if it's that much of a deal breaker, you're not gonna be happy with the outcome, so you might as well just be truthful from the start.

Interviewer: ...How does that relate...to the instance where you knew your teacher just wanted to do one thing, and even though you believed something else, you wrote what he wanted?

Fiona: ...That class was...an intro class....I'm not a philosophy major....I think, really, his objective for the class was to get us to think certain ways about...certain things we were writing, and if that was his objective, then I think that's unfortunate, because I think that [there] could've been a lot more done in the class, but if that's the objective, then that's what I'm gonna do.

Interviewer: Mm-hmm. Do you think that it compromised your integrity at all?

Fiona: A little bit....To some extent, but nothing that I'm...gonna lose sleep over.

Writing something she did not believe was acceptable when Fiona did not really care about the class, or when she did not respect the professor, so the only thing that counted was the grade, the outcome. This was far from ideal in her experience, but she felt it a reasonable accommodation to the circumstances.

Students even justify cheating, at least in the abstract, out of "need." If education is regarded by students at elite universities as putting in a certain effort to attain the desired end—a good grade, a degree, fun—then knowing how to achieve that goal is a measure of their competence. As Rachel explained:

I wouldn't say that the ends justify the means. I think...you should stay within the law, but I can understand why a person would do the cheating thing....If people who are worried about their grades and stuff, and if they're doing really poorly in a class, I could see why they would be tempted to cheat, and I could understand why they would, because they want to do well.

...And I think that's the problem with grading people too hard, because they aren't concerned with what they know and what they can do. It's more,... "Oh my gosh. I have to get this grade."

Connecting with others and projecting—performing—a self are very absorbing projects. Such a self looks to the consequences of the action—comfort, getting along with others, pleasing professors, meeting others' expectations—as the aim of action. Since the focus of the performance self is on outcomes, anything, even cheating, might be an option if it is seen as "necessary" for achieving the desired end. Plagiarism makes sense in this context, since the self as unique and consistent originator of thoughts is not a consideration, the relationship between words and self is loose, and the self is always changing anyway.

What Is Integrity? Being True to Yourself? Achieving Goals? Respecting Others?

The notion of integrity is related to the idea of self (for a discussion of academic integrity, see chapter 5). One dictionary provides three different meanings of the term: "(1) firm adherence to a code of especially moral or artistic values: incorruptibility; (2) an unimpaired condition: soundness; (3) the quality or state of being complete or undivided: completeness."[43] A similar term, "integral," has to do with being entire, complete, whole. These views of integrity accord well with the model of authentic selfhood.

An authentic self might agree that integrity means the absence of division, wholeness. As Parker Palmer writes: "The divided life, at bottom, is not a failure of ethics; it is a failure of human wholeness....Living integral lives is daunting. We must achieve a complex integration that spans the contradictions between inner and outer reality, that supports both personal integrity and the common good." Examples of a divided life include when "we refuse to invest ourselves in our work, diminishing its quality and distancing ourselves from those it is meant to serve" (as when students only go through the motions in completing class assignments);

or when "we conceal our true identities for fear of being criticized, shunned, or attacked" (as when Edward didn't wish to appear too nerdy or too cool); or "we hide our beliefs from those who disagree with us to avoid conflict, challenge, and change" (as when Fiona wrote a paper that accorded with her professor's viewpoints, not her own). Palmer's aim is to achieve inward and outward unity. When we can answer "yes" to the question "Is this person the same on the inside as he or she seems to be on the outside?" then the person is said to possess integrity.[44]

A performance self sees things differently. When asked about integrity, Saint U. students were eager to discuss it, having taken (required) philosophy classes and being surrounded by the discourse of morality and religion. Yet most of their responses revealed numerous contradictions as they mulled over the abstract meaning of integrity and then recalled situations in which compromise was necessary. (In this these students are no more contradictory than students elsewhere, or for that matter than non-students.)

Their attempts to explain integrity yielded the same few definitions: "acting according to your own views," "being honest." For some it meant something like generalized good behavior. Most connected integrity explicitly to ways of treating others—something not reflected in the dictionary definition—and even how others regard them. They often provided examples of behavior that they believed illustrated integrity.

Julia, who had been talking about how much she changed in various circumstances, gave a classic definition:

> *Julia:* I think ultimately...when we say that somebody showed a lack of integrity we just mean that they were inconsistent somehow....Because they say they believed one thing but they did another thing. So it's not so much that they violated some absolute of what's integrity and what's not; it's just that...they were hypocritical.
>
> *Interviewer:* ...How do you exhibit your integrity?
>
> *Julia:* ...Well [sighs], I'd say it's a very conscious thing. I have to think about it, and make sure that I'm acting with integrity because...it's really easy to not [laughs], 'cause...it's more comfortable sometimes. But I would say that I try and show it by...talking the talk and walking the walk type thing....If I say that I think something is wrong, and I know that I think something is wrong, then I'm gonna want to

make sure that I speak up about it. If I see someone doing it, or hear someone talking about it, or if I think to myself that something is important to me, or I tell someone that something's important to me, then I try and make an extra effort to...be committed to whatever that is. So I guess I try and show it by being consistent.

Another student, Alexandra, connected integrity with upright behavior in general, even at football games:

> I think integrity...someone who's honest to themselves will be true to oneself,...being loyal to your own values,...morals and values that you say you believe in, just sticking to those and...trying not to waver if at all possible from that....
>
> I think [integrity is people] being respectful of others and respectful of themselves,...presenting themselves or acting in a...manner...that shows some class....Representing yourself in a manner that you would want people...[to] think of you...and also representing yourself in the way that you want the university—if we're talking specifically about [Saint U.] students—to be perceived....I know a lot of times during football seasons, we talk a lot about class and...the student body and how we're represented or how other schools' students represent themselves by their actions....Entire student bodies can get pegged in one way or another by certain people's actions.

For Alexandra, integrity is general good conduct, including how one is viewed by others. Integrity can be a collective as well as an individual attribute. Another student, Amanda, defined integrity similarly:

> *Amanda:* I think it's respect and respectability at the same time....I think integrity has a lot to do with strength of character, yet openness to other people. You can't be totally self-righteous, 'cause too much strength of character would be self-righteous, but...I think you still have to respect other people. Having good balance with that.
>
> *Interviewer:* How do you exhibit your integrity?
>
> *Amanda:* I try to uphold respect by being a truthful person and honest but not...painfully honest, which I think is a big part of respect....It has to do with honesty and telling the truth but not...harshly, because that's not really having any respect for anybody involved....I think a lot of it has to do, in college in particular, with how you handle yourself around your friends...or...how you handle yourself in

social situations when you're out at parties, out at bars. Just talking about me personally. I think that has to do a lot with the way I express integrity because...I don't really take crap from people....I hope I'm creating respect for myself...and not just being a bitch,...but at the same time,...I look out for my friends....I like to respect other people's opinions, and I encourage it.

Integrity thus has to do with honesty (but not to the point of being "painfully honest"), with respect for oneself and for others, often including acting appropriately in social situations. Being "self-righteous," speaking too honestly, or showing too much strength of character is to be avoided. Others' opinions must be respected.

Another discussion of integrity arose in connection with what students write on college applications, a form of self-presentation, a performance, and a genre of writing. We discovered that a good number of students had shrewdly indicated interest on their applications in a relatively obscure major in order to increase their chances of admission. Reactions to this strategy were mixed. "Monkey Friend" mentioned a friend who had expressed an interest in "Jewish Studies" on a college application "'cause she knew that if she wrote that, she would have a better chance of getting into UCLA, and she actually did get into UCLA and ended up studying Jewish Studies, which is...a little ironic." Asked, "Do you think it's okay that people write things like that even though it might not be true?" she answered:

I know personally I would not do it, 'cause I think [I place]...some sort of...emphasis on being true to yourself, even on applications....You just have to question your intentions if you know for a fact you would not be happy at any other school that you were applying to and you had to do this one thing to get you in, well, maybe you'd look back and you'd be like, "Well, do I deserve to be in this school?"...I never really felt that pressure [to deceive] when I was applying, so maybe that's why I was unaware. But I guess there are people who will say, "Maybe I'm interested in this subject and maybe this will help me get in." And I think that's fine. But if you're like, "There's no way in the world I would ever study this," then that would be wrong.

In this case "Monkey Friend" rejects the idea of falsely stating an intended major mostly because it would be ineffective, in the sense that she would not end up in the right school and would be unhappy. The goal is to find a school at which to be "happy," so if lying gets someone into the wrong school, this would be wrong—that is, ineffective—as strategy. She does introduce the notion of "some sort of emphasis on being true to yourself," as an authentic self would, but moves along quickly to the issue of consequences.

Another student, Michael, explained that although he would never identify an insincere choice of major on his application, in fact he had not been fully straightforward. "I'll be honest with you," he told the interviewer. "I put 'Catholic' on my application. I'm not a baptized Catholic....My mother's Jewish and my father's Catholic, and I figured it wasn't a complete lie, but it couldn't hurt at the same time."

Though these students, who chose to attend a Catholic university, had unformulated but heartfelt guidelines about honesty, the boundary between lying and truth telling was not firm. This was especially true of their attempts to achieve their goals.

Greg, a senior from Pittsburgh on his way to medical school, saw integrity as striking a balance between one's own needs and the needs of others. While it is "gracious," he said, to temper what you say in certain people's presence, "I don't think you should change your whole demeanor, your whole attitude to appease them." Acting differently or holding back certain viewpoints according to the situation detracts from a person's integrity "a little bit," he acknowledged, "because it's not who you truly are." Greg defines integrity as "doing or saying, acting...what you believe or say[ing] what you feel because you feel that way. Not worrying about what anyone else...how you think they're gonna react, what you think their viewpoint is...saying honestly and truthfully...how you feel and you don't care at all what the response is." He exhibits integrity

through many channels...related to academics...doing my own work, not cheating on tests...abiding by the honor code here. In regards to social relationships,...[integrity means] trying to be as honest as possible with people even though I'm not always,...because I don't wanna hurt people's feelings or make them think less of me, [so] I hold things back, and so that's how I act with integrity even though I'm not always truthful; I try to weigh the benefits and burdens in my mind of what would be the best outcome of telling or doing something for somebody.

Students are conscious of competing values in their lives, from consideration of others' feelings to achieving social comfort to attaining academic success. While few students would sanction genuine crimes, they gauge their behavior against the probable outcomes of various acts.

Integrity for Greg is measured by consequences; for him, the internal impetus for behavior is less significant than the context in which it will be performed. Reluctantly, he admitted that he would write something untrue on his college application if it helped level the playing field:

> Personally I would do it because...the environment definitely influences your decisions, and so since other people manipulate the system,...if you...failed to adapt to that, then you would be the odd man out.... All the other people are doing it, and...you know they're blatantly choosing this major to get into the school while as soon as they enroll they're gonna...pick a different major.... I don't think it's a[n] honest thing to do, but I'd do it. Absolutely. Because...I think you have to look at the larger perspective for you personally.... Say you really wanted to come to this school and it was between you [honestly] picking a major and getting in....I would...pick a different major just so you could get in, so you could achieve your goal,...whatever it may be. You might see this university as...the ideal place for you to achieve your goal and so,...yeah, I don't agree with it, but I would do it.

Similarly, Greg would not cheat on tests, but mainly because it is too easy to get caught. He sees society as increasingly corrupt, and unyielding honesty as too naïve in such a context:

> With the state of...academics where it is now, where...so much of an emphasis is placed on just GPA, test scores, things of that nature, I think you have to...somewhat adapt to that environment or else you're gonna be left behind. Yeah you're gonna be that honest guy,...you didn't do as well but, hey, you're very honorable. Hey, that's great, good for you. But...is it gonna...help you get to the point where you wanna be with your life?...You're gonna have to make some tough decisions in your life. You know, have...moral dilemmas and you're gonna have to be able [to] answer them in a way that benefits and burdens...your decisions.

He explicitly sees the problem as one of weighing alternatives:

> There'll be times when difficult decisions are to be made, whether to sac-
> rifice your principles, your morals, to achieve...certain goals, whether
> it be...sales or...making a profit in a company or satisfying...a cus-
> tomer or a boss or something like that. And so...I think...weighing
> the goals and outcomes...is on the same scale as...your moral integ-
> rity, and I don't think you could take away or put too much emphasis
> on one or the other. Rather you have to...make small changes so as
> not to...affect the overall balance of...your moral integrity and your
> personal beliefs and other things.

These students might be considered realistic about the many forces
that must be put in the balance as they interact in the world with others, a world they see as competitive and peopled with others unfairly
advantaged by improper behavior. The question of principles and morals versus goals, one's own values versus others' views and opinions, is
not simple, and students generally avoid uttering platitudes about one
at the expense of the others. Cheating and plagiarism, like other forms
of immoral behavior, may be criticized yet resorted to on occasion,
depending on "need." Thus integrity, wholeness, independence, and
individuality are recognized as competing with the exigencies of a situation and the actor's desires, as well as with others' perspectives and
needs.

Plagiarism and the Performance Self: Does It Matter Where Words Originate?

As we have seen, contemporary students, who are preparing to be
contemporary adults, place a great deal of importance on collaboration
and collective action. This collaboration is, of course, forbidden in the
individual-centered educational system, which tests students as individuals,
asks them to write as individuals, and assumes that knowledge, desire,
and expression are specific to the individual.

One form of plagiarism is the sharing of written work. Many faculty
members encourage collaboration at certain stages of learning. Some
clearly specify when collaboration is permitted and when it is forbidden,

while others assume students will understand that it is prohibited unless explicitly allowed.

Students have thus absorbed mixed messages about collaboration and solitary endeavor. The solitary author for them is not necessarily the default case. Even looking at computer screens has become, in part, a social activity, as friends cluster together and watch one person type a response to a physically absent but communicatively present friend.

The performance self is more prone to cheat and plagiarize than the authentic self, given its focus on results rather than on the expression of a singular personal essence. Whose words are spoken is irrelevant; what matters is that the words fit the requirements. As long as the job gets done, what does the source matter? Despite their elders' rejection of it in formal contexts, unattributed intertextuality is a strategy that is employed consciously and frequently by what has been termed the "millennial" generation.

Of course the authentic self is an ideal type, more honored in the breach than in the observance in much of everyday life. Nevertheless, among certain professions and segments of society it remains a powerful figure, particularly in academia. Products of the twentieth century and its preoccupation with authenticity, professors and administrators still believe that ideally, original products derive from authentic beings, core selves unmediated by social demands. An authentic soul can be like no other, and its words must be entirely its own. The twenty-first-century American self is a very different being, made up of fragments of text—images, lines, plots—collected from an astonishing array of available sources. Without an understanding of a single, unchanging self, the notion of "owning" an expression or viewpoint is foreign. For the performance self, identity has to do with selection and consumption rather than with creation, with sampling rather than with composing. For a performance self, intellectual property is a quaint yet meaningless notion.[45]

Multiple selves, multiple screens, multiple platforms, multiple usernames, studying with AIM on, Facebook accessible, the cell phone at their side, and surrounded by virtual and actual friends, even when today's students perform alone, they are with others. Given such permeability of boundaries, there is a tendency to practice self-division and to separate oneself from one's utterances. For students it does not matter much whose words go into a paper, because in their experience it is impossible and unnecessary to trace anything to a singular point of origin.

Driven by competition, the marketplace, and the morality of success, students seek to write the script for their assorted activities. They need to know how to perform in biology class with Professor Cell and how to write in anthropology class with Dr. Stickler, how to swear with their soccer teammates and how to joke with their roommates. For this generation, altering according to context, playing expected roles, is acceptable, even appropriate, a way to achieve the goals of being liked, fitting in, getting on. It is done knowingly. Students can discuss this life of alteration without feeling that they are admitting to a compromise.

Sharing and sociability are valued, solitude and selfishness deplored. Feeling that others' ideas are available for their use, students live in a world where people use whatever is needed for the task at hand. No one involved in a group project would ever say, "You can't use that phrase; I invented it." Accusations of plagiarism are at odds with the positive value placed on working collectively on producing a joint product, making a team effort.

By better understanding group values and the new category of selfhood as shared intertextual performance, the academy can more effectively uphold its beleaguered standards of originality and attribution. And students must learn that if they wish to succeed, they must grasp the concept of authority and its rules so they can perform according to them. In the next chapter we look at the broader social and educational context within which this generation of students arrives and must learn to function in college.

4

Growing Up in the College Bubble

The Tasks and Temptations of Adolescence

> In a culture that emphasizes the autonomy and self-reliance of the individual, the primary problems of childhood are what some psychoanalysts call separation and individuation—indeed, childhood is chiefly preparation for the all-important event of leaving home.
> —ROBERT BELLAH ET AL., *Habits of the Heart*

WHEN students are asked what they are doing in college, their answers vary considerably, whether we question them about goals for their college experience in general or their aims for a particular activity or assignment. Life at today's universities and colleges presents young people with a challenging array of options. One thing is clear: class work no longer holds a central place among students' priorities (if it ever did). They are absorbed in a wide variety of activities, mostly centered on the business of achieving adulthood while taking advantage of their opportunities to remain children. The intellectual component of that undertaking is dwarfed, in terms of time and attention, by the immediate and more pressing concerns of social life, clubs, and other factors.

In this chapter we look at the very broadest context into which college fits—the place of adolescence in the human lifespan—and then at the day-to-day balance of what students frequently characterize as the "work hard, play hard" mandate. For students who see the academic side of things as a chore to be completed as quickly as possible, cheating is a pragmatic option with few evident shortcomings. But even those who value academics are torn by a host of distractions. College has changed since I was a student, and maybe since you were one, too.

The University and Adolescence

> Every class-stratified society has its processes for recruiting people into the different classes, and education has increasingly become a major means for this recruitment throughout the world.
> —ALICE SCHLEGEL AND HERBERT BARRY III, *Adolescence*

In many cultures late adolescents leave home for what anthropologists call a "liminal period"—a time set apart from the ordinary cycles of family and work life, removed from their original place—in order to return transformed.[1] College builds on this human tendency to initiate adolescents into the often esoteric knowledge required for adulthood. From their teachers, American college students gain complex factual, vocational, intellectual, and ethical knowledge, and from peers the knowledge of secret rites (beer pong, fake IDs), sexual initiation, traditions (football, dorm lore, preferred teachers), organizations, and other practices.

Because of the complex nature of the liminal period, several contradictory processes are going on at the same time. Children are being turned into adults; they are being taught the mores and values of the larger society so they can carry them on; they are being separated from the larger society to form bonds with "age mates" that will endure as they become adults. In the meantime, pranks, rebellion, rule breaking, defiance, and utter disregard for regulations are rampant. In college as in initiation rituals in all cultures, the initiates are in tension with the larger society. Each social segment fulfills its roles, adults as disapproving observers and enforcers or as trusted counselors, and students as the wild rebels busy remaking themselves.

So although those who observe the prevalence of plagiarism and other forms of misbehavior among contemporary students may be appalled by their cavalier attitude toward authority, norms, and learning, from a broader perspective this mismatch, this struggle, this tension is built in to the very roles that these groups play: grownups set guidelines; the young resist them.

Residential college is the province of soon-to-be but not-quite-yet adults living in a not-quite-real world. College students are at an age when people in many other eras and societies, and indeed in less advantaged segments of our own society today, would already be engaging in productive and reproductive activities.[2] Marriage in the mid-teens has been common; a "generation" used to be considered twenty years, the average span of time assumed to separate a mother and her first child.

"Adolescence," both the term and the concept, was invented by G. Stanley Hall in 1904. He, like many others of his day, had noted an increase in delinquency and unruliness, especially around sexual matters, during the teenage years; until then the recognized age categories were simply "child" (up to twenty-one) and "adult." Hall's description of adolescence now seems both familiar and strange: "Girls are far more prone to overdo; boys are persistingly lazy and idle. Girls are content to sit and have the subject matter pumped into them by recitations, etc., and to merely accept, while boys are more inspired by being told to do things and make tests and experiments."[3] Heated controversy persists about the universality or cultural specificity of adolescence as a cross-cultural stage of development.[4]

Margaret Mead's classic book *Coming of Age in Samoa* derived explicitly from her and her teacher Franz Boas's efforts to disprove Hall's claims about the inevitability of a period of Sturm und Drang during adolescence. Mead returned from her nine months among young people in Samoa reporting their condition as one of blissful nonchalance rather than the violence and misery Hall assumed to be natural and universal. Mead concluded that the turmoil Hall observed stemmed from particular features of American society, and from a lack of understanding that would later be summed up as the "generation gap." The concept of adolescence may also be a consequence of the intense age segregation that has characterized U.S. society since the beginning of the twentieth century and the rise of universal compulsory education.[5]

Continuities exist between Hall's and contemporary psychologists' views of adolescence, as Alexander Siegel and Lori Scovill point out:

> From Hall's time to the present, we have realized the gregarious and impulsive nature of adolescence. We know and accept that adolescents are neither children nor adults and that they have specific developmental needs. Since the time of the Puritans, as a society we have been worried that "idle hands are the devil's workshop" and have been concerned with the havoc that those idle hands might wreak....Generations of

adults have voiced a collective need that adolescents control their "instincts and impulsive behaviors." We have designed institutions...for their socialization and the internalization of our values. We have also tried...to provide adolescents with constructive outlets to satisfy their developmental needs.

From flappers (1920s) to bobby-soxers (late 1930s to 1940s) to teenagers (1950s) to generation-Xers, certain adolescent developmental needs have remained constant (and are the stuff of textbooks): adolescents want instant gratification, need to test the limits of authority, need to engage in a modicum of outrageous behavior, etc. Adults, in turn, also have collective needs to put limits on them, to "control" their impulses, to socialize them. This much has been constant in every era.[6]

In the past, guidance was provided by adults within their own families or in the larger community, but those roles have since been taken on by schools and other institutions.

Developmental psychologists now identify a new stage of life in industrialized societies, called "emerging adulthood"[7] or "late adolescence."[8] They regard the tasks of this period as those of developing intimate relationships, leaving home, separation-individuation, and identity development or self-development. This period is tied up intimately with the development of higher education.

Shaping the Modern University

> I believe that education...is a process of living and not a preparation for future living.
> —JOHN DEWEY, "My Pedagogic Creed" (1897)

The American university is a strange beast. Growing out of the German and English institutions of higher education, the earliest universities were largely training facilities for clergy, and almost all were rooted in particular Christian sects, although since their founding the most prominent have lost their religious affiliations. At first most served wealthy white men, though there were a number of illustrious institutions for women or blacks. Over time the mainstream institutions added a wider variety of students to their clientele. The most visible changes came with the forced integration of the University of Mississippi, "Ole Miss," in 1962, when the National Guard escorted James Meredith onto the campus on the orders of President Kennedy, and with the widespread coeducation movements of the early 1970s.

A much less publicized change had occurred earlier in the twentieth century, however. As Jerome Karabel points out in his hefty study *The Chosen,* the elite three universities—Harvard, Yale, and Princeton—began to consider extracurricular activities (as evidence of "character") in their evaluations of applicants as a way of excluding Jews, whose academic credentials tended to be high but who were not "one of us." By focusing on extracurricular credentials, it would become possible to include only those who were versed in tennis, boating, horseback riding, and other exclusive activities. Over time, this emphasis on outside activities came to dominate the concerns of prospective students, and subsequently of students already in college.

College is regarded, at least by those in the privileged classes who expect their children to attend selective institutions, as the final phase of adolescence, although in actual practice, for many upper-middle-class Americans adolescence now extends into the twenties and even into the thirties, ending only with the establishment of a family of one's own and a stable career. For many in the working classes, who may not even complete high school, adolescence often ends a good ten years earlier, with marriage, pregnancy, and hard physical labor.[9]

For students aiming to achieve prominence, attending a selective college is viewed as a necessary step toward their eventual success. As childhood reaches its climax, they are still working hard at growing up, at being accomplished, at gaining confidence. Many of their struggles are an outgrowth of their teenage years prior to entering college. We will see how this helps explain why some students are willing to engage in plagiarism.

Selective Colleges and the Student Profile

Education is a numbers and letters game. Students assess their chances of entering a particular institution of higher learning by comparing their own achievements in an alphabet soup of measures—GPA, SAT, ACT, AP—with the figures published by those institutions: acceptance rates, average scores, average rank, average yield, graduation rates, and so forth. The figures construct a profile of the institutions and the students who attend them. Some students are haunted all their lives, not only before they enter college but even after they graduate, by their high-school test scores.

Harvard College accepted 7.1 percent of all applicants in 2008 (down from 9 percent the previous year); Yale accepted 8.3 percent. MIT accepted 12.5 percent in 2007. Saint U. accepted 25 percent in 2008. By comparison, a highly regarded state university such as the University of Michigan, Ann Arbor, accepted 42 percent in 2008—regarded as an extremely low rate—and Indiana University South Bend—a decent regional branch of a state system—accepts 77 percent of freshman applicants. "Selective" and "highly selective" colleges and universities tend to be seen as the most desirable and prestigious. Although most students in the United States do *not* attend such schools—only 3 percent of college students attend schools that admit fewer than one-third of their applicants— these set the tone in terms of preparation for entry into higher education. These schools also attract the bulk of mainstream media attention. Some colleges have increased their prestige by deliberately lowering the percentage of students accepted, for example, by advertising in order to increase the number of applications so they can refuse more of them. That in turn increases donations as the schools rise in the rankings.

Another statistic frequently broadcast as revealing each institution's exclusivity, selectivity, desirability, and impressiveness is its average SAT scores. In 2006 Harvard students' average scores were 725 (math), 716 (critical reading), and 719 (writing), though Harvard does not itself advertise or post these figures. (By contrast, average national scores in 2006 were 503, 518, and 497.) MIT's average math score was 753; Brown's average writing score was 704. Saint U.'s were 676 (math), 653 (critical reading), and 663 (writing). Indiana University South Bend's were 473 (math) and 467 (verbal).[10]

Formerly called the Scholastic Aptitude Test, the SAT is now referred to only by its initials or, if pushed, as the Scholastic Assessment Test, since its writers acknowledge that it does not measure "aptitude."[11] This lengthy test—it now takes three hours and forty-five minutes in one sitting—has been criticized from many directions: it favors white, middle-class students; it fails to predict achievement in college; it is correlated most closely with the student's socioeconomic status.[12] Dozens of selective colleges have stopped relying on it. The test was changed substantially in 2005 after the president of the University of California system, Richard Atkinson—himself a psychologist and an expert on testing—threatened in 2001 to abandon it.[13] Rather than risk losing its 1.5 million annual customers, the College Board revised the test completely, incorporating some of Atkinson's criticisms. He had pointed out that the best measure of college readiness was achievement, as already assessed on the SAT-II (subject tests) or Advanced Placement tests. The SAT now includes a writing component, and the math section has been made more difficult.

For most elite college–bound high school students, the SAT is the primary mountain they must scale in their attempt to gain admission to the college of their dreams. Parents pay thousands of dollars to enroll their children in test-preparation courses. Some students take the SAT test several times, usually increasing their scores slightly with each sitting: the College Board, which creates and scores the tests, claims that second-time test-takers' scores typically rise 30 points and third-time test-takers' 54 points.[14]

The SAT was originally proposed as a way to measure not merely achievement in high school but also "aptitude," for the purpose of enlarging and thus democratizing the pool of eligible college students.[15] During its first years it was used by only a small proportion of high school students, but by 2006, 48 percent of the 3 million students finishing high school, about 1.5 million students, took the test.[16] A student's scores on the SAT are not raw scores but are "norm-referenced," or evaluated in relation to the results of other test takers. A score of 500 is by definition the mean; the "standard deviation" is 100. Students with a perfect 800 may have missed a question or two.

As the proportion of students taking the test increases, they no longer represent an elite group, and so it is not surprising that scores have tended to fall. In 1996 the tests were "recentered" ("re-normed"), or given a new meaning.[17] The earlier score of 500 was the average for the elite group of test-takers in 1941; the new score of 500 was the average for the broader group of test takers in 1996. Scores rose approximately 100 points, so a 650 in the 1970s would be equivalent, roughly, to a 750 in the late 1990s. Like grade inflation, this "recentering" compresses the highest scores, making it more difficult to detect differences among the top students.

Average and median SAT scores are scrutinized carefully to discern meaning about social trends and the quality of our educational system. If the scores drop one year, is this caused by a change in the test or by a change in the scoring of the test? Is it a reflection of a change in the number of people who took the test or of expansion into a less highly achieving population? Does it reflect poorer instruction? Poorer learning? The influence of video games on time spent reading? In 2006 a sudden drop in scores was deemed "not explainable" by the College Board, though most observers saw it as a result of the new test's being forty-five minutes longer than it had been, a charge that the College Board emphatically denied.[18]

Many argue that the best predictor of college success is success in high school, as measured by grades and class rank.[19] But since grades have become so inflated (more on this momentarily), universities do not completely trust the data from high schools and seek independent corroboration of students' excellence.

At the same time that SAT scores rose, the number of students graduating from high school increased from about 2.5 million in the early to mid-1990s to about 3 million at the beginning of the twenty-first century.[20] If the top students are all competing for the same one hundred colleges—as they appear to be—it is no wonder they perceive the process as unpredictable and treacherous. Indeed, public information about competitive colleges emphasizes their increasingly selective nature. In April 2007 and again in 2008 the *New York Times* reported the most competitive admissions years in modern memory, as Harvard rejected more than one thousand applicants with perfect SAT math scores, and Princeton rejected thousands of students with perfect GPAs. Although these highly selective schools might have acceptance rates as low as the Juilliard School's 7 percent or Stanford's 9.5 percent, nationally the acceptance rate for four-year colleges is 70 percent.[21]

Despite the fact that there is space in one college or another for virtually anyone who wishes to attend—there are over seven thousand institutions of higher learning in the United States, most with less than grueling admission procedures (and sometimes, as for community colleges, entirely open enrollment)—highly selective colleges and universities are disproportionately desirable. People find them so for a variety of reasons, from availability of specialized courses, to opportunities for cultivating high-profile contacts, to ego gratification.

Someone planning to attend a highly selective college—one that accepts fewer than one-third of applicants—must begin to prepare early. In some cases the preparation starts at birth, with parents enrolling children in preschools that have been successful in placing students in the grammar schools that feed into the selective college-prep secondary schools. It is not easy to enter these preschools. When a 2003 fund-raising auction at the Ninety-second Street Y in Manhattan yielded $1.4 million, it was suggested that some givers were aiming to secure a place in its desirable preschool program for their toddlers.[22] IvyWise, a private, for-profit college admissions counseling service, has a branch called IvyWise Kids, which can even help parents place their infants in selective preschools.

Certainly being born into a family with both wealth and cultural capital—say, with parents who graduated from the target university, as well as the means to fund SAT preparatory courses, or trips abroad, or math tutors, or dance classes—is the best option, but this is one that children can't arrange. (The prevalence of the wealthy at highly selective schools is lamented whenever affirmative action, multiculturalism, and diversity are debated.)[23]

The selection process, then, becomes increasingly self-fulfilling. Good students from good backgrounds who attend good schools are almost guaranteed to get into "good" colleges. The high school segment of that process is regarded as key.

Since the 1990s approximately 7 percent of public high schools in mostly affluent residential areas have given students 5 points (on the normal scale of 4.0) for receiving A's in honors or advanced placement courses, resulting in what are called "weighted" grade point averages; as a result, a small number of elite students graduate with a GPA over 4.0, in other words, better than perfect. These students are happy, because they feel that they have been deemed exceptional. The colleges that accept them are happy, because they can boast about the number of students with 4.0 averages that they enroll—or, even better, that they reject. (Rejecting "perfect" students reveals how very extraordinary their pool of applicants is.) The high schools are happy, because their best students have records that can gain them acceptance at the best colleges. But the practice has many negative consequences: it causes a concentration of credentials to be lavished on a small number of students, a lack of comparability of grades among different schools, and, particularly relevant here, students who view themselves as perfect and thus above reproach. Critics charge a "mirage of meritocracy" and "stratification among the haves."[24]

I once had a pre-med student who gave himself 11 points on a 10-point class presentation. (I like my students to develop self-critical skills.) He also admitted that he lied on his medical school application, stating that he wanted to practice general medicine when in fact he aimed to select a super-specialty like his wealthy neurosurgeon father. Clearly he had learned somewhere about inflated grade scales.

But the general cynicism runs even deeper. I recently heard of a selective private college-prep high school in which A's begin at a grade of 89 rather than the standard 93. That way more students can get A's—including the 5-on-a-scale-of-4 type of A—and then they can graduate with extraordinary GPAs and go on to highly selective universities and colleges, which satisfies their customers and draws in even more parents and children with the same high-priced aspirations. (Many private schools decline to rank their students, and savvy guidance counselors direct their best students to apply to slightly different lists of colleges, supposedly so as not to compete against one another, but also so that colleges do not have the opportunity to detect that almost *all* students at All-Superior Country Day are A students.) You pat my back, I'll pat yours. And we'll all get rich together. (Tuition at All-Superior was $22,000 a year in 2007 for its high school students.)

Applying to College: The Singular
Affirmation of Being

High school guidance counselors are notoriously overworked, often reputed scarcely to know students' names at the biggest public high schools, though the workload can be intense even at private schools. Students focused on admission to particularly selective colleges who do not feel that they can rely on the advice provided by their school's counselors can turn to a new breed of consultant: "college application counselors." These professionals are often former admissions agents who devote themselves to helping individual students prepare for the college application process. They advise them about which courses to take in high school, which activities to emphasize, when to run as club officers, how to spend their summers, and which schools to apply to; they even "edit" their essays. Alexandra Robbins, in her terrifying account of ambitious high school students, *The Overachievers,* reports on one such counselor who "fired" her client. The client was not single-minded enough to tailor her life to the counselor's recommendations, and would not have been certain to be admitted to the most selective colleges, thus threatening the counselor's record of success—her main selling point.[25]

One counseling service offered parents an on-line nine-question "quiz," clearly intended to frighten them into choosing to buy the service. My favorite two questions are (1) How many colleges have acceptance rates under 35 percent? Answer: One hundred! (And presumably these are the ones you want.) and (2) What percentage of high school valedictorians did Dartmouth reject? Answer: 40 percent! (So if you want your child admitted—and you do, or you wouldn't be taking the quiz—you need us!)[26] Prices are available after an initial consultation. *Business Week* reported on one family that spent $30,000 on college consulting for its two children—the implication being that their story was far from unusual.[27]

Because colleges can no longer be certain that applicants' essays were written by them alone, the SAT writing sample has taken on added importance. Huge discrepancies between the polished essay submitted with the student's application and the essay written under controlled conditions can raise suspicions about the likely intervention of a professional editor. Private admissions counselors also give their clients sample tests under actual testing conditions, and offer them feedback and pointers for improvement.

A student who is accepted by one of these highly selective institutions has been very successful at every level prior to college. Whether groomed at a private prep school or enrolled in any of the country's more prosperous public high schools, such a person has been not only a top student but also a varsity athlete, perhaps captain of a team, has participated in community service for years, likely at a church or synagogue or through a community organization, and often has some experience in the arts, probably playing an instrument in a band or orchestra. This combination of academic, athletic, community, and artistic achievement constitutes "well roundedness" and is a prerequisite for admission. It is clearly not sufficient, of course. To get into the absolutely most selective schools, a student really has to stand out. She has to have published books of poetry, or to have won not just the ordinary prizes for science research but international prizes, or to have written symphonic music that was performed by a regional orchestra. She cannot merely have worked at a nonprofit organization but must have founded one. Climbing mountains is not enough; one has to have climbed "fourteeners" for charity and used the money to aid inner-city children. In 2007 an article in the *New York Times* called such students "zoomers"; when they actually get to their highly selective colleges, they often find the class work easier than at their fancy college-prep high schools.[28] This contrasts with the experience of the majority of college students nationwide, who require remediation in one or several subjects.

At an orientation session for prospective students that I attended at Stanford, the polished student leading the session mentioned that the application had room for only twelve activities. Some parent-child pairs in the room gasped. The student presenter, representing the admissions office, suggested that Stanford was interested more in depth than in breadth. This is not the approach taken by students with ambitions for the Ivies or the "New Ivies." Most of these students, supported by their wealthy parents, pile on the activities. Students in college report that their high school activities were selected almost entirely with an eye to their college applications. One student lamented that she could never do what she really wanted, only what would impress a college admissions board.

Today's college students have been groomed to be successful, clever, and above all calculating: "Will this look good on my résumé?" When I began my research for this book, I asked some students if they had selected activities just because they looked impressive on their college applications, if they had joined clubs they weren't interested in just so they could list another item when they applied to college. As I tried to describe the process, the students informed me that there was a perfectly good term for it: *résumé padding*. It wasn't a term I'd have known at eighteen.

I went to a meeting at a high school where parents were pushing for a certain kind of block scheduling because, as one parent put it, "colleges look to see that the children have done arts and music, not just academics." The argument was not, "My child wants to have a chance to do ceramics because she likes it"; everything must revolve around the sacred moment of college application.

At one high school meeting, in which a new International Baccalaureate program was introduced, the new math program for IB students was mentioned. In the senior year, students would take one semester of calculus and one of statistics and probability. Several parents immediately protested:

"My daughter is already in precalculus as a sophomore. Do you mean there will be nothing to take as a senior?"

"Do you mean my son will have only *one* semester of calculus in high school? What if he is planning to study science and math in college?"

One mother tried to lay their fears to rest: "I was worried about this, too, so I called some top engineering and science programs and asked what they would think about a student who had only one semester of calculus. They said, 'We really like the way IB students are prepared. But if you're really concerned, your child can take calculus at a local college during the summer before they start with us.' And that was Princeton!"

Not satisfied, another parent at the meeting later called another university about their standards. I heard about it from the incredulous professor who received the call.

The parental involvement, the focus on credentials, the utter panic about piling on advanced courses as early as possible, is in many ways the cornerstone of parenting and of childhood in the early twenty-first century. Some parents talk about which high school "they" are attending: "We're at 'Central.'"

I was a very good student in the 1970s; I took some AP classes but didn't worry much about what this meant for college admission. My parents knew a few of my teachers, but they certainly didn't know the content of my courses. This new approach to parenting has transformed the meaning of childhood and of education. Each phase of education is in thrall to the next, and parents see it as their job to stand over the process, cracking the whip.

For decades, countless books have been pointing out the dangers of pushing children. From David Elkind in *The Hurried Child* (1981) to Richard Louv in *Last Child in the Woods* (2005), experts and social critics have been urging parents to allow their children time and space for imagination, for free play, for making their own mistakes. They lament the way children's lives are filled up by organized activities, by schedules, by being driven around, by lessons, by technology. These passionate pleas for a more innocent and free-ranging childhood is in stark contrast with the experience of the "zoomers," who have been trained, by nearly two decades of coaching and rehearsal, to consider, always, the written record and the next step.

Mental health experts such as Madeline Levine are extremely worried about these students. In *The Price of Privilege: How Parental Pressure and Material Advantage Are Creating a Generation of Disconnected and Unhappy Kids,* Levine shows that many of the affluent children who will arrive at highly selective colleges exhibit alarming rates of eating disorders, self-destructive "cutting" behaviors, suicidal tendencies, substance abuse, and other manifestations of depression or anxiety disorders. She attributes this epidemic to affluent parents' insistence on perfection in achievement and the single-minded pursuit of their children's accomplishments. The children end up lacking a sense of self, as well as a sense of warm emotional connection to their parents, who may speak to them only to grill them about their activities and evaluations of those activities.

David Brooks wrote in 2001 of the "organization kid," having looked at the daily activities of Princeton's extraordinary students—the elite in training. He writes of the students' contentment at being organized and supervised by their parents, with whom they invariably have close relationships.[29] The "helicopter parent" phenomenon, first mentioned in 2002, has by now become a cliché.[30]

The reshaping of childhood has psychological effects, to be sure. But this kind of decades-long preparation for college entrance has transformed education itself, and as we shall see, it in part explains the decisions some students make to "cut corners" as they pursue their college career.

Welcome to the Total Institution

In the end, the students claimed, even the fun of college life was a learning experience. And with this claim, the dichotomy between formal education (work, learning) and college life (fun, relaxation) collapsed entirely for the students. In the end, you learned from everything that happened to you in college, the students asserted. And, anthropologically speaking, they were not far from wrong.

—MICHAEL MOFFATT, *Coming of Age in New Jersey*

American students' views of college education derive in part from their preparation for the college application process, as well as from the current conception of childhood, with its focus on credentials and tasks, its emphasis on building self-esteem, its inflated rewards, parents' overprotection and overinvolvement, and students' habit of piling on activities to which their commitment is superficial. Furthermore, students are affected by the character of residential colleges as "total institutions," where social life and extracurricular activities absorb much of their time and attention.

A consistent impression of this aspect of higher education comes from accounts such as that by Barrett Seaman—a college trustee, journalist, and Hamilton College alumnus—of twelve colleges and universities, called *Binge: Campus Life in an Age of Disconnection and Excess,* or Cathy Small's *My Freshman Year,* describing student life at a large state university. Earlier accounts include the pathbreaking *Coming of Age in New Jersey* by Michael Moffatt, who enrolled in the 1980s as a first-year student at Rutgers, or *Making the Grade: The Academic Side of College Life* by Howard Becker, Blanche Geer, and Everett C. Hughes, which examined the University of Kansas in the mid- to late 1960s. More recent works show similar trends, such as Stuart Rojstaczer's *Gone for Good: Tales of University Life after the Golden Age* (about Duke), Peter Sacks's *Generation X Goes to College: An Eye-Opening Account of Teaching in Postmodern America,* William H. Willimon and Thomas H. Naylor's study *The Abandoned Generation: Rethinking Higher Education* (drawing on their experience at Duke and Middlebury), and Ross Gregory Douthat's *Privilege: Harvard and the Education of the Ruling Class.*

Although Saint U. has some particular characteristics, and students tend to choose it because they like its mix of athletics and academics, its "laid-back" feeling, its status, and its sense of community, it is quite similar in most respects to many other selective schools.

At Saint U. and elsewhere students generally adhere to a "work hard, play hard" schedule: one pattern is to focus on schoolwork four days a week for several hours each day. Many students don't work as hard as faculty would like them to or believe they do: faculty expect thirty hours of studying a week; students put in on average about eleven. Students do not necessarily read the material assigned to them. Many are motivated primarily by their desire to earn high grades, so they often select classes that are easy and take strategic measures to minimize their workload. Increasing numbers of students nevertheless have startlingly high grade point averages; and they reward the instructors who give them those high grades with positive teaching evaluations.

Rather than working hard, many students spend time instead "relaxing" (especially males, who put in a great deal of time playing video games). But they "play hard," too. It is common for students to "party" on Thursdays, Fridays, and Saturdays. Even those who don't engage in it themselves tolerate a wide range of "partying" behavior among their peers.

Carrying on the patterns established in high school, many students also participate in a wide range of activities outside class, including sports, exercise, political groups, social action groups, musical and theatrical ensembles, tutoring, and other interest groups, including ethnic or religious identity clubs.

Students report that their goals for college include the obvious: career preparation, fun, "changing" (including growing up), being with other people, friendships, prestige, exposure to different cultures, and independence from family. They say that success is connected with achievement, with having a comfortable lifestyle (in other words, money), though few state outright that they seek to become rich.

These, of course, are generalizations. Actual college life at Saint U. takes place within what many students refer to as the "bubble." By this they mean its isolation from the world around them, a good instinctive definition of Erving Goffman's brilliant term, "the total institution." Many students who venture off campus do so for one of only three or four purposes: to go to bars, to purchase alcohol, to seek medical care, and to shop. Among students, the town in which the college is situated has the reputation of being dull, violent, dangerous, impoverished, and generally not worth their consideration. Most students know only the path to their usual haunts, especially to and from the bars by taxi, or to and from the airport. Some engage in "service"—tutoring low-income children, working at the center for the homeless, teaching Sunday school.

The campus provides everything students could need. They buy winter clothing emblazoned with Saint U. iconography as the temperature plummets during the fall semester. There are twenty-four-hour study and eating spaces, as well as two large dining halls reputed to be among the best in the nation. There are fitness centers of every variety: tracks, weights, aerobic equipment, pools, and even a separate facility for faculty and staff who prefer to exercise away from students. There are films shown in a variety of venues, concerts, lectures, clubs, social action opportunities, religious services and exploration, laundry facilities, a bookstore, several branches of the library, computer centers and a computer store. Like other residential colleges, Saint U. is indeed a "total institution," engendering loyalty and dependence while limiting a resident's sphere of judgment to within its confines. As Goffman explains:

> A total institution may be defined as a place of residence and work where a large number of like-situated individuals, cut off from the wider society for an appreciable period of time, together lead an enclosed, formally administered round of life. Prisons serve as a clear example, providing we appreciate that what is prison-like about prisons is found in institutions whose members have broken no laws.[31]

Clearly universities are different from prisons, mental institutions, nursing homes, and monasteries. Goffman writes: "There are institutions purportedly established the better to pursue some worklike task and justifying themselves only on these instrumental grounds: army barracks, ships, boarding schools, work camps, colonial compounds, and large mansions from the point of view of those who live in the servants' quarters."[32] Saint U. is very much a total institution in this sense. All of the needs of individuals are cared for by a centralized staff (more on this in a moment); they live, work, and play together within the geographic boundaries of the setting.

Saint U., like all universities today, has an ever-growing body of administrators and staff, in addition to the more visible cadre of faculty and students. Besides maintenance workers, cooks, electricians, and so forth, there are provosts (full, associate, assistant), vice presidents (full, associate, assistant), directors, and deans (full, associate, assistant), scattered among offices dealing with, in addition to academics, student affairs, public affairs and communication, university relations, general counsel, business operations, finance, investment, and athletics. The school has more than 750 faculty members and 1,400 executive, administrative, managerial, and service personnel, plus nearly 800 clerical and staff members to support them.

None of this is unique to Saint U. In the past, admissions officers compared paying for college to buying a car. Now it's more like buying a house. In 1996 the *Philadelphia Inquirer* wondered "Why College Costs So Much."[33] The article answered the question, in part, by highlighting the increase in administrative personnel. At the University of Pennsylvania, between 1980 and 1996, student numbers increased by only twenty-nine (in a student body of approximately twenty thousand), while administration and staff increased by 1,820. As the article pointed out, universities discovered that raising tuition made them more desirable, like other luxury goods; tuition since 1980 has been rising at twice the rate of inflation. Colleges have also increased their fundraising efforts; they spend more than ever on (necessary) financial aid; and many spend lavishly on new facilities, services, and amenities as well. A tour of any campus is bound to include a number of buildings under construction or renovation. The better endowed the school, the more cranes and construction crews one sees, although the oldest ones, like Harvard, are often forced to expand beyond the central campus.

All residential schools have health centers, counseling centers, alcohol and substance abuse centers, sexual abuse prevention centers, "learning centers" (often remedial), computing centers, career centers, and diversity programs, in addition to the athletic facilities so proudly displayed to visitors and prospective students. Many include performing arts centers, museums, off-site botanical gardens or environmental laboratories, or even farms, increasingly organic. Some have day care centers, and a few have lab schools. All of this diversification requires organization, oversight, reporting, and fundraising, and gives rise to competition for resources.

Between 1975 and 1993, nationally, the increase in the number of administrators was extraordinary (83 percent), especially compared with increases in undergraduate enrollment (28 percent) and faculty (22 percent).[34] In 1996, for every dollar spent on instruction, colleges spent forty-five cents on administration, up from twenty-seven cents in 1950. Nationwide, approximately half of all faculty positions are "adjunct," meaning temporary, without paying benefits, and without offering the possibility of tenure.

All universities now employ an enormous phalanx of people with training in higher education administration or in various kindred fields: social work, substance abuse prevention, psychology, student activities, "advisement," and so on. In many ways these professionals know the students much better than faculty do, and are regarded as more central to the university experience. They are responsible for scheduling extracurricular (now more commonly called "co-curricular") activities and for keeping students safe and happy.[35]

Higher education functions more like a big business than it used to.[36] Universities are occupied—some would say overly so—with fundraising and partnerships with private investors. For this reason college presidents are now regarded more as chief executive officers than as prominent academics.[37] Derek Bok, president of Harvard from 1971 to 1991 and interim president from 2006 to 2007, has written passionately about "our underachieving colleges," a result not of inadequate funding but of misplaced or unclear views of the goals of higher education. These residential schools aim not merely to convey "knowledge" or to prepare students for employment but to minister to their every need—physical, intellectual, spiritual, moral, and social.

At Saint U., as on many other residential campuses, social life among students absorbs much of their time and attention. Without fraternities or sororities, and without any specialized housing, students are thrown together from their first moments on campus, and much effort is made to get them to interact. The "Frosh-O" (freshman orientation) program includes mixers and getting-to-know-one-another activities intended to convey several messages: college is about fun; fun is about other people; you need to learn about how Saint U. does things and to do it our way. The nonsanctioned "Dis-O" (disorientation), a forbidden "antidote" to Frosh-O, includes a lot of drinking and hazing activities, like running through campus naked. It is not officially permitted but nevertheless takes place every year.

The point of all this initial activity is that new students are socialized by older students into the mores of Saint U. There is pressure to participate, to share, to join, and to conform. Many students report that by junior year they are tired of this pressure and opt out. Students who go abroad, usually during their sophomore or junior year, often return without the same feeling of belonging to campus life; retaining their broadened perspective, they move off campus, a little less engaged than before. But for those who live on campus, within the confines of the institution, it provides everything they need—or at least everything that they are permitted.

What Am I Doing Here?

That the place of academic concerns is not necessarily dominant within the vast, entertaining total institution is evident from what students say about their experiences in college and their reasons for attending. When students at Saint U. were asked about the latter, they generally answered that going to college was always expected of them, and they chose this particular college for its "traditions," its "athletics and academics," and its "reputation." Some liked the atmosphere; some had parents or elder siblings who had attended and had been groomed from infancy to follow them. Other selective schools place a similar focus on "legacy" students, and on those who seek the luster of attending a particular school.

Kaitlin, an enthusiastic finance senior, told an interviewer: "I've always wanted to...go to [Saint U.]....My dad went here....I have pictures of me when I was...two...wearing cheerleading outfits and stuff like that....I only applied [to Saint U.] and [to] Ohio State, and if I didn't get [in], I'd be kind of devastated....I've just always loved [Saint U.], and I'm very happy I chose it now."

Unlike Kaitlin, Lauren had no family connection to Saint U., but like many students she was lured by the balance she found here between work and play:

> I loved the campus and I liked the people....It struck me that it was a really good school, but the people were still really laid back....They just...struck me as the type of people that I could get along with, so I just...felt like I belonged here....They knew how to work hard and then they would play hard. [During the week] you work hard, and that's cool, but then on the weekends...you take your time off....At a lot of really good schools they just study all the time. That's boring.

This theme of a "balance" between working and playing hard is common in the interviews. Another student, who gave himself the pseudonym

"John Stamos," was honest about the importance of status and about college as one of several "steps," each leading to the next. Asked why he chose Saint U., he answered:

> I think [attending a selective school like Saint U. is] the type of thing you just have to do...to maintain—I don't wanna say status—but to maintain where you think you fit....I've always considered myself one of the smart kids, and...that was important to me....It's important to me to know things. It's important to me to be quote-unquote smart. That sounds awful [chuckle]....But I think that knowledge is important to me, and to feel like I'm ahead of the game in a sense is important to me. And to move on to the next step, whatever it is...is also important.

Maria, by contrast, was not initially committed to Saint U. She was "pretty skeptical about leaving California, just 'cause [Saint U.] was so far away from home and it was cold, but I came to visit and I just fell in love with it. I loved the campus, I loved the school spirit, I just loved how I felt, and it felt right." Having been here a year, she was pleased: "I really like it here....It's challenging academically, but I love the football, I've never been as into football..., and I've made some really great friends." One thing that particularly appealed to Maria was the university's religious affiliation: "I love that religion incorporates into a lot of things, and I can just go down to...a dorm at night and go to Mass and stuff like that. Can't really find a lot of things that we have here at other colleges." Although religion "wasn't a huge component" of the Saint U. experience for Maria, "it was definitely a plus....The main thing for me was academics, but...I think it just adds that whole community thing, and you're not really gonna get that where there isn't religion involved."

Some students regarded Saint U.'s simultaneous focus on athletics and academics as "well rounded," and suggested that only Stanford and Duke were similar. Many students spoke about the school in reverential terms, mentioning its unique "tradition" and its emphasis on "working hard, playing hard." Such expressions, also heard at other universities, become part of the marketing and branding strategy used both by administrators and by students themselves to justify their choice of university.

I was interested in learning not just why students chose Saint U. but why they were going to college at all and what they hoped to gain from their experience. Many of the students answered that question in terms of long-range success, from getting into good professional or graduate schools, to finding good jobs, to forming broad social networks. Occasionally a student would speak of the importance of value formation and of "changing." One was frank about her goal of marrying and having children. But in interviews, students scarcely ever volunteered anything as old-fashioned as "finding themselves" or "figuring out who they are" as a reason for being in college, though they might have agreed if asked. Their goals had to do with action, with finding a place, not with finding a self.

Statistics on entering college students in the United States from a wide range of schools show that the percentage who consider "developing a meaningful philosophy of life" essential or very important fell from 80 percent in the late 1960s, when it ranked first among all college goals, to only 43.1 percent in 2002, ranking sixth. Meanwhile, those who saw as essential or very important "being very well off financially" measured 73.6 percent in 2002, the top value, having risen from 45 percent (fifth or sixth) in the late 1960s.[38] In 2005 the top reason to attend college was "to learn more about things that interest me" (77.7 percent), followed by "to be able to get a better job" (72.2 percent), "to be able to make more money" (71.0 percent), "to get training for a specific career" (69.4 percent), "to gain a general education and appreciation of ideas" (65.4 percent), "to prepare for graduate/professional school" (58.1 percent), "to find my purpose in life" (51.7 percent), and "to make me a more cultured person" (42.5 percent).[39]

Like many of his classmates, Dave equates academics with grades and degrees; college is about learning, but mostly in terms of social relations and self-knowledge:

> *Interviewer:* In your mind, what is...the advantage to going to college?
>
> *Dave:* Well,...obviously job opportunities open up much more....Just the whole college experience is a lot of fun....I have friends back home who...either don't go to school or go to really small community colleges, and...they're not really learning anything....I think they struggle a lot more because...you don't get a sense of community. [At Saint U.] you learn to discipline yourself. It's kind of... a transition period, so I think it helps out a lot.

Interviewer: That's really interesting: you named a couple [of] things...like advantage in the job market,...social life, and stuff like that, and one thing you didn't mention was academic life.

Dave: To me,...academics are really important, and...getting a good education is really, really important. But...it seems to me...it's important to society and to myself. I'm not really concerned about...how good my grades are as long as I'm doing the best I can, and...it's interesting to learn...things that I'm interested in, but...I think that a lot of people, especially at [Saint U.], are so concerned with...what they're gonna do [after graduation], what field they're going into,...they're already thinking about, "I have to get my degree in this and do this 'cause I need to make this amount of money," and I think that's...one of the problems, and I don't really like to focus on that much.

Similarly Patrick described his motives as purer than others':

I think a lot of people come to college, especially a college like [Saint U.], where the student body is going to be comprised of really competitive, credentialed students,...people who actually care about their transcript, essentially,...how well they look on paper....I think a lot of people show up here saying, "I'm gonna whup ass at this school, I'm gonna get A's, and I'm gonna make money," instead of showing up here and saying,..."By the time I leave this place, I'm gonna be an educated person,...a person who is smarter, who has...a much more refined analytical framework,...who actually...grows socially."

He elaborated:

I think that the numbers game is...important for prospective employers to judge you...relative to others, but...I also think that at the end of the day, the people that are gonna...look back on their educational experience and be more satisfied aren't gonna be the people who are like,..."I got straight A's in college." It's like, "Hey, what do you remember from your theology class?" "I don't remember a goddamn thing, I learned it for the paper, and wrote it down, and that's it."...I think especially in the business school, this might just be my bias, but from what I've seen,...it's more about learning a trade than getting an education,...being programmed for a trade rather than being rounded and developed as a person.

113

In Patrick's experience, students in the business school grew less than those in other programs, and he considered this a waste.

Amanda, who plans to go to graduate school, found herself at Saint U. for no particular reason other than prestige ("I thought the point of college was to go to the most impressive-sounding place you could go to"). But she has come to credit her college experience with forming who she is:

> Events I've [experienced] in college have been totally responsible for...shaping the way I see the world and shaping...my life. Who I am now. So...looking back at college,...it's made me who I am now....You couldn't really have everything that's happened to me in college and...not have me now....I think now the purpose has been for...personal development.

When the interviewer asked what she thought about the idea of "finding oneself" in college, Amanda agreed that it happens to some people, but she did not see it as something that can be deliberately sought.

Fiona, a serious student who described herself as a "dork," characterized her view of success as differing from what she perceived to be the mainstream:

> I think that, unfortunately, some people label success as getting a certain job, getting into a certain college, having a certain lifestyle, and I don't think that that's important. I think that you can succeed in so many ways that are so different from what you originally thought you wanted to have,...to say that you've succeeded, and I think that, unfortunately, not everyone recognizes that.

Asked about the point of going to college, Fiona answered thoughtfully:

> [In] the strict[est] of senses, there are jobs that you cannot get or certain lifestyles you cannot achieve if you don't have a college degree,...so there's that level of it. But in another respect, I think that being in the college environment as an eighteen- to twenty-two-year-old,...there's something to be said for being in a community of people that are [in] your age group,...in an intellectual setting where you're asked to learn, and learn new things, and think in new ways, and go through that experience together....And...at a university or college setting there

are people who are teaching you who are...very committed to what they're telling you....They've made this their life's work, to become experts in [a] certain area, and to pass that knowledge on to other people, and so there's a lot to be said for...growing intellectually in that environment because that's what this environment is for,...teaching new things, getting new experiences.

And then, just being in a social community, on another level, of people that are your age and going through a time in your life which,... whether it's completely natural or whether it's...constructed by society,...it is a time in our lives that can be really confusing,...really hard. You're...starting your life...away from your parents,...who've been taking care of you. You're starting to think, "What am I gonna do with my life?" And to be in a community of people that...are at that same point I think can provide you with a lot of support. And...you have...a social environment,...to have fun, and to grow in that respect,...because if you don't grow socially, I think you can run into a lot of problems in your adult life.

Asked to think about what he had accomplished at college, Evan, a senior, responded:

Just by graduating I think you've done something very, very special....You know, you've come to one of the premier universities in the world, not just in the United States, but in the world....Just by graduating...with a degree in biochemistry or...whatever degree that may be just that piece of paper that says...you achieved something that...not the average Joe could achieve every day....I think that makes you feel special....Other than that, when you look back, I guess...you see you established...not just close friendships but almost a brotherhood with everybody you live with....You grow up in a dorm with them....Some people come [to college] and...they think they're mature, but I don't think anybody realizes when you live with everybody you attend school with, when...you become a man or a woman outside of your own household, outside of your comfort zone,...you mature a lot more than you think you do....I think this is a great place for that.

Clearly for all these students, there are multiple reasons for going to college, or to any particular college. They mention career considerations and are quite realistic about their accomplishments, but they also recognize their growth as human beings interacting with others. Matthew acknowledged that grades matter for graduation and for finding a job, but they don't reflect someone's work ethic or professional capabilities. As for life after graduation, success would mean "doing what I love:...family, work...spiritual success,...if you could call it that."

Asked, "Before you got to school here..., do you think your ideas...were pretty well formed?" Jenna answered:

> No I don't think so. I think maybe I had begun thinking about things when I was in high school to an extent, but I don't think I had any way to put them together. I think...that...in college I ended up getting really passionate about...social justice things, stuff like that, and in high school I wasn't involved in anything like that....I think in college...there was some [kind of]...structure to put it in for myself,...or just being surrounded by so many other thoughts and perspectives.

Although Jenna appreciates how much her ideas have developed in college, she is aware that she has "a lot more growing to do."

Greg, a pre-med student, spoke at some length about the point of attending college. Comparing current students with those of the 1960s and 1970s, he observed:

> I think there [was] more independence, back in the [sixties and seventies], especially with the...hippies and...[the] sex and drug revolution, so I think there [was] a lot more free-spirited thinking and just overall...free will, so to speak....Riots and protests and things of that nature,...you don't see that at all in the United States now....I think everyone is sorta in this...factory game plan. Like go to high school. Go to college four years. Get a 9-to-5 job.

Another thoughtful, earnest student, Sawyer Jackson, summed it up this way:

> College [is]...supposed to prepare us for life...sorta like that window of opportunity...to...meet other people...from all over the world, learn from...the brightest, smartest in the world,...learn about how you could shape your life into...something that can benefit other people.

The range of responses to the question of why these young people are in college revolved mostly around helping them become independent, preparing them for careers and for life, opening them up to the world, and introducing them to friends they hoped to keep throughout their lives. Such goals align well with what developmental psychologists regard as the tasks of young adulthood.[40]

Work Hard? Classes, Grades, Choices

If we wish to understand students' behavior with regard to plagiarism and cheating, and the anxiety surrounding these issues, it is important to keep in mind students' perception that Saint U. affords a "good balance" between academics and other aspects of campus life—the "work hard, play hard" ethic. But exactly how hard do they work?

Students at Saint U. frequently talk about their burden of taking five courses per semester. This would indeed be a full-time job if they were held to the official standard of putting in two or three hours outside class for every hour in class. Five courses at three credits per course entail fifteen hours of classes a week, and should require thirty to forty-five hours of preparatory and homework time, a total of forty-five to sixty hours a week. But as I mentioned earlier, almost no students put in this kind of time, nor is it required. Numerous students in our interviews claimed that they did "no outside reading"—that is to say, no reading outside class—yet had a GPA of 3.5 or better. One senior majoring in business boasted that she never did any homework at all. She did do some preparation between classes while on campus, but as soon as she got home to her off-campus apartment, she just sat around. Even an excellent student planning to go to graduate school told me that she and all her friends regard assigned reading as a "suggestion." They assume their professors know that students aren't actually doing the reading. I heard one student shout a recommendation of a popular course to another across a sidewalk.

"What's it like? Is it easy?" his friend shouted back.

"I never went to one class and got an A."

Saint U. students are not unique in their disdain of hard work. According to one source, the amount of study time U.S. college students report spending is (on average) eleven hours a week—that is, just over two hours *per week* for each class.[41] An article in the *Chronicle of Higher Education* argues that at Duke University, considered one of the premier institutions of higher learning in the country, "many.... students only go through the motions academically." The author, a professor of hydrology, laments the lack of genuine intellectual engagement of his students. "The hardest thing for students at Duke—and at most elite institutions—is getting in," he writes. "Once admitted, a smart student can coast, drink far too much beer, and still maintain a B+ average." As at Saint U., Duke students enjoy the multiple dimensions of campus life, but this rarely includes a focus on ideas:

> Our students like that Duke isn't intellectually demanding. We are known for our unique combination of laid-back academic standards, very tough admissions requirements (except for legacies, children of wealthy families, and athletes), significant Greek life, and top-notch basketball. That's why most students come here. Our typical student is bright, personable, and focused on a career in business, law, or medicine.
>
> But there are problems with that niche. It's pleasant for the type of students we attract, but is making students comfortable what education is about?[42]

I have read hundreds of student evaluations of teachers when hiring new colleagues. Some questionnaires ask how much time the students spent on the class. The average seemed to be about four hours per week per class, even at first-rate universities. Sometimes students responding that they worked as little as three to four hours complained that the course had too intense a workload or had too much reading for them to finish.

At Saint U. the "working hard" dimension of campus life tends to run in binges, with Sundays reserved for preparation and writing. Some students, however, do focus on academics, and spend most of their time on it. Engineering and science students are known for their hard work. Ward, for instance, an electrical engineering major who admits that the class work is tougher than he had expected it to be, works most of the time during the week, relaxing only for meals. "Pretty much my only break is [for] food," he says, chuckling, "so when I get to the dining hall I completely forget about all the work and just relax for that good hour that I have to eat and talk with friends, [and then] get back to work." Even on weekends he mostly just stays home. His first year he went off campus frequently to see friends, but now, during his sophomore year, he mostly hangs out with friends in his dorm, watching movies. The interviewer asked why. "I think it's the workload," he answered. "I just really don't care by the end of the week, I just wanna stay home and sleep and not do anything."

More commonly, however, students seek to fill their time outside their schoolwork with other activities. Minimizing their workload is a key consideration in selecting classes. Jessie, a sophomore, was quite frank about this:

> *Interviewer:* What are your decisions...when you're deciding on classes?...Do you take a class based on who's teaching it or what the subject is or...how easy it is?...What are your classifications for class?
>
> *Jessie:* Requirements [chuckles]. And then from there,...if I have a choice, professors. And I usually talk to friends that have had the professors before. Tell me a little bit about them. What did they like or not like about the professor.

Jessie recounted the choice she had made for a required sophomore seminar. One class really interested her. Even better,

> a friend of mine had taken it and the same professor was gonna be teaching it, they were gonna be using the same textbooks, and she said overall it was a really easy class. They were gonna talk about what they did during their childhood the entire time. So I was like, "Okay. Considering that I'm taking organic chemistry and biology and statistics, it'd be nice to have a really easy class" [laughter]. So I...opted for that.

Amber, a student in the honors program, admitted, "I don't like to work, I like fun, so I tend more toward the 'party hard' side of things." She dropped one class her freshman year because she was failing it. Still she had to struggle to focus on academics rather than partying and drinking.

"John Stamos," introduced earlier, was thoughtful and articulate about the trade-offs between learning to learn and learning to achieve:

> *Interviewer:* You are more interested in acquiring tools...—cognitive tools, intellectual tools,...academic tools—that you can use later on than you are in...actually experiencing...the reading of a book or...listening intently to a lecture.

John: ...Absolutely. I'd say undeniably....Everybody takes notes in class and everything, but...I'll make sure I get down everything the teacher says,...and part of it is because then you don't have to read the book [laughter]. The three hundred pages of the book...I could save myself that agony of going through a book I don't even wanna read if I take down everything [the professor] said. But there are times where...I wish that I could just step back and kind of enjoy what he has to say....I know that's one thing I regret to some degree, but...no matter what I did, I would have to take notes anyway....There's one class where the teacher has Power Points and he talks...and he refuses to put his Power Points on-line....That frustrates me, because I wish he would just put it on-line so then I could listen to what he has to say instead of having to furiously write what is on the slide....Definitely there are classes where I try to take something out of them, but I don't think you're incorrect in saying that my primary objective in class is to...learn things as...sort of a tool, something that I can take with me, even for better understanding of stuff or even to use at some point.

The interviewer asked if the professor was correct in assuming that students like John, "who are gonna do...the minimum amount [of] work to get [by]," would not attend class at all if the slides were posted:

Right....There's a lot of people who wouldn't come to class....In this class, it's a class that I would go to anyway, 'cause I'm legitimately interested in what he has to say. But there are certainly other classes where I would not...if I felt like [the lesson] was solely based on the slide. But I feel like there are ways to get around [the problem],...in that if [the professor] would make it so that his slides covered the bare materials and he talked about important things, you wouldn't have to furiously copy notes. You could listen and copy what you need to copy and still have the bare minimum written down already so you weren't wasting time....

I feel like a lot of classes are just a lot of wasted time....You feel like you're just doing the same stupid things over and over and over again.

Clearly, if students are going to "waste time," they want to do it on their own terms. Kustin boasted about his relaxed senior year:

Kustin: This year's been kind of unique for me. I've only got...three technical classes and a fourth, but it's an accounting one, so...in a given week, I'm pretty idle actually [chuckles]....For most of the day actually—I don't wanna give the specifics—but, yeah [laughter],...I'm pretty idle. Which is good. You know, senior year is supposed to be laid back at [Saint U.].

Interviewer: Really? Do you really think that?

Kustin: That's...my philosophy of it...anyway. I figure,...[it's] my last semester, might as well cool things off and end with a nice easy...

Interviewer: ...What is your philosophy of life as a student?

Kustin: ...Basically it's work as hard as you can and once you reach your level of...peakness, basically...you can cool off a bit,...take some time off to relax.

Interviewer: ...What does it mean to work as hard as you can?...Give me some concrete examples of times when you worked really hard.

Kustin: Well, when you sit at the library,...actually study for an exam and really go for it. That's really working hard, especially when... a grade basically depends on how hard you work.

Interviewer: ...How do you know when it's acceptable at some point...to relax?

Kustin: ...Basically I...reached all my requirements...for my major. There's no point to move on and...go to a different subject or other major. Doesn't really matter for...what I'm going for in mine.

Interviewer: ...What makes a good student?

Kustin: Probably...has very high ethics,...morals. Somebody who works really hard in their classes and strives for...good grades.... Someone who just wants to learn for learning's sake.

Although he says that a good student is someone who engages in learning for its own sake, Kustin has missed much of the focus on classes that would qualify him as such a student. In contrast, studious Michelle says that what makes her unique is being the "dork":

Michelle: I'm always the one that's like, "Guys, I can't go out tonight. I have to study." Or...I'll make stupid...engineering jokes that no one else understands.

Interviewer: That's funny that you call yourself a dork but you also in the beginning...said that you feel like you go out too much.

Michelle: Yeah...well, see—that's the difference between...my friends and the engineers....I think I'm [in] between....My friends are the ones who go out five days a week, and then engineers usually go out...one day a week. So I'm more like two or three. So it's...kind of like [I] have to find the place in the middle that most suits me....

Interviewer: So you're...the token engineer among your group of friends....

Michelle: Yeah, I'm the one who gets made fun of all the time [laughter].

Interviewer: Really? For—

Michelle: I don't mind it though—

Interviewer: —working too hard?...

Michelle: Oh...just anything....I'll make...a science joke and I'll think it's hilarious and everyone's like, "You are such a dork."

Focusing on academics outside class makes a student a "dork." This is, then, not the norm for today's students. The era when it was considered cool to sit up all night discussing Nietzsche and Marcuse is long gone. It is no wonder that faculty, who tend to be of that idealized earlier generation, lament the absence of ideas in student life.

Interestingly, Cathy Small, the anthropologist who enrolled as a freshman at a large public university and wrote (under the pseudonym Rebekah Nathan) about her findings in an important book, *My Freshman Year,* disputes the frequent complaints about student disengagement. She claims that "many students privately think about course material even while following scripted discourse that downplays their intellectual lives."[43] There was much of that scripted downplaying of intellectual life in my interviews. Fiona, for instance, was adamant: "I love to read for fun; I'm never gonna tell anyone that." When Small asked students at her university to record what they talked about among themselves, fewer than 5 percent of their conversations could even loosely be regarded as connected with academics, and even then, the discussion was mostly about grades and assignments.

Students view their homework burden in a variety of ways, mostly bolstering the view that it is not excessive or onerous. Kaitlin, the finance major whose parents had always prepared her to attend Saint U., describes her schedule:

Kaitlin: Well [laughter], I sleep to the last possible minute before my classes. Um, I work [at a job] two days a week....I work there just six hours a week, so mostly I just get up kinda early, 9:30....Go to class....Since I don't have a car and I live off campus, on Mondays, Wednesdays, I get here at 9:30 and then I leave at 4:15, and...I have...a forty-minute break where I go to the library and kinda get some of my work done, 'cause believe me, not much...gets done at my apartment these days....Then after I go home at 4:15 I just [laughter] sit around, watch—keep in mind for three years I wasn't like this, but I'd say the academic part of [Saint U.] has necessarily become secondary to me this year....

Interviewer: Has it been replaced by going out more, or has it...kind of just been you—

Kaitlin: ...No, I definitely go out a lot more than I ever did....Me and my two roommates, we don't [do] anything, we just...sit there, listen to music....We don't do homework....The TV's never on, I don't know what we do. But we've become really good friends with two of our neighbors....We just hang around just doing stuff with them....On Tuesdays, Thursdays,...I have class all day till 3:15 and then I go home....Obviously if something's due, I'll do it, but really, I get a lot of my work [done] at the library. One of my class[es] normally gets out early. I'll just go to the library and get my work done then.

Kaitlin regards one of her major accomplishments as learning to manage her time.

Kaitlin: I remember freshman year, my first...semester finals,...I pulled...three consecutive all-nighters. One was an all-nighter for theology....Now, I would be like [laughter],... "I have a theo final like in two hours; maybe I should open a book." [I] had no idea how to manage my time....I've certainly learned...if I should get something done, I know I have to go to the library....I have [to] read by myself [because of]...my apartment and distractions....I certainly think over the four years, that's...one of the biggest things I've learned in college,...time management and...learning what's important and what's not.

When the interviewer pressed her about her study habits, Kaitlin offered a good bit of detail:

Kaitlin: I'm really efficient in what I do....One thing that my friends can't believe,...I'll just sit down if I...have a five-page paper—I'll just do it in two hours. I'll write it, I'll proofread it, and I'll never look at it again. So...in that way...I can wait to the night before, and it's not like I'm up till 6 in [the] morning doing it, because I just get things done quickly....

Interviewer: What about...your other friends and...their study habits? Are they all pretty much in the same mindset right now...?

Kaitlin: Yeah, no, most of us are in the same kind of boat....On IM,...all our away messages,... "Should be studying, but I'm...running around the parking lot, or doing something stupid."...I hear all the time, in my classes or in the hallways,...senior business majors [are] always like,... "I don't need to go to class anymore, I'm a second semester senior."

From the accounts I've quoted it is clear that for most students, the focus of their college experience lies principally outside their classes. Michelle, who goes out only two or three times a week and makes science jokes, has to label herself a "dork" to acknowledge that her seriousness is out of the ordinary. For students who don't care about the content of courses, or who only go through the motions of learning, plagiarism and cheating are strategies like any others, aimed at producing the best outcome (high grades) without impinging on what they really want to do with their time—socializing and relaxing.

Students might engage in cheating for any of a number of reasons:

- It makes things easier.
- It helps them attain the grade they desire.
- Class work is not their primary priority.
- They have a number of obligations and goals to meet.
- They are surrounded by other students who scorn the "nerd" or "dork" mentality.

Many students who are earnest and are deeply involved in their academic work would never engage in any of the activities that are considered plagiarism. But they constitute a minority. The rest may be quite susceptible to the reasoning in this list. Let's take a closer look at their thinking to understand why.

Motivations for Learning versus Motivations for Cheating

The role of academics—classes, learning, reading, writing, discussion, intellectual discovery—in the college experience is fundamental to students' views of plagiarism, since, unlike underage drinking or other matters of conduct, for them, plagiarism belongs entirely on the academic side of things.

As we have seen, although some students do work hard and concentrate on the courses they are taking, thinking and caring about them beyond their time spent in the classroom, a large number even of accomplished students consider intellectual labor a means to an end. They mentally calculate exactly how much effort they need to expend to gain the desired reward: their grade, and ultimately their degree. Education specialists distinguish *intrinsic motivations* for learning (a love of knowledge for its own sake, or a need for knowledge in application) from *extrinsic motivations* (good grades, teachers' or parents' praise, a diploma, a job). Students who value the work of learning for its own sake are less likely to cut corners, to rush or cheat, because they savor the experience itself. Whatever faculty and administrators may consider the point of education, however, in students' eyes grades are one of the primary focuses of their attention, and they may take whatever measures present themselves to ensure a good grade without the requisite investment of effort.

Since the late 1960s, students' grades have been rising higher and higher. At many very selective colleges at least half the grades recorded are an A or A–.[44] Harvard granted almost 90 percent of its graduates some sort of honors in 2001.[45] Numerous articles in the *Chronicle of Higher Education,* the *New York Times,* and the *Economist,* as well as scholarly publications, have both documented and lamented this trend, though a few have defended it. Many academics, including at my own institution, discuss the topic very seriously. Stuart Rojstaczer of Duke has documented on his Web site, gradeinflation.com, a sharp increase in the average grade and discusses several possible explanations for it. He rejects the explanations linking it to improved student quality or to affirmative action, seeing it more as stemming from the 1980s emergence of consumer-based education and declining of both intellectual rigor and grading standards.

Some prefer to call the trend "grade compression" instead of "grade inflation," which would have grades going ever higher. When the majority of grades are A, A–, or B+, they provide little meaningful information. Biostatician Valen E. Johnson, a prominent opponent of grade inflation, considers the trend "a crisis in higher education," influencing everything from the selection of courses (students choose easy classes that will yield high grades), to students' evaluation of faculty, to avoidance of entire academic divisions such as natural science and mathematics, to a lack of comparability in the meaning of grades in different fields.[46]

Grades reward students; teaching evaluations reward teachers. Teachers who are known to give high grades are popular, while those who give a broader range of grades are avoided, or receive less positive course evaluations from students. Many who study teaching evaluations argue that there exists a clear correlation between average student grade and the evaluation students make of their professors.[47] Several faculty members admitted to me that although they would like to grade more strictly, "I need higher teaching evaluations" or "I have to wait until I have tenure/ am promoted to full professor before I dare make students unhappy." Students share information, often at the speed of light. "Harsh grader" makes the rounds of student networks faster than a professor can explain her grading. Who wants to sign up for that class next semester when there is a nice, friendly, soft-touch professor available instead?

Just as there are a number of reasons for grade inflation, a number of possible solutions to the problem have been proposed, sometimes by individual faculty members and sometimes by administrators. One Harvard philosophy professor, Harvey C. Mansfield, decided to give his students an "ironic" grade—the inflated one they had come to expect—as well as a genuine grade that reflects his actual assessment of their achievement.[48] Duke considered a similar proposal whereby students would receive two grades for each course: the grade assigned and the average grade for the class. An A in a class in which the average grade was A would be less valuable than an A in a class in which the average grade was a B–. The proposal was rejected by the faculty.[49]

Many faculty deny that skyrocketing grades are a problem, arguing instead that students are just getting better. After all, the SAT scores are rising; high school GPAs are stratospheric. Shouldn't excellent students be acknowledged for their excellence? Johnson disagrees:

Grade inflation and, perhaps more important, differences in grading philosophies, distort student and faculty assessment. Students tend to select courses with teachers who grade leniently, often learning less along the way. Uneven grading practices allow students to manipulate their grade point averages and honors status by selecting certain courses, and discourage them from taking courses that would benefit them. By rewarding mediocrity, excellence is discouraged.[50]

When students make choices on the basis of likely numerical reward rather than on content and learning, the entire educational enterprise is devalued.

Even students who are committed to education often think in terms of grades. Pre-med student "Fluffy Fernandez" explained that she was not purely interested in academics—which she equated with grades:

> *Fluffy:* I wanted to go to a school that...had high academic standards, but...I didn't wanna go to a school where it was just focused on that. I feel like...I would never fit in 'cause I'm not purely academically minded [laughter]. I don't like to go to class, and...I don't think that the grades are the most important part of college....Most of my classes are just preparing me for the next step in my career [medical school]....And so if I get the material through the lecture, I don't feel the need to go back and review all of it again. I understand it the first time....
>
> *Interviewer:* How much do you think...you're actually learning right now as...actual training, or is [it] mostly just—
>
> *Fluffy:* ...Just kind of pre reqs....When I'm in the ER or whatever, I'll have to know the basic knowledge to actually do something.

After a detour on applied versus theoretical knowledge, the interviewer again asked the question about motivation, and Fluffy's friend Annabella chimed in with a sigh:

> I guess I mainly do [assigned work] because something's due or I have [a] test;...that's when I'll buckle down and do it. But...for some of my classes, like for this class I'm taking now, the professor gives us...news articles from the newspaper that relate to what we're talking about, and I...really like reading that....I read that for enjoyment and amusement. It makes me...wanna read more....I guess now that I'm in my

major,...it's stuff that I'm actually interested in versus stuff that I just
have to memorize, like vocab, which I still have to do.

Like Annabella, students can become excited about the material when it is
useful for practical purposes or simply because it engages their interest.

Asked directly about positive experiences in classes or with particular
professors, pre-med and psychology junior Heather responded:

> My freshman year philosophy class...was actually an awesome
> class....[Her professor] is a really excellent philosopher. Really...inter-
> esting guy, and I think he...took the right approach on the class....He
> never told us his personal opinions, which obviously I'd say...most
> philosophy professors try to do, but he presented the material in a
> really clear and concise way, really...challenged us to...integrate it
> and...know it and understand it and then also spent a lot of time
> teaching us some philosophical theories that would...challenge us
> to...improve ourselves...and our lives,...just some theories that
> say...no one should...have excess....And...you should give...until
> you...can't give any more, and...some interesting...life philosophies.
> I thought...he was a really good teacher. And then...my freshman
> year seminar also....I had [a different professor], and she is fantastic.
> And basically it was...a really eye-opening class. It was about...va-
> grants and rebels in French literature and film. It was...really obscure,
> but she exposed us to some really...cutting-edge...writing and some
> really...revolutionary stuff. And then [she]...had us to her house for
> dinner and discussion and stuff like that. She...kinda went above and
> beyond, and she mostly teaches...graduate classes, so for her to
> take...such an interest in this...freshman seminar was pretty cool.

One thoughtful senior, Bill, admitted that he worked a lot less than he
should have during his time at Saint U. but pointed out that many other
students similarly procrastinated, cut corners, and did only what was
required:

> *Interviewer:* Does...putting off [working]...affect the way in which
> you eventually do the assignment or the paper or whatever?
>
> *Bill:* Oh sure, yeah....Obviously the more time you spend on [an] as-
> signment, the better quality that the assignment's gonna be....
>
> *Interviewer:* Let's say you put something off...because you want to
> do something else. Do you think you would be likely to use fewer

sources—outside sources—that you would...be likely to...turn in fewer pages?...

Bill: ...Yeah,...that's always obviously true because there's just not...the time to go find more sources, and...you're gonna work on a book or a paper—well, you could produce a book—a "sources cited," it's...five pages long.

The interviewer then asked Bill about his social life and other claims on his time:

Interviewer: How many nights a week would you say you go out? Where does that fall in terms of your priorities?

Bill: I think it's a large priority....Most of my socializing isn't...restricted to going out to bars....It's usually hanging with friends in the dorm....I usually try to eat...meals with...people every day, and...I eat twice a day....I usually will try to do something. Go out on a Friday or Saturday night....depending on how much work I have....If I don't have work to do, then I'll...for sure go out....Maybe...every other week...go out [one] other night.

Bill spoke candidly about the many distractions that prevented him from doing all that his professors expected:

Bill: My main priority is academics. I find myself trying to refocus my energies into academics. [It] is easy to get distracted from academics...not finishing the readings or...you're not putting in the time you want....I've had very few papers that I've turned in that I've been [chuckles] really proud of.

Interviewer: Why is that? Well, first of all, is that okay with you?...In retrospect, do you look back on four years—

Bill: ...If I could do it again, I would definitely take more out of all my classes, and I would definitely produce better papers....Usually my papers end up being...better-quality work than I usually thought I had handed in, but...I think there's also a...large grade inflation at this school,...but...the classes I have turned in the best papers are the ones that teachers...graded harshly on some....I usually...do what's expected of me in the course [chuckles]....I rise when I'm expected, but I have...other goals....The reason I'm here...is to learn....I feel better about myself if I'm doing better in a class....And...it's really easy when you're not expected to do

[much] work to blow it off. Because...it is hard to...do all the readings in every class and all the work.

Interviewer: Yeah. How often...would you say...you do all the readings, you do all the work, and everything that's mentioned in terms of an assignment?

Bill: ...It's surprisingly not very often [laughter]....I usually do selective reading or skim it.

Interviewer: Is that based on interest or just on the demand of the course?

Bill: ...I think that you have to say it's both, because obviously I think you can find time for anything....I generally don't like...courses where other students aren't interested in the material...'cause...it brings the whole class [chuckles] down...

Interviewer: Do you think that instructors in general at this school would be surprised to know how much or how little students... engage themselves in the material?

Bill: I don't think they'd be surprised....They're smart people, and I think it's pretty obvious when people haven't done the reading in the class....Most undergraduate students don't do all the readings. So it's sometimes surprising that teachers won't call them out on it.

Interviewer: Okay, so let's think about this idea of...cutting corners.... To what extreme can that be taken?...What sort of things have you observed?...How far do you think an average student will...push... cutting corners to make work easier or less demanding...?

Bill: ...One...thought that...comes to mind...is reading books. I've been in some courses where I've...Cliff-Noted books....And...I think a lot of students do that and...don't feel very bad about that....

Interviewer: Did you...feel [bad] about it when you did it?

Bill: Yeah, I felt bad,...definitely....I feel bad because...you're not challenging yourself....

Interviewer: Did you feel like it was ethically wrong to do that?

Bill: ...I don't think that's a case where anything's ethically wrong....You're just cheating yourself.

Bill rarely completes the assigned reading. He cuts corners and has a hard time focusing on what he regards as his primary obligation—academics. He hopes his teachers regard his papers as "quality" (measured by a good grade). He is tempted by his social life, the lure of relaxation, and pro-crastination. And he is surprised that teachers let so many students get away with so much evident laxity.

And so the reasons, or at least the rationalizations, for cheating mount up. If a student pulls a paper together carelessly, at the last minute, as Bill and Kaitlin do, there is no opportunity to check with a faculty member about whether a particular passage must be cited or to give careful consideration to issues of attribution. A due date remembered at the last minute could easily result in a desperate grasp for some solution to the problem at hand.

Students who put their intellectual development at the center of their college experience regard paper writing as valuable and worthy of exertion, while those whose interests lie elsewhere attempt to breeze through the task. Although most care about the extrinsic aspects of coursework—especially grades—they often find no intrinsic value in the work itself.[51] The goal of making course content matter, though, competes with all the other claims on students' attention: the habit of extracurricular involvement, the mandate to "play hard," and the view of education as merely a hoop students must jump through on their way to what really matters.

The Co-Curriculum: A Life Full to Overflowing

The lives of contemporary students are crammed with a variety of activities that compress schoolwork into a very tiny window. In 1989 just over 65 percent of college freshmen participated in volunteer work. In 2001 the figure was more than 80 percent. Alexander Astin and his colleagues observe that "increasing numbers of secondary schools are *requiring* students to perform community service as a graduation requirement,"[52] and students without volunteer work on their college applications are likely to appear self-absorbed and undesirable. Once in college they often continue this participation, both as a habit and because they believe it will burnish their credentials beyond college. A good number, of course, are also doing what they believe in. At Saint U., where Catholic social teaching is emphasized, a majority of students remain active outside the classroom. In 2002–3 approximately 3,338 students out of an undergraduate body of 8,000 participated in groups such as Amnesty International,

Big Brothers/Big Sisters, Circle K, Habitat for Humanity, and the World Hunger Coalition. In 2001, 54 percent of Saint U. seniors did one to two hours a week of volunteer work, and 13.6 percent put in three to five hours.[53]

Donald, who was a very good student in high school but had a difficult transition into college, including a problem with drinking, describes his busy week in detail:

> It just doesn't seem...like there's enough hours in the day....Like,... right now I currently only have twelve credits, but I do extracurriculars such as SIBC, which is the Student International Business Council, and I...am a Frosh-O [freshman orientation] commissioner, so we've been working on that, putting stuff together for next fall. I am involved in...Big Brothers/Big Sisters. I make time for my little brother on the weekends....And...I work at [the Student Center] for a couple [of] shifts a week;...it's a work-study program....I pick up a shift at Sbarro, shift at the [convenience store], so work in there. I go to see a TA [teaching assistant] during the week. I have a class at [our sister campus], so that takes a little bit of time out of the day to take a class over there. But it just seems like I'm never really able to get in swing or start my homework until like 8 or 9 o'clock.
> ...[I'm] usually drained from the events of the day. So I get back from dinner,...lie down, take a nap, hop in the shower, and...I finally start my homework,...go to the library around 8 o'clock, and...I try to work hard over there.

Melinda, a senior business major, said that her time spent abroad made her wish that she had been more of a "scholar" during her earlier years at college, having discovered that she really liked learning. Asked if she felt pressure to be around people and to participate in activities, she answered:

> Yeah, definitely!...Like the whole communal aspect of...dorm life, and the one million clubs and activities that there are, and...the whole [Saint U.] family...there's a definite pressure to be social....Some people that I know that aren't particularly social, it's kind of hard for them, because they feel like they should be going out...whenever they really just...want to stay home and watch a movie or something....But it's a good thing, too, to get people out there, and participating in things.

Some students handle the whirl of activities and commitments without difficulty. The 2007 Saint U. valedictorian, who was moving toward the priesthood following graduation, had done service work for six of his eight semesters, taught English in Uganda, and studied abroad in Tanzania and Poland—while earning a 4.0 average. But like Donald and Melinda, many students wear themselves out trying to juggle schoolwork, employment, engagement in clubs, volunteer work, exercise, social engagements, and "relaxation." A senior told me she suddenly realized one day that she was becoming "stressed" from doing a lot of activities as if automatically when she really had no interest in them. She dropped them all and felt much better.

Play Hard: Drinking and Partying as Rites of Passage

At Saint U., as at most selective residential universities, "partying"—which generally means drinking—is a topic that commands a lot of attention.[54] Students enjoy discussing social rituals in class, and drinking is always a feature. Students have a schedule for "partying": it begins on Thursday night and continues on Friday and Saturday. During football weekends in the fall, all of Saturday is devoted to drinking. Almost nobody drinks on Sunday, which is reserved for schoolwork.

On most campuses students do everything they can to avoid early classes. (Even at my 10:30 class, students are always rubbing sleep out of their eyes, and when I taught at 9:30 they straggled in practically in their pajamas.) Friday classes are shunned altogether, to the point where some schools have simply eliminated them entirely. An effort was under way several years ago at Saint U. to require Friday classes, both to dissuade students from drinking on Thursday and to utilize classroom space more efficiently, but the idea was dropped. And not only because of student opposition: faculty also enjoy having a three-day weekend, and departments often use Fridays for meetings or colloquia, since this is the only time when most faculty are not teaching. The phenomenon is national. Katie Hafner, writing in the "Education Life" section of the *New York Times*, explains "How Thursday Became the New Friday."[55] Even where they are not banned outright, veteran faculty know better than to offer courses on Fridays; only freshmen or sophomores end up taking them. Although having Fridays off frees some students to schedule paid work or volunteer activities, mostly it allows the partying to start on Thursday night.

What are "parties?" we asked students. They are events of various sizes at which people drink. The hosts buy enough liquor to provide approximately five drinks per student. When the alcohol is used up, the party is over. Food is never considered part of the event, unless there is a theme (say, a Superbowl party). In fact, some students see eating as a way of preparing to drink: they increase their food intake so they'll be able to drink more without getting sick. Some women acknowledge that they diet all week so the calories from alcohol they consume on the weekend won't cause them to gain weight.

Often students "pre-party" or "pre-game": they drink shots of hard alcohol in their rooms to get into the party mood before going out. Campus alcohol experts are especially concerned about "shots" because it is so easy to drink them quickly, raising the risk of alcohol poisoning and other "high-risk" drinking behaviors.

Partying isn't to be confused with dating. In fact, today's college students largely do not date—if by "date" we mean an arranged activity between two people interested in pursuing a relationship with each other. Alcohol use is associated with the infamous campus "hook-up" culture, in which students get drunk and then engage in sexual behavior that does not entail any hint of commitment or a future relationship. The potential for misunderstanding is great; it is almost always under the influence of alcohol that date rape and other forms of sexual assault occur.

Students have been drinking on college campuses for decades, if not centuries. What is different now, it seems to me, is that at places like Saint U., drinking has become a scheduled activity in its own right, participated in by even the best students, and perhaps by the majority of undergraduates. Nationally the proportion of incoming freshmen who drink fell from 75–80 percent in 1981 to 50–55 percent in 2001;[56] don't forget that in 1981 many freshmen could drink legally, as the national drinking age had not yet been raised to twenty-one. But once on campus students become extremely competent drinkers. Experts are alarmed at the amount of alcohol—expressed in terms of blood alcohol content, or BAC—students can consume without showing severe effects such as unconsciousness or poisoning. While the legal limit for driving is a BAC of .08 percent, many students show levels of .15 percent or even .22 percent or more. One expert notes that these levels would leave him thoroughly incapacitated; it is only someone who has built up a tolerance for alcohol who can function at all after drinking so much.

Not all students are able to function while drunk, of course. Every year in the United States approximately 44 percent of all college students engage in binge drinking;[57] almost 30 percent miss a class because of alcohol; 21 percent engage in unplanned sexual activity (half without protection); 29 percent drive after drinking; and 1,700 die.[58]

Most students are tolerant of other students' drinking even if they don't engage in it themselves. Maria "doesn't have a problem with it in any way" even though she doesn't enjoy the "parties," which she describes as events where "you just go and you drink beer in a room full of people." Asked what she thinks about the "work hard, party hard mentality," Maria answered that at Saint U. it was more accurately a case of "work hard and then drink hard," adding:

> If people want to spend their weekend de-stressing and drinking and having fun, that's fine, but it's when you overdo it that it becomes a problem. If you're drinking more than twice a week, then...you might wanna consider your priorities and how it's affecting your work....I know people that party...four or five times a week and they're doing fine in school, and I just think, how is that even possible when I feel like I have all this work and couldn't even imagine doing that.

Maria is among the nondrinkers. In contrast, Donald spoke about his rocky transition to college, explaining it as a consequence of too much drinking. The dangers were clear to his dormitory adviser but not, at the time, to Donald:

> I went out too much [during his first semester]....Thursdays became like...the weekend was perpetually three days long....It was tough that last month and a half of school, kinda catching up with everything....I managed to...salvage some grades here and there, but...I was...so drained from the weekend on Sunday that...I only had...a good three workdays in the week.

Donald admitted that he just "wasn't a very good Friday afternoon worker.... Especially in the fall. Who's gonna wanna go to the library? Who's gonna wanna do anything?... And then... Saturdays would [be] college football time,... and you always go to the games, watch the games on TV."

Saint U.'s alcohol policy is a mixture of law and custom, which seems to be the case on almost every college campus. In 1984, under pressure from the federal government, the minimum legal drinking age was increased to twenty-one in all fifty states.[59] Thus students at traditional residential colleges are almost all too young to drink legally; yet a great deal of drinking occurs, as administrators fight a losing battle to contain it.[60]

Ironically, raising the legal age to twenty-one may actually have contributed to the prevalence of underage drinking. In the United States, the principal marker of the transition from childhood to adulthood is driving, which occurs at sixteen or seventeen in most states. The threshold age for drinking, however, does not coincide with this or with other legal markers of the age of majority: people can marry at sixteen or drop out of school at sixteen; they can buy cigarettes, vote, or join the armed forces at eighteen; but they cannot buy alcohol until they reach twenty-one.

The main argument for raising the drinking age was to reduce drunk-driving fatalities among teenagers, and on this count the experiment has been successful. But culturally, symbolically, and psychologically, the change in the law has given alcohol among the young the allure of forbidden fruit. It has become a primary marker of that transition to adulthood which they all seek—and dread. Drinking on campuses has skyrocketed. Not just at Saint U. but on all residential campuses, it has become a significant activity for a significant proportion of the students. There can be no adult guidance or modeling because the law makes it impossible for adults to be present when students drink.[61]

American society, with its roots in Puritanism, is ambivalent about pleasure, consumption, and the body. Whether eating, drinking, or spending, we tend to binge in extravagance, followed by purging (cutting back, dieting, going to the gym). Alcohol has been condemned, constrained, and otherwise placed off limits. It serves as a good topic for comedy because of our strong ambivalence about it as sinful but enjoyable.[62]

Joseph Gusfield writes of drinking as a symbol of the American culture that contrasts work and play as one of the dominant distinctions in modern industrial life. He points out all the ways that our "comportment" must be different on weekdays and on weekends, when leisure is our goal and our focus is on "spontaneity, disorder, relaxation, freedom, equality," as opposed to work.[63] This describes perfectly the defiantly student-centered, adult-free drinking culture of Saint U. and many other campuses.

Students generally deplore the regulations forbidding access to alcohol and develop sophisticated skills for evading them. Tim, an honors program student from Texas who turned down the University of Chicago because he preferred the social life at Saint U., articulated the general student attitude: "[Drinking] is against the law, but...I kind of feel like...we are in college, we are in a place where we're supposed to be growing into adulthood, we should be given the chance to be responsible....I understand why the university is [forbidding] it,...but I don't necessarily agree with them."

What students say about the regulations is essentially that they must respect their power even while they attempt to circumvent them. Fake IDs are almost universal, and cultivating friendships with older students who can procure alcohol legally is viewed as essential. One of the main unofficial activities of the first-year students' orientation period is to be initiated into the marvels of getting drunk. Students lament the punishments inflicted when they are caught breaking the rules. They complain about having to be profiled by alcohol and drug experts. They deplore the high fees they have to pay as fines. A few accept the legal limitations, but many more simply refuse to follow them. Students and administrators alike agree on one thing: that drinking laws are widely flouted—at Saint U. and virtually all other campuses.

Like most of their activities on campus, drinking and partying occur in groups, among students who live near one another in their dorms or know one another through some student activity. At Saint U., as at most residential universities and colleges, social interactions occur almost exclusively among age mates, as students band together in opposition to the "adults." Resisting the group's expectations would be considered antisocial and would mark a student as an outsider. It is very hard for a young person to withstand the pressure of group behavior, with all its expectations.

When these pressures include maximizing time for personal and social interests, then academic work is done only to the extent necessary to finish the required assignment and move on to the next activity, the next party. Here again we find fertile ground for cheating.

Clouds in the Campus Sky: Anxiety and Economic Realities

Although students often sing the praises of their college years, the "work hard, party hard" story has a dark side. Saint U. is no exception to what some specialists have identified as a "campus mental health crisis": a doubling of reported cases of depression, a tripling of the number of students contemplating suicide, and a quadrupling of sexual assaults since 1988. Almost half of all students become clinically depressed at some point, and about half regularly binge drink.[64]

Students are anxious about their academic and social performance. They are exhausted from keeping late hours and packing in so many activities. Worries about their appearance lead to anorexia and bulimia, and often excessive exercising. They have brought with them from high school an obsession with grades and external rewards for their accomplishments, and this only adds further pressure in the already pressure-packed college environment.

As David Brooks points out in his article about Princeton, "The Organization Kid," today's best students are serious about time management. They uniformly carry planners and check off the items on their lists: classes, paid work, community service, dormitory activities, sports, clubs. Social engagements may also be recorded. In other words, they continue to pursue the "well-rounded" profile that was the goal in high school and earlier.

I have had an honors program student break down in tears in my office because she was on the verge of getting an A–. The students in the honors program have had excellent grades and test scores all their lives. This student was a wreck. Her face was tight, her hair pulled back so sleekly that it hurt to look at it, her thin body—with its fashionable, expensive clothing and jewelry—was almost shaking with fear and the effort of self-control. I recommended that she *pursue* an A–, precisely so that she could break her perfect record and release herself from its bondage. The following semester she told me that she had indeed received an A– and was much less worried about everything. Her career plans included going into the family business, where nobody would ever ask her again about her grades. Why worry about them? Nevertheless, just prior to graduation, she seemed uncomprehending that her major department would not confer honors on her despite her 4.0 average in that field. With so many students getting such high grades, I explained, a mere 4.0 was not enough for a degree with honors. Her department required a graduate class and a thesis, too.

This habit of perfection brings us students who are unaccustomed to taking risks. What they want is to be handed the formula for success. When we give assignments, we can no longer issue an open-ended invitation to write about a work. The students find that "confusing." (Or it yields self-indulgent ruminations about their own experience.) In the early phases of the first of three courses she took with me, Rita complained that one of the assignments was "unclear." She wanted detailed instructions so as to ensure getting an A. In subsequent classes she was happier when I gave those instructions.

Students are not entirely wrong to worry about their records. They have to get good jobs immediately after graduation. The average graduating senior in 2007 had incurred $20,000 in debt. In one survey of recent graduates, 49 percent reported that their total credit card and student loan debt exceeded their annual salary, and 60 percent admitted losing sleep because of it.[65] Concerned about a level of debt that was making attending college prohibitive for students from non-elite backgrounds, Congress has held hearings about college costs.[66] The average price for a public four-year college was $15,100 in 2003–4 and $29,500 for a private four-year college. The average student had a loan debt of $3,200 for *each year* in a public and $6,100 for a private institution.[67] The average total debt at four-year public colleges in 2004 was $15,399; at private New England colleges it was $23,491.[68]

This affects more than the students' bank accounts. It makes them afraid to pursue postgraduate education other than professional school with job prospects guaranteed.[69] It makes them averse to doing service work after graduation. It forces them to take jobs they don't like, to live with their parents, to delay buying a car or a home, to postpone medical or dental procedures—and even to delay having children.[70]

It also drives them increasingly to seek paid employment while enrolled as students. In 1970 only 33.8 percent of full-time students were employed, most of them (19.3 percent) less than twenty hours a week. In

2005 fully 49.1 percent of full-time students were employed, 21.1 percent between twenty and thirty-four hours a week. Nearly a tenth—9 percent—of full-time college students worked thirty-five hours a week or more, compared to only 3.8 percent in 1970.[71] This too is a severe drain on students' attention and time.

These financial factors make college even more of an economic prelude to adult life than it has always been. In the 1990s jobs were plentiful. Students boasted of earning six figures the day they graduated. By the early years of the twenty-first century, however, students had become anxious about finding a tolerable job. This anxiety is shared by our society, which worries about the fate of our brightest young people. And it is manifest in the choices made by those young people, who can't afford to fail.

Plagiarism as a Necessary Means to a Necessary End

In these circumstances plagiarism might strike many students as a logical option: for those who are focused entirely on external goals such as high grades, a degree, or admission to the next level of education; for those who are in college to have fun; for those whose notion of education involves checking items off a list rather than reveling in a process of discovery; for those who are busy with other activities and obligations; for those who lack the ability to earn the rewards to which they feel they have a right. Clearly, not every student regards education as a means to an end, and not every student plagiarizes. And the more than half of all students nationwide who admit to some degree of plagiarism do so for a variety of reasons. But for those who see their college education as just another hurdle to jump on the way to a bigger goal, plagiarism is another means among many for accomplishing their mission. Everything that shapes their college experience points them in that direction, including the way the larger society regards adolescence and the purpose of education. Thus we can only partly blame the individuals who cheat: they have absorbed the cultural messages about competition, success, multitasking, and the bottom line.

Plagiarism, as we have seen, includes a variety of very different behaviors: buying papers (a rare but dramatic instance); using a friend's paper; falsifying a bibliography; wholesale copying into one's own paper without citation; and borrowing a phrase or an idea without crediting the originator, whether intentionally or inadvertently. Although about 60 percent of college students report that they have engaged in one form or another of plagiarism, only 2 percent admit to buying a paper.[72] Given the range of practices lumped together as "plagiarism," it is difficult to generalize about students' motives. Some express supreme disrespect for institutional guidelines, while others simply haven't mastered the conventions of citation.

When asked why students cheat or plagiarize, one student suggested that it has to do with changes nationwide in who goes to college. It used to be only wealthy people, or brilliant poor people who loved ideas and understood what universities were about. But now, she said,

> everybody has to go to college if they want to continue to live the way they were raised, if they were well off, or to alter the way they lived if they were poor. Most jobs that college students get...used to be done by people [just] out of high school,...but now they need a college degree to get those jobs. For 85 percent of [Saint U. students], they are just checking off their classes and their degree on a list, but don't really come here to "dig," to look into things intellectually or even emotionally.

She was only warming up:

> When students get to the first day of a course, the first thing they look at is the course requirements, to see how hard or easy it is. They aren't in it for learning. So if someone borrows a fellow student's paragraph because she forgot to do the assignment, it isn't really anything, because they both know the answer and came up with the same thing, and aren't trying to get anything different out of [the task].

"John Stamos" similarly explained that students plagiarize to make their lives easier:

> *John:* They wanna get their paper done quicker and they want it to be to a certain level....I think to some degree a lot of people if they sat down [to] think would not be confident that their ideas were that good....So they feel like they need some kind of substantiation...[of] some idea that they feel really has some legs to it...instead of having the confidence to go through with their own thing.

Interviewer: What about...deliberate, some might say premeditated, plagiarism? Do you think [it] happens often?

John: Uh, yes I do;...enough that it's an issue, I would say....I think a lot of people do it...even in the sense that they have other people...write parts of their paper....Or they have other people do certain...parts of their work for them....That's obviously more serious....I know in principle it's wrong, so...it's not something I've done on a major work, but I guess you could say copying to some degree is [something I've done].

Similarly, Crystal related how her roommate, whom she characterized as "always" cheating, got into trouble for plagiarizing, though with inconsequential results:

Crystal: [My roommate's] friend...took a class, a philosophy class,...in the spring, and then my roommate took it over the summer,...and then she had the same professor....She had to turn in a paper, and instead of turning in her paper, she just used her friend's old paper from the spring semester. And the professor obviously knew what happened because he [had] changed the assignment, and my roommate didn't realize that [laughter]....So he was just like, "This is the assignment I gave in the spring semester. Obviously you got this from somebody. Tell me who you got it from and I'll make it easy on both of you guys." So she told him her friend's name and they both got in trouble. But she didn't get in too much trouble.... I was surprised.

Interviewer: What actually happened?

Crystal: Well, she had to go to...an honest[y] committee, but...it was kinda ridiculous 'cause...she flat-out admitted to me, "I took her paper and turned it in." And...she admitted that to her parents, but...her parents...[called] the school and [were] just like, "She didn't understand. She...was just trying to get help."...Her parents totally bailed her out....She basically got...a slap on the wrist, like, "Don't do that again." But in terms of plagiarism, I know that she has...never taken a test that she has not cheated [on]. Or has never done a paper on her own....We would have disputes about that 'cause she was just like, "If you can do it, why not?" and I'm like, "It's wrong" [laughter].

Interviewer: Why did she feel that [she should cheat]?

Crystal: Well, she was an athlete, so I think she felt pressure because I guess she always felt like she wasn't as smart as other kids were. I mean,... she'd be like, "Crystal there's no way I'm gonna do good in the class," like, "I can't do this," like, "...I'm gonna have to call somebody and...take the on-line quiz with them."...So I don't know if it was she just didn't wanna try or she just held herself back or what but—

Interviewer: And you said you had disputes about that?...

Crystal: I remember one of the times,...the professor wasn't going to be there for the test. And she was like, "Oh my God, I'll help you make a cheat sheet." And I was like, "No, that's okay [laughter]. I don't need to cheat. It's fine."...She just thought it was ridiculous that I would have opportunities to cheat and not cheat.

Interviewer: And why didn't you?...

Crystal: 'Cause I feel like it's lying....

Interviewer: Obviously your roommate cheats for reasons, but do you think those reasons are common...?

Crystal: I think people would cheat because they either don't wanna do the work or they don't feel confident enough that they'd get an A on their own.

One pre-med student talked about her experience studying abroad in Mexico, which she characterized as "relaxed" compared to Saint U. The interviewer asked if academic dishonesty occurred more in Mexico because students were less serious and less grade-conscious. She answered: "It's hard to say. It just depends on the situation...on how important [it is] that...you needed to get a good grade." The inference is that if someone *had* to get a good grade, the decision to plagiarize could be justified.

In college, students who are pre-med or business majors are known for their relentless pursuit of grades, which might mean cutting corners or doing whatever else it takes to end up with an A. In classes graded on a curve, students argue that cheaters hurt their classmates because their high grades skew the results. In other classes, most students say that cheaters hurt only themselves, though some perceive them as harming their professors as well by destroying trust and respect.

Given the casual attitude toward classes that Kaitlin observes in many classmates, as well as in herself, it is not surprising that she also knows a number of students who cheat:

> *Kaitlin:* One friend in particular,...she doesn't like it here but...her parents wanted her to go here, and...she's very well off....She doesn't have a job, she's not really worried about finding a job, so...she just doesn't care enough...about her GPA, so she's like, "Why put in the time on something I don't care about?" and so she just cheats...every opportunity she gets....
>
> I would never...cheat on a test,...but...for homework I definitely would....I feel like homework, like collaborating or something,...I don't see that as a big deal....If we've got...homework, my friends and I get together, or...in group projects,...sometimes people are just like, "I am so busy right now," and they don't [do their] part of it, and...their name's on it but...they didn't do any of it. And..., I understand that's gonna kinda come with the territory eventually....But certainly I think...getting a test...in advance [is wrong], or blatantly looking at someone else's paper during a test,...but I guess I'm a little more lax on cheating than others would be.
>
> *Interviewer:* ...How about...paper writing?
>
> *Kaitlin:* ...I just don't write that many papers, so I don't know....Obviously I wouldn't trade someone else's paper I have from another semester. It would be cheating. But...I would be much more willing to...give a paper to someone than...give a test to someone,...'cause a test,...I feel like that's blatant cheating, but...a paper,...I know I can't physically turn in the same paper, so I will have to have done... some work, so in my mind maybe I'd rationalize it differently....
>
> *Interviewer:* Where do you think the crime is in cheating?
>
> *Kaitlin:* ...By you putting your name on the test, it inherently implies that...that's your work, that's your thought, and cheating obviously is not....I think it's kinda that whole thing where you're taking someone else's work and counting it as yours. If you give it credit, then obviously it's fine, but if you're putting your name on the test and then not acknowledging that "Oh,...the answers are really my neighbor's," then...that's where it lies.

Other students remarked on the severe penalties for cheating, and most said it wasn't worth it. Yet Henderson, who had organized what he called "cheating rings" in high school, spoke of how easy it was to cheat:

Henderson: In high school...I [felt] bad sometimes [because] I'm smarter than other people. So I used to help other people out. While here, I'm not afraid to cheat, but other people are terrified to cheat....People are afraid to get in trouble....Like, [at] my high school there was, like, six people that were competitive about grades. I wasn't even one of them even though they tried to be competitive with me 'cause I was above them. But I don't care about grades at all. But everybody here's so competitive and people don't wanna help other people out. People don't wanna share their information....I know that there's definitely ways to cheat....I don't know if this is common at college—but people here are hardcore on plagiarism....People...won't even talk about what they wrote their essays about or anything like that. That's not a form of cheating, but...I'm definitely against plagiarism.

But...on a multiple choice test,...I know ten different ways to...use sign language or just use systematic taps of the hand or the feet or...blinks of the eye. I've done all different kinds of stuff... involving signals and then relaying the information across.

This is my favorite method that I've come up with....So they have...all these desks and...you just sit, and you don't have to sit at the very back because...I imagine a professor's a little fishy about the people sitting in the very back,...but if you sit...toward the back, just kinda sit in the corner and have somebody sit kitty-corner behind you, and I could just sit there and put my fingers over the edge of the desk—one finger, two finger, three finger, four finger, representing A, B, C, D—and I could just go there and flash a person all the answers down a Scantron sheet or down a multiple choice test, it doesn't matter....And then I had...[an] economics test,...but...that's where I had a professor that...was unbelievably hardcore about cheating. He made us take off our hats and he said if he saw anybody looking at anything other than the desk in front of him, he would take their test away and give them [a] zero. So there's definitely teachers that...[take] extreme measures to prevent it.

There was nobody else who confessed to cheating on such an elaborate scale. But while Henderson wondered at the lack of cheating at Saint U., others considered that any was too much. "John Stamos" wished that there were greater enforcement of rules. One aspect of the honor code, now abandoned, was that teachers were supposed to demonstrate trust in their students by leaving the room during examinations, a practice that left "John" scornful:

> I think the university has a responsibility to its students to prevent cheating, especially on a test. For some reason, that is the most serious one, at least in my mind.... When a student cheats on a test, the university has the responsibility to find that out.... A kid sitting there with a cheat sheet? That should never happen. You're just letting people take advantage of you.... The symbolic trust factor—the honor code doesn't have to work both ways in this. There isn't an honor code, like,... in the city.... There isn't..., "We won't put any policemen out there, this way you guys don't rob anything." ...
>
> I think it's appropriate to have the teacher in the class at least with one eye open.... I find that the teachers that leave the room probably have more kids cheat in their classes than won't. And in the end that's the most important result.

For this student, unlike Henderson, cheating involves criminality and is preventable only through the visible enforcement of authority. Also in contrast to Henderson, "John" believes that students at Saint U. are not so cutthroat that they would refuse to help others with their work, which he sees as appropriate. The reason he deplores cheating is that it gives the cheaters an unfair advantage. "It's not something that I'd make [a] big deal out of," he says, "but it's something that certainly frustrates me,... knowing that there are people that are doing that."

The rules prohibiting cheating and plagiarism are variably enforced by college authorities, and students embrace them to the extent that they accept their validity on the one hand or decide on the other that the danger of being caught is not worth the risk. The odds are good, however, that many students will cheat and most will get away with it.

COLLEGE STUDENTS live in a world they did not make. They did not choose to be forced into an exhausting series of activities in high school. They did not make college admissions increasingly competitive. They did not cause the era of postwar economic expansion to end just as they were born. They did not invent the college experience, which includes their transformation into independent adults, their preparation for a job or career, their exposure to the wider world than that provided by their childhood. They did not design the academic program of requirements, credits, testing, grading criteria, and degrees. They did not write the laws making drinking in college illegal—and thereby an emblem of risk-taking and adulthood.

None of us makes the world we live in. Our task is to navigate within it. We have choices, of course. We can opt out of the entire credential-emphasizing educational system through home schooling or at private schools that eschew such standards. We can choose to limit our consumption and make most of what we need. We can turn down invitations to participate in social events while we stay home alone and study. But insofar as there is a "mainstream" American culture, and insofar as higher education partakes of it, the emphasis on credentials, careers, stamps of approval, evaluations, socializing, and multitasking is an intrinsic part of that culture.

Independent, thoughtful preparation for its own sake may be the goal of professors' assignments, and some students clearly do produce such work. But as the national figures on work effort and plagiarism attest, this is not the norm.

Up until now I have refrained from addressing solutions to the plagiarism "problem." An anthropologist's task is first to understand. I have aimed to illuminate the broad context within which students lead their lives. We have looked at the admissions standards of highly competitive colleges, the nature of student life, the multiple goals that college students are attempting to realize, the attention paid to academics and grades, and the pull of social activities including drinking. In a number of ways, students may be pushed to plagiarize by those who wish most fervently that they not do so.

In the next chapter I examine how some administrators and faculty have attempted to hold back the plagiarism tsunami, showing why most of these efforts have failed.

No Magic Bullet

Deconstructing Plagiarism

> We must, therefore, quit our roles as jailers and instead take care to
> prepare an environment in which we do as little as possible to exhaust
> the child with our surveillance and instruction.
> —MARIA MONTESSORI

> Selfhood and the good, or in another way selfhood and morality, turn
> out to be inextricably intertwined themes.
> —CHARLES TAYLOR, *Sources of the Self*

IT would seem at first glance unacceptable that about three-quarters of
undergraduates commit actions that are regarded as serious breaches of
academic ethics. Most college faculty and administrators feel that something has to be done. The standard approach is to attempt to transform
students' behavior. Yet how to transform which behavior depends on what
kind of problem plagiarism is. We need to address that question before we
can determine what kinds of solutions might be feasible and effective.

Morality and Rules: A Quiz

Violations of morality are sins.
Violations of rules are crimes.
Violations of healthy behavior are symptoms of illness.
Violations of procedure demonstrate imperfect mastery or incomplete
   socialization/education.
Violations of norms could indicate conscious rejection of those norms
   or the application of cultural relativism.
Which kind of violation is plagiarism?

5

The two dominant approaches to preventing plagiarism call for either treating plagiarism as a sin or treating plagiarism as a crime. I have come to believe that neither approach can possibly be universally successful, because the values that create mandates against plagiarizing are in flux, and few students feel passionate concern. A third approach treats one type of plagiarism, the cut-and-paste kind, as a necessary, inevitable part of the educational process.

In considering this question we must recall the wobbliness of the definitions of plagiarism, the historical development of both the idea of authorship and the forces that are eroding or changing it, and the numerous disagreements regarding its nature. We must also recall the movable feast that is the contemporary residential college, in which students regard assigned writing as only one of dozens of obligations and temptations.

Codifying Honor

What questions are moral, and how do we know? I have become consumed by this question. To look at the problem cross-culturally, some questions are moral in some places but not in others. For instance, in India caste contamination is a moral issue, but in cultures that do not share the notion of caste, it is not. Witchcraft accusations among the Azande may involve morality, but only for those who see witchcraft as a realistic possibility. How do we decide if the question is one of culture or one of morality? If I don't think something is moral, is there some other stance from which I can be regarded as wrong? In the United States, failure to recognize murder as morally wrong is considered a sign of mental incapacity. But presumably during the Nazi era those carrying out the orders to kill Jews and others deemed less than fully human (people with cognitive deficiencies, homosexuals) did not regard their acts as murder. Does it all come down to cultural relativism?

If students regard copying homework as a strategy for completing an assignment under time pressure while their teachers regard it as a question of morality, who is right? If the law regards underage drinking as a crime while some regard the law as unjust, who is right?

Honor codes approach the problem of cheating and plagiarism as a matter of ethics and morality. They appeal to students' desire to do the right thing, and assume that with appropriate social pressure to uphold this value, students will do so. Donald McCabe is the best-known advocate of this approach; his work with the Center for Academic Integrity has also acknowledged how complex this question is, especially because students—like all people—hold competing values.[1]

Honor codes typically require students to affirm that they will practice virtuous conduct as members of the university community. Duke students, for instance, pledge the Duke Community Standard:

1. I will not lie, cheat, or steal in my academic endeavors, nor will I accept the actions of those who do.
2. I will conduct myself responsibly and honorably in all my activities as a Duke student.[2]

At the University of Virginia, which has one of the oldest honor codes in the nation, students pledge, "On my honor as a student I have neither given nor received aid on this exam/assignment."[3] The university publishes statistics on the number of students investigated for infringement of this pledge. In 2005–6 seventy students were investigated. Of these, fifty-one were accused, and nineteen cases were dropped. Six students left the university after admitting their guilt. In 2004–5 sixty-four students were investigated. Eleven left with an admission of guilt.

The United States Military Academy at West Point directs simply, "A cadet will not lie, cheat, steal, or tolerate those who do."[4]

Haverford College sees its code as a philosophy, not a list of rules:

Students are expected to take full responsibility under the Honor Code for their conduct and integrity in all academic work, including homework assignments, papers, and examinations, and to confront those who do not. In return, Haverford students are trusted with a greater degree of freedom in their academic pursuits. Self-scheduled, take-home, and/or unproctored examinations are a routine part of the Haverford experience.[5]

During a week-long orientation period, guided by "Orienteers," students at Haverford discuss plagiarism and originality. On a bulletin board in April 2007 I saw a piece a student wrote about Malcolm Gladwell's controversial *New Yorker* essay on the virtues of plagiarism. The student grappled with the nuances of giving credit for influence and celebrating innovation while attempting to uphold the honor code strictly. Haverford students are even prohibited by their honor code from discussing grades with one another.

The College of William and Mary declares first that "a person's honor is his or her most cherished attribute" and then states: "Under the Honor Code of the College of William & Mary, it is expected that all students will demonstrate honesty and integrity in their conduct. Acts of intentional lying, cheating, and stealing are deemed reprehensible and cannot be tolerated. A person who has violated the Honor Code must be sanctioned for compromising the community of trust and honor."[6] Then follows a thirteen-page document spelling out what each of the terms means and what procedures are to be followed if violations occur.

Many universities are careful not to specify what they mean by honorable conduct, on the assumption that students might seek to follow the letter rather than the spirit of the law and find loopholes that were not enumerated. In contrast, some are very explicit about what they mean. Western Michigan University, like many others, prefaces its pledge with a paragraph about honorable and ethical conduct: "Western Michigan University (WMU) is a student-centered research university that forges a responsive and ethical academic community. Its undergraduate, graduate, and professional programs are built upon intellectual inquiry, investigation, discovery, an open exchange of ideas, and ethical behavior.... This includes exemplifying academic honesty, integrity, fairness, trustworthiness, personal responsibility, respect for others, and ethical conduct."[7] Then follow a definition of plagiarism and explicit instructions about how to provide credit, down to the level of how a single footnote or endnote suffices, usually, to provide credit for a series of connected sentences.

Stanford University's "Fundamental Standard" has stated since 1896: "Students at Stanford are expected to show both within and without the University such respect for order, morality, personal honor and the rights of others as is demanded of good citizens. Failure to do this will be sufficient cause for removal from the University."[8] Stanford's honor code explicitly states that faculty will *not* proctor exams—something that the students interviewed at Saint U. (which uses a "modified" honor code) felt was extremely foolish and undesirable:

A. The Honor Code is an undertaking of the students, individually and collectively:

1. that they will not give or receive aid in examinations; that they will not give or receive unpermitted aid in class work, in the preparation of reports, or in any other work that is to be used by the instructor as the basis of grading;
2. that they will do their share and take an active part in seeing to it that others as well as themselves uphold the spirit and letter of the Honor Code.

B. The faculty on its part manifests its confidence in the honor of its students by refraining from proctoring examinations and from taking unusual and unreasonable precautions to prevent the forms of dishonesty mentioned above. The faculty will also avoid, as far as practicable, academic procedures that create temptations to violate the Honor Code.

C. While the faculty alone has the right and obligation to set academic requirements, the students and faculty will work together to establish optimal conditions for honorable academic work.[9]

Saint U.'s code of honor pledges simply, "As a member of the [Saint U.] community, I will not participate in nor tolerate academic dishonesty." It is followed by thirty-four pages of procedures that are invoked if "academic dishonesty" is detected.

These codes all specify that students' work should be characterized by "honorable conduct," "integrity in academic work," "honesty and integrity," "original work," "their own understanding," while "lying, cheating, stealing," "receiving [or] giving aid" are deplored.

We've seen in this book that some students knowingly "cut corners" and violate regulations because they run out of time but still wish to succeed. Others question the worth or even the possibility of originality. Still others value cooperation over independence. If students do not regard their behavior as dishonorable or dishonest, is this merely self-serving justification, or is it possible that there is genuine considered reasoning behind what they do? Should we regard these students as immature in their moral development, or could it be that their morality simply differs from that of the academy?

Academic Integrity

If the notion of academic integrity—and its negative other, academic dishonesty—is to serve as the cornerstone of all efforts to inculcate student morality, it is useful to recall how students regard the underlying notion of integrity. As we saw in chapter 3, students consider integrity to be a general virtue, like being honest and upholding moral principles, tempered by the need to consider other people's feelings (also a moral principle). Some define it as a sense of wholeness and a refusal to compromise.

Academic integrity is defined by the Center for Academic Integrity as "a commitment, even in the face of adversity, to five fundamental values: honesty, trust, fairness, respect, and responsibility."[10] In the sense that it requires ethical behavior, it is related to other forms of integrity; but insofar as students understand that it means using only permitted sources in their academic work, it stands alone, like a stone mountain in a Chinese landscape painting: students have nothing to relate it to. Saint U.'s student handbook on the Academic Code of Honor does not define academic integrity at all.

The connection between *integrity* in general and *academic integrity* is not obvious to most students. Asked directly what it means to have academic integrity, a senior struggled to answer:

> *Brian:* I guess that would be [working] toward the academic moral good, which would be…honesty, no cheating on papers. I don't know what else there is in academic integrity; that's all I can think of, so it would be, I guess, striving toward that.
>
> *Interviewer:* Do you see that here, a culture of integrity?
>
> *Brian:* Um, yes and no. I'd say yes, based on the, I guess, the quality of people that are here already, generally has upstanding morals, has goals not to be dishonest, not to cheat on tests, to do well on their own accord….But I think there still is a long way to go in the fact that reading through the [student newspaper], the number of

reported cases of academic dishonesty or stuff like that isn't really reported, so I don't know if we're upholding the other end of the bargain, which is... holding the other people accountable....

I think confronting at the very least—not necessarily turning them in and sending them to jail, but I think there's a lot that goes overlooked here, that people just pass off as, "Oh, well, I was just helping him on his paper" or whatever, or "helping him on the test," rather than, "No, you were actually cheating...."

I don't know if we've made the definition more fluid, but I think in practice... certain professors will say, "Do your homework on your own, I want you to do your homework on your own." If it's not explicitly stated, I think most people would say, "Oh, it's all right [to work together]."... It's kind of like bending the rule if you wanted to, but I guess it's still cheating, it's still doing what the professor said not to....

Academic integrity in a lot of the Arts and Letters [departments] is more [a question of] plagiarism, right? Ideas and who you attribute them to.

As a math major, Brian knew the abstract definition but did not appear especially invested in its execution—as long as students were not sent to jail. The lack of accurate information about the actual consequences for violations of academic integrity codes is striking.

Students echoed the official line about universities being built on trust and about the importance of originality,[11] but few seemed to go beyond the superficial justification offered by faculty, who may themselves not have examined these guidelines carefully. Alexandra's definition of academic integrity was as vague as Brian's, as was her understanding of the consequences of breaching it, though like many students she resented other students' success if built on a foundation of cheating:

Alexandra: I guess when I hear "academic integrity" [I think of] the honor code. Not cheating. Um... being original with your ideas, giving credit where credit's [due] if you're citing or quoting or whatever. Um, I guess that's just the basics of what I think of—the things you're reminded of every time you take an exam or write a paper.

Interviewer: Once you break that honor code, that stays with you. I mean I don't know exactly what happens, but I'm assuming it goes on your record or something.

Alexandra: I think it does go on your record—

Interviewer: You probably lose the respect of the teacher. I don't know if you lose the respect of your friends—I mean, I don't know if you have any experience with that, whether academic integrity can be lost and whether you lose respect in people's eyes.

Alexandra: ...I think in some manners it can. I know some people who have cheated on exams or completely used papers of their friends, and I...definitely lost some manner of respect for that just 'cause you feel like you're getting cheated if you're doing all the work. Not just because of that....Obviously there's morals and values that go along with that, but at the same time, it's very irritating if you're busting yourself and doing all your own work, which is what you're supposed to be doing in college. You're supposed to be challenging yourself and learning and...going through these hurdles and working really hard, and if someone else just goes and swipes someone else's work,...it's frustrating....I guess in some manners it's hard to gain that [respect] back, because once you've done it [cheated]..., there's nothing you can really go back to change about that or to remedy it.

Alexandra sees cheating as unfair to those who uphold the proper guidelines. At the same time, she knows that many students rationalize their ethical breaches in a variety of ways:

Alexandra: I think a lot of people try to justify things to themselves,...whether it be justifying consumption of alcohol or justifying...cheating or justifying...I don't know—avoiding problems. You justify things a lot. We try and make a reason for why you don't wanna deal with it or why you couldn't do something or whatever....I think it happens a lot, and it's probably not healthy.

Student Solidarity and the Hierarchy of Values

Morality often sounds like a cut-and-dried set of propositions: avoid stealing, never lie, and so forth. In practice, however, people weigh relative goods. A code of behavior may be a rough guide for a new situation, but in practice we frequently invent more rules as we go along.

While in the abstract students subscribe to the ethical principles embodied in the notion of academic integrity, other principles—including some celebrated by colleges themselves—sometimes compete with their understanding of the concept, leading them on the one hand to cheat or plagiarize and on the other to accept their classmates' infractions.

In the competition among values, friendship and the desire to help out far outweigh the abstract pull of academic integrity in most cases. In *Coming of Age in New Jersey,* Michael Moffatt shows how ardently students pursue "friendliness" as a social value. No student he interviewed would turn in a friend for violations of academic integrity; at most a student might lose respect or grumble behind the other's back. Friendship and friendliness—student solidarity—are virtues that take precedence over adherence to the academic code of honor.[12] These are the same virtues that are fostered and celebrated by the institutionalized bonding and the "Saint U. Family" rhetoric that attract so many to the school.

Alexandra is aware of the pressures for success that may provoke students to act dishonestly in doing their schoolwork ("I think a lot of people—especially when it comes to academic integrity or lack thereof—...[cheat] a lot so that they can get those grades and move on to whatever the next step is, whether it be law school or med school or whatever....I think there's a lot of pressure to go into a profession"). But she is clear that confronting friends is a major taboo:

> Unfortunately I think people are more likely to gripe and moan about [a breach of academic integrity] to their friends...as opposed to confronting it. I think part of that is...people don't necessarily like confrontation [and] want to avoid it as much as possible, especially if it is one of your friends that you know that has done this....I haven't [ever confronted] the people I know who have been less than honest with their work.

Despite administrative claims that students should turn in other students who cheat, this is almost never done on any campus. Rachel put it succinctly: "I feel like there's this unspoken code—I don't know if that's right—that you don't rat other people out...because...they're your...classmates....You don't wanna make that person angry at you because…I don't think anyone wants to be a mean person.…I think you want to be liked."

Similarly, "John Stamos" insisted that he would not turn in a friend, even for cheating on tests, which he believed to be a much greater offense than copying homework. Material theft, however, is another story:

> *John:* It would bother me if I copied just because I was lazy, I didn't even try to do it and whatever. But if somebody has a test the day before and they're studying for that test and that's why they don't have their homework done, I'd give them my homework to copy, just so they had an answer in class. That wouldn't be a big deal to me.
>
> *Interviewer:* Why would you not turn in your best friend for cheating?
>
> *John:* Because he's my best friend.…My loyalty to my friend outweighs…that sense of, "Well, this wasn't fair,"…and I guess it's just a hierarchy…of values in that sense that my loyalty would outweigh my sense of fair play.…Now, that being said, if you were stealing hundreds of thousands of dollars…from clients or whatever, I [would] certainly pull him aside and be like, "Listen, either you gotta stop this and give that money back or fix this, turn yourself in, or I'm gonna have to turn you in," because I would draw that line.…It's just a personal weighting system I guess. I'm not adhering to any strict sense of principles.…But him cheating on a—I don't know—math test, to me wouldn't be as bad as him stealing a hundred thousand dollars [chuckles], if that makes sense.

In what John calls a "hierarchy of values," friendliness and solidarity are moral imperatives that command a student's attention far more than loyalty to abstract principles of academic integrity.

Students are influenced by a number of considerations when they forgive fellow students'—or their own—transgressions: pressure, stress, and competition; lack of meaningfulness of a task; ease and temptation of the transgression. In each of these cases, students evaluating someone's behavior can understand it and even overlook it, although they might simultaneously recognize it as "wrong." As analysts have shown in other contexts, even in the case of murder, people are often willing to forgive the transgression if there are mitigating circumstances.[13]

Rules: Some Are Made to Be Broken
(but Which Ones?)

> Unjust laws exist; shall we be content to obey them, or shall we endeavor
> to amend them, and obey them until we have succeeded, or shall we trans-
> gress them at once?
> —HENRY DAVID THOREAU, *Resistance to Civil Government,*
> *or Civil Disobedience*

The second approach to preventing plagiarism is to treat it as breaking a rule—as a crime rather than a sin. At many universities, regular
revisions are made to procedures, sanctions, oversight, enforcement, and
prevention, and faculty and administrators are prompted to be ever more
vigilant in enforcing the regulations surrounding academic integrity.

Turning to a new weapon to aid the policing approach, many schools
now rely on electronic plagiarism prevention resources such as the popular Turnitin.com. Faculty submit to this Web site all student papers, or
at least those they suspect of having been plagiarized in part or entirely.
(At some schools or in some departments this procedure is universally required. At others it is up to individual discretion.) They receive an "originality report" demonstrating whether any part of the paper matches
existing works in the database.[14] Students are scared into following the
rules because they know they will be penalized if they are caught—and
caught they will be. Here the emphasis is on law and enforcement. Yet
students are surrounded by many rules, some of which they embrace and
others they ignore.

We all follow rules in our lives, but there are different kinds of rules,
and we follow them—or violate them—for different reasons.

We drive through intersections when the light is green and we wait
at them when the light is red. We do this because we recognize that it is
necessary for streams of traffic to be physically regulated. We learned this
rule early on, even playing games with it ("Red Light, Green Light"). We
speak of "having a green light" when things are going well with a project.
This is a basic traffic rule, and we follow it for our own safety at least as
much as for its legality. People do violate it. They hurry through a yellow
light just as it's about to turn red—a violation out of self-interest. They
ignore traffic lights when streets are empty in the middle of the night,
when the legal stricture still holds but there is no danger—a violation

through reframing the rule. They ignore the rule when they are drunk or distracted—an inadvertent violation because of impairment. They may fail to observe a light when they are learning to drive—a violation through imperfect mastery.

We self-report our income and our tax obligations each April. Some of us do this because we are afraid the Internal Revenue Service will come after us if we don't—compliance through fear. Some do it because they accept the burden of paying taxes as the price of living in society—compliance through acceptance. Many do it out of routine, dutifully obeying what is asked of them—compliance through socialization and superego. People also violate this rule, for a variety of reasons: they willfully underreport income and overreport expenses to lower their taxes—a violation out of self-interest. Some do not report income or pay taxes because they do not have the money—a violation based on conditions. Some do not report because they forget or are disorganized or are not able to fill out forms—a violation through lack of skill or concentration. Some reject the legitimacy of taxation and do not pay as a form of protest—a violation through principled resistance.

When speaking English, we put subjects before verbs and objects. We say, "The woman paid her taxes," but we generally do not say, "Her the taxes woman paid." We do so because this is how the language works; the reasons lie in the development of English from its Germanic origins. Most people are not aware of this rule, unless they study linguistics or have learned foreign languages or teach grammar. Some may violate this rule because of lapses in knowledge or attention—a violation by mistake.

We eat to perpetuate life. The reasons for this rule are biological and have to do with metabolic functions. People follow this rule, often embellishing it in countless, culturally variable ways. People violate it as well. They stop eating to lose weight; they stop eating as a form of political protest; they stop eating (often at the end of life) deliberately to end their period on earth or passively because their body is shutting down.

We put our napkins on our laps. In the United States this rule has to do with etiquette and table manners. People explain it as a way of protecting clothing from dropped food. This rule is learned from parents reiterating it regularly. People follow it, more or less, when they wish to be "proper" but not when they perceive their situation as casual—a violation of context. They violate it because they forget—a violation of imperfect mastery. They violate it because they prefer having their napkin on the table—a violation from questioning the rule.

We marry and remain faithful to our spouse, a rule that has historical, cultural, religious, moral, psychological, and sociological reasons. We follow it because we agree with the rule, because we have no reason to do otherwise, or because we fear the consequences if we violate it. Yet people do violate it in great numbers. They have affairs because of love—violations based on passion. They have affairs because they are unsatisfied in their marriage—violations based on need fulfillment. They have affairs because they and their partner agree that this is acceptable—violations based on rejecting the rule.

I could go on forever, but you would stop reading long before I felt satisfied. So I will state my point: people do all kinds of things for all kinds of reasons, including violating rules. Maintaining academic integrity is an academic rule. Violating various forms of academic integrity is common. The question, though, is what kind of rule is academic integrity, and what kinds of violations are there? Rules about academic integrity—don't cheat, don't plagiarize, give credit, work independently—are not monolithic. Different reasons govern each one, and different responses are appropriate for violations of each one.

Clearly academic integrity is not a biological drive. It is not practical, a matter of safety, like stopping at a red light. It is not entirely arbitrary, like placing a napkin in the lap, not on the table. It has a specific historical development and a specific context within which it makes sense.

The rules of academic integrity rest on these foundations:

- A college education is valuable, so rules should be followed. (Don't cheat.)
- Independent work is preferable to collective work. (Work alone.)
- Intellectual property is a social good that needs and deserves protection. (Give credit.)
- Words have individual origins that can and must be traced. (Be original. Give credit.)

Plagiarism may be a violation of any of the following types: questioning the foundations; weighing a different value over this one; imperfectly mastering the conventions; or knowingly violating rules just because we can.

Students may see the rules governing academic integrity as moral principles they embrace. But they are equally likely to see them as akin to other rules and laws that they may follow reluctantly or disregard because they challenge them. The laws regarding drinking, for instance, are routinely flouted at almost every college and university in this country, with the complicity of staff and administrators (see chapter 4). And laws regarding music downloading, a form of sharing intellectual property, are so broadly disregarded that it is worth taking a look at the phenomenon.

Free Music? An Intellectual Property Tale

When we asked students about downloading music and videos, they generally said, "I know it's not legal but, yes, I do it." Or "I know we're supposed to think of it as stealing, but everyone does it." Many justified it explicitly in a moral calculus that included such claims as "The record companies don't need my fifteen dollars as much as I do" or "I couldn't afford to pay for CDs" or "I know the artists need to get paid, but the record companies are so rich." Few students refused to download out of moral scruples.

Jessie was an exception (though she benefited from the willingness of friends to engage in behavior she felt was wrong): "I think even if I could [download] I wouldn't.... I have respect for the music industry, and I think it depletes it in some sense...It's not like I'm worked up about [my friends'] downloading music or anything like that. And I can't lie. I have to be honest. I have asked some of them to download music for me, but...me personally, I wouldn't do it."

Several students, however, had been caught by the university illegally downloading music. Like all universities, Saint U. has strict regulations governing computer usage and monitors transactions occurring on its networks. Students who have been caught are much more reluctant to continue to download music.

In the 2006—7 academic year the recording industry began enlisting universities throughout the United States in a crackdown on "illegal" downloading—or at least tried to.[15] Universities supply their students with peer-to-peer networks that facilitate various kinds of open communication within intellectual communities. A side effect is that they can be used to share music. Record companies have been pressuring universities to prosecute students, although only a handful of universities have agreed that it is their responsibility to monitor students' computer use on behalf of the industry.

In May 2007 Ohio University announced that it had come up with software sensitive enough to detect the illegal use of peer-to-peer file sharing while allowing legal uses to continue.[16] The previous year a University of Richmond survey showed that 34 percent of students "illegally" download music, 53 percent of them using their university's computer networks. A documentary produced by the Intellectual Property Institute at the university's law school brought up many of the same questions students raise in terms of rules. Some wonder why software exists to facilitate the downloading of music and movies if this activity is illegal. Some ask the empirical question whether musicians are harmed (losing CD sales) or helped (publicizing their music) by sharing files. (The jury is out on that.) And some question whether preservation of property rights is in the end a moral issue. What about Marxist notions of property and class? What if a person regards those rights as illegitimate? Is copying files a matter of civil disobedience or more like shoplifting? When you take a purse off the rack, it's not in the shop anymore. When you copy a song, it's in both places.

In his book *Free Culture* Lawrence Lessig points out the absurdity of a situation in which, as of 2002, 20 percent of the population, some 43 million people, download music, making them guilty of a felony.[17] It is clear that civil society and the law are completely at odds on this issue. But since the recording industry, like other "big media," can't possibly police the entire society, they focus on scapegoats, such as college students. Lessig tells the story of one student, Jesse Jordan, who was forced to give up his life savings of $12,000 because he was detected gaining access to music files. A freshman at Rensselaer Polytechnic Institute, Jesse had discovered how to modify a within-university search engine—using entirely legal components—to give him access to more than a million files. It turned out that about a quarter of them were music files. The Recording Industry Association of America served him and several other students (whom he did not know) with a lawsuit, demanding from Jesse alone at least $15 million for copyright infringement. The association agreed to settle with him for his savings, as long as he admitted his fault.

He wanted to resist this pressure, but his uncle, a lawyer, advised him that fighting a suit against such a powerful adversary would cost at least a quarter of a million dollars. So Jesse gave all his money to the RIAA. What about the other 42,999,999 people who download?[18]

This is a matter in which technology is moving very quickly and the students move right along with it, but the legal and ethical concerns are a bit slow to change. Students reject the rules made by the state and by the university because the gains to them in doing so are great. A library of five thousand songs, free? Who wouldn't want that? And the chances of being caught are small, so this behavior persists.

This aspect of the rules orientation toward plagiarizing is very much in flux. With iTunes, Apple Corporation has figured out a way to charge for downloading songs which has been successful and is perceived as equitable by the industry and consumers alike. But students do not generally accept the recording industry's arguments. This is evidence of a significant lack of settled notions regarding intellectual property. It remains a hotly contested issue, whether in terms of music, software, movies, clothing designs, or writing.

Is the sanction against plagiarism like the rules and laws that *everyone* breaks a little, such as downloading music—or speeding, or underage drinking? Are these moral issues? Is it a matter of morality to follow all rules? Or is it rather moral, and mature, to assess them and break those we deem wrong?

To the extent that, in the view of students, plagiarism is forbidden simply as an arbitrary rule whose logic is opaque to them, but which carries tremendous consequences if violations are detected, it is followed out of fear rather than conviction. But that isn't what we want from the experience of higher education.

We cannot solve this perennial philosophical puzzle here and now. But we can admit that there is no simple answer to it. That's the honest—moral—thing to do.

If we regard rules against cheating and plagiarism as akin to other rules, we need to discover whether students follow them because they embrace the underlying principles or because they fear the consequences of breaking them. Many administrators at Saint U. and elsewhere are concerned about the patchy enforcement of rules and demand that faculty members explain why they fail to bring charges. If self-reported cheating and plagiarism rates are in the 60–80 percent range each year, then why do most universities report relatively few cases of academic dishonesty? If Saint U., with almost 8,000 undergraduates, hears about 40 cases a year, then does this mean that at minimum, 4,760 cases are getting away scot-free? Are faculty oblivious? Do they not care? Are they too preoccupied with their own careers? Are the procedures too onerous? Are faculty ignorant of the definitions and procedures? Students are especially scornful of rules that are unevenly enforced, as this is patently unfair.

Most administrative attention to preventing plagiarism has focused on values, morality, rules, enforcement, and other such bureaucratic or ideological approaches. There are a number of reasons why these approaches fail:

1. Students have only a vague sense of what is meant by the moral quality termed "academic integrity."
2. The notion of academic integrity is in turn dependent on eighteenth-century concepts of genius and originality, which as I showed in chapter 2 are waning.
3. The notion of academic integrity is dependent on twentieth-century concepts of authenticity and singularity, which I showed in chapter 3 are being superseded.
4. Students employ a "hierarchy of values" in which concern for relationships is especially prominent—a concern fostered by the very institutions that are also attempting to enforce academic integrity.
5. Students are mostly concerned about success and achievement, a bottom-line mentality that has permitted them to enter the highly selective institutions that are also attempting to enforce the norms of academic citation.
6. Students are engaged in a number of activities that have nothing to do with academics—yet another aspect of life encouraged by college admissions procedures and by the structure of college.
7. Rules regarding intellectual property in general are in flux and cannot serve as a solid model for norms governing schoolwork.

Those engaged in day-to-day interactions with students might not be surprised to find that a third approach to preventing plagiarism revolves around the practical matter of inculcating the appropriate and desired academic skills, especially with respect to citation and quotation. But for this approach there are no shortcuts.

Teaching Citation: Who Owns Ideas and Words?

> Students' patchwriting is often a move toward membership in a discourse community, a means of learning unfamiliar language and ideas. Far from indicating a lack of respect for a source text, their patchwriting is a gesture of reverence.
>
> The patchwriter recognizes the profundity of the source and strives to join the conversation in which the source participates. To join this conversation, the patchwriter employs the language of the target community.
>
> —REBECCA MOORE HOWARD, *Standing in the Shadow of Giants*

In addition to the top-down approaches of plagiarism prevention represented by honor codes and rule enforcement, a third approach treats academic integrity, especially the mandate to cite sources, as a set of academic skills to be learned. This notion of academic integrity has both philosophical and practical dimensions: students must be persuaded of the value of citing—something that is far from self-evident—and instructed over time in how to do it. Furthermore, citing one's sources is a historically and culturally specific mandate; it must be explained and discussed.

The nuances of citation are very complicated, as we have seen, even though we summarize them by saying, "Give credit."[19] Faculty who teach writing and composition—the usually unsung heroes of this story—struggle to educate their students about what citation means and how to avoid plagiarism.[20] Unlike administrators and faculty who merely announce the guideline—"Cite your sources"—these writing teachers admit the paradoxical nature of drawing a firm line between what is original and what is borrowed. But even sensitive composition teachers can't (and don't) simply deliver a once-and-for-all lesson about citation.

As Jean Crocker and Philip Shaw demonstrate, there are vast differences in expectations with regard to citation and quotation among faculty in different disciplines. In engineering, for instance, quotation is not considered desirable, while in the humanities it is expected. They acknowledge a continuum between acceptable and unacceptable practices, with a gray area in between. Most legitimate is "quoting a paragraph by placing it in block format with the source cited." Most illegitimate is "copying a paragraph as it is from the source without any acknowledgement."[21] Paraphrasing, patchwriting, and cutting-and-pasting lie somewhere in between. But despite the apparent clarity of this model, students may find illegitimate strategies successful—even educational. Crocker and Shaw propose thinking in terms of intersecting axes, with one scale between *legitimate* and *illegitimate* and another between *most* and *least effective.*

John Swales and Christine Feak, addressing themselves to graduate students, devote two pages to "Some Notes on Plagiarism" and provide an exercise to help students draw the line between acceptable original work and plagiarism. Later in the book they discuss "theories about the role and purpose of citations in academic texts," but this kind of discussion is almost unprecedented.[22] Most of the time students are simply expected to absorb and accept the mandate to cite quotations or paraphrases, without being given reasons why.

Brian, the senior math major introduced earlier, was very thoughtful about the absolutist explanations of plagiarism, and echoed much of what writing teachers such as Crocker and Shaw discuss:

> *Brian:* Part of my question on plagiarism is where we draw the line on it. So there's obviously a continuum. Clearly if you go on-line and find a paper and just print it out and write your name on it, clearly that's wrong. But I think there's a lot that goes on that may just be ignorance, in terms of not properly citing things or ideas or where ideas are based off of. And...I guess I don't even know where the gray area is on this. I want to write a paper on topic X and we're sitting at lunch and we chat about this topic. If you maybe come up with an idea, or you help me in that direction, and we talk about it more, do I need to cite you in that because you helped in the idea process, or could [I] say, "No, it's kind of my idea still"? I don't even know what the answer is to that.
>
> *Interviewer:* That leads to an interesting question:...Can you own an idea? And is anything original?
>
> *Brian:* ...I think you can [own an idea]. Yeah. Again there's a gray area around that. I think there's a definite black area and then there's a gray area. The definite black would be something like a lot of inventions. Those are totally ideas on designs and things....You came up with that idea, you can own that, you can own the patent on that, that's fine. But other things like the lunch conversation, that's [a] gray area. Can you copyright something like that?
>
> *Interviewer:* And that's hard when we have more and more sources now, you know what I mean?

Brian: Yeah, like Google. Shoot, you can find anything you want in there.

Interviewer: And when it's in a book, it's a lot more official looking than something on the Internet.

Even when asked to consider the possibility of "ownership," students sense—properly—that the notion of owning ideas or expressions is difficult to pin down. With the ease of copying and modifying material from the Internet, students recognize the availability of material and are less concerned about protecting than about sharing. Blogs, for instance, encourage the free circulation and expression of people's viewpoints. The freeware, open source, Creative Commons, and wiki movements in technology celebrate mutual creativity and circulation.[23] Since students are generally not earning money through their work, the economic downside of sharing does not seem worth considering.

Cite Me! In Praise (or at Least in Defense) of Plagiarism

In 2004 in the *New Yorker* Malcolm Gladwell celebrated "being plagiarized" for the validation it conferred on him as a writer.[24] His ideas were taken and made more widely known by a playwright who had read an article of his and used his characters. Although Gladwell was not credited, he was pleased to have his work appreciated. The playwright, explained Gladwell, regarded Gladwell's articles as "news" that she could draw on for inspiration rather than as texts that required acknowledgment.

Learning through imitation is very effective. Art students do it all the time. Rebecca Moore Howard was the first to point out that students learn to write by what she calls "patchwriting," defined as "copying from a source text and then deleting some words, altering grammatical structures, or plugging in one synonym for another," which is academic misconduct only in a system that valorizes the singular, identifiable writer.[25] This system in effect rejects the kind of apprenticeship that had Bach transcribing Vivaldi, for instance, or artists learning to draw by copying the Old Masters.

Cross-culturally, examples of literal, humble transmission of words and phrases outnumber examples of each generation starting afresh and creating something brand new. The young, with their astonishing ability to memorize and mimic, are always expected to learn from the old, to defer to them, to memorize and chant and recite until the rhythms are embedded in the psyche and soul, until the person is now socialized and can act properly, having embodied the wisdom of predecessors. Countless studies in a wide variety of traditions demonstrate the value placed by most human beings on oral transmission of tradition, from Jewish and Christian scriptures,[26] to folktales throughout the world,[27] to Greek traditional transmission,[28] to Samoan oratory.[29] Even written texts may rely primarily on collecting previously written fragments, as in incorporation of traditional texts in the Chinese classical histories.[30]

Not only are the skills developed in learning to cite very narrowly defined, but as linguist Ron Scollon's work on plagiarism demonstrates, the rules are also culturally specific and variable.[31] Authority for ideas and words, in some cultural settings, cannot reside in the student but must be found in the tried-and-true wisdom of predecessors, those valorized through credentials and publication. How could a student have the audacity to claim originality of thought or expression?

Writing specialists, whether teachers of composition or analysts of literature, know that integrity is a slippery concept that cannot be conveyed in a single precept uttered once and for all. "Thou shalt not copy" cannot possibly describe the actual functioning of practitioners of the writer's trade.[32] From first-year students struggling to write a convincing argument that their teachers will find "original" yet that completely fulfills the requirements of the assignment, to well-known novelists (such as Dan Brown of *The Da Vinci Code*) relying on research produced by historians, all writers (and musicians and artists and playwrights and filmmakers) take the legitimated work of others and do something with it.[33]

Of course, writers see practical and professional benefits to being quoted by name. Academics increasingly rely on "citation indexes" in various databases, including Google Scholar, to demonstrate their scholarly impact. Researchers rely on getting complete citation information so they can track down sources and use them themselves. Students whose readings are all presented by their teachers and whose writing goes into a vacuum, unread by anyone but a single instructor, cannot be expected to understand the pragmatic reasons for which citations are demanded. (Some innovative writing teachers ask students to cite one another, to ease them into the citation process.) Even those who do understand and accept the legitimacy of stringent citation rules struggle, as we saw when the English major Callista ruminated on the challenges of being original and unique while incorporating other sources as her teachers required. When professors minimize the complexity that thoughtful students recognize, they drive students to abdicate involvement in the citation process.

The professorial insistence on citing sources is often seen as arbitrary and puzzling to students. Even one of my senior research team members, majoring in a field that requires a lot of writing, admitted not understanding why she had to give a page number for a quotation from a journal article, since inclusive page numbers were given in the bibliography. She had accepted the basic guidelines about citation but could not quite grasp all the nuances of their execution.

Students must be shown how to cite, how to refer, how to use quotation marks for direct as opposed to indirect quotation. This is a matter of learning through classroom instruction, for which few faculty members other than composition and writing teachers tend to be very carefully trained.

Students can recite the guideline for giving credit to anything that is not "common knowledge" such as that there are twelve months in the year or that George Washington was the first U.S. president. But what about technical terms defined in textbooks? What about the selection of certain texts to answer the question posed by the professor? Should the professor get credit for the question? For the syllabus?

Strict admonishment—"no copying"—is inadequate, whether as timeless morality or as universal practice. It is not even what we want. At a conference on plagiarism, a law professor argued that enumerating examples of plagiarism made enforcement more difficult. He believed that a simple statement of the guidelines ("Give credit where credit is due") was preferable. Everyone in the room, especially those who work regularly with undergraduates, pounced on his statement as simplistic. Perhaps from a legal perspective such an approach could work, but from a pedagogical one it would surely fail.

Students need to be taught the genre requirements of academic writing.[34] They need to be shown how to do what we, their teachers, are asking of them and to see how it differs from their ordinary practices of including snippets of insight or cleverness out of the sheer joy of it.

Academic writing has a much less obvious joy to it. You might say it's an acquired taste—that most never really acquire.

Thoughts across the Skin's Edge

What is it that we are trying to accomplish through our teaching? Are our students principally supposed to *learn* something? Does this *require* independence and originality? If they copy homework, is it possible that they are still learning? If they rush through it at 3 A.M., are they learning at all? In a world where basic facts are often a Google search away, why do we still insist on individual, independent mastery? A TV game show allows "lifelines"—people contestants contact for answers. Collaboration is increasingly accepted everywhere. Why not in college? Most of our students will not become scholars and academics. They enter our world for a short time, with goals quite different from ours. Do they need to be original in everything they do? Is that even possible?

Treating academic integrity as a constellation of skills, taught largely through the long apprenticeship of higher education, seems to me the most promising approach for getting undergraduates to follow the rules of academic citation, but the one with the least likelihood of finding a shortcut. This simply means teaching students—*really* teaching them—what academic integrity involves, why professors value it, and how exactly to carry it out. At the same time, those teaching it must understand the precarious position of claiming an absolute knowledge of academic integrity and its others. The lines are drawn with great uncertainty and differ around the globe. The best we can do is understand our own practices with greater clarity, look honestly at our own work, and then sort out how to convey this knowledge to the next generation.

Given the nuances of citation and their entanglement with issues of educational goals, originality, intertextuality, selfhood, and individuality, it is clear that students cannot simply be handed a brochure and be expected to get it. The message has to be broadcast over and over, by many sincere people who have given it much thought.

As long as contemporary students regard their university years as simply a stage of life that must be endured—and this may be a hard reality for academics to accept—there will be a fight for their attention. Scaring them into honoring the rules of attribution is unlikely to succeed. What we ultimately desire is for them to *want* to learn. We can do this only through genuine engagement with the tasks we demand of them, through understanding the full context within which these tasks are undertaken, and through the equivalent of cross-cultural (in our case cross-generational) communication. This means we must listen, not only preach.

When we look closely at what is expected of students writing as apprentice scholars, we see that the academic standards for proper citation are fraught with contradictions; they are a recent invention and perhaps will be short-lived, coinciding with technological, artistic, and social movements. Furthermore, they conflict with the mores of quoting that apply in students' lives outside the classroom, where they celebrate their freedom from the need to cite.

Our notion of the originality of utterance as the product of the unique, isolated, authentic self had its peak in the 1960s and 1970s. Students today have been immersed in a culture that revels in trying on different personae. There is no inviolable connection between words and the self that produces them. Sharing freely and taking others into consideration are paramount values. Performing has become natural. These students are not wedded to the integrity of their own writing and do not necessarily assume that others are either.

Students focused on education for its own sake—like a majority of faculty—would give their attention to the process of learning and to producing assignments that increase that learning. They would aim to model their behavior on that of their teachers. Instead, what we find is that many students don't especially value the process of classroom learning; they are focused on attaining other ends, so any process will do. As adolescents seeking opportunities to grow up, have fun, and be comfortable, students at residential colleges minimize their academic load and maximize their engagement in other activities. This is nothing new, but it represents a significant mismatch between faculty and administrators on the one hand and students on the other.

As we have seen, when administrators and faculty attempt to solve the quandary of plagiarism, they tend to attempt either moral suasion or stricter enforcement of rules. Each of these approaches aims at one aspect of the problem but overlooks the fact that students need to be taught the proper skills in a subtle and ongoing fashion.

The rules of citation, like all rules, arose in a particular environment, and that environment—consisting of ideas about writing, selfhood, identity, and socialization—is changing while the rules endure. That is not a bad thing. But it places the burden on the enforcers of those rules to recognize that our students do not share all of our assumptions about the world. If we want *them* to understand what we ask of them, *we* need to understand it first.

Conclusion

What Is to Be Done?

Grown-ups never understand anything for themselves, and it is tiresome for children to be always and forever explaining things to them.
—Antoine de Saint-Exupéry, *The Little Prince*

A child is not a vase to be filled, but a fire to be lit.
—François Rabelais

THIS book has examined students' words and, presumably, thoughts about the enterprise of being a college student who writes in the twenty-first century. I have suggested that those of us who are educators trained in the twentieth century must try to understand how students today are different from us in order to grasp their motives for and attitudes toward plagiarism. Whether there is indeed an epidemic of plagiarism, educators and the public perceive the existence of such a scourge. This too can be explained largely as a result of substantial transformations in what it means to be a person and a student over the past several decades. I do not suppose that all educators trained twenty, thirty, or forty years ago are the same, nor that all contemporary students differ entirely, and in entirely the same way, from their elders. There are, however, a number of different cultural *emphases,* and these can account for the choices and value judgments made by students.

Given that I consider the most common approaches to the topic of plagiarism to be inadequate, it is only fair that I make my own suggestions about what we—educators, parents, writers—should do about it. I begin with the most concrete and practical and soar into the ether with my wish for grand social change.

The fundamental law is that we be honest; students are excellent detectors of hypocrisy. Hypocrisy begs for uncovering. If academics demand an impossible standard from students—not drinking until twenty-one, citing every instance of influence—then it is the duty of youth to reveal its impossibility, with both increased infractions and lack of respect for those who demand the absurd. But even honesty, frankness, and patience may not suffice.

I had a recent experience with plagiarism that shows how, even with the best of intentions, I still struggled to convey what was required. But my response—coming after I had done a lot of research on this project— was less anguish and judgment, as before in such cases, than a sense that what was needed was *instruction*. I believe my response was more effective than it would have been years ago, when I might have applied the academic "death penalty," in Rebecca Moore Howard's apt phrase, and had the student expelled.[1] This time around I saw the academic miscreant as more of a lost soul than a hardened criminal.

I HAD ASSIGNED what I thought was a cheat-proof take-home final examination in an advanced linguistic anthropology course: Design a research project based on the course we've finished. Explain where you would carry out your research, why, and how. Connect your project with course readings and ideas.

I received the usual range of papers, from a six-page explanation of a modest application of course principles (How do people pronounce things in one place and another?) to an ambitious attempt to understand people's ideas of the self by recording those who live alone and might speak aloud to themselves. Everybody's paper fit more or less completely, in style and quality, with his or her previous work.

One paper, however, stood out. It went into a great deal of detail about nuances of tribal differences in Africa and described challenges for development. Only peripherally did it even begin to mention language, and then not in any terms or ideas that the course had covered. There were strange phrases and odd old sources cited. I stuck one phrase into Google and, *voilà*!, to my horror, an entire paragraph turned up, verbatim. I called the student in and asked how she could explain this. I didn't really mean "How can you explain it?" I meant "I'm accusing you of plagiarism," but I did hear her explanation: "I've been working thirty hours straight and threw the paper together. I often collect quotations to use in my paper and I must have forgotten to put quotation marks around it."

I half believed her. I did believe that she was exhausted and overwhelmed and that it was difficult to find time to write the research proposal. I did not believe that this was the first time she had been "confused" about the origins of pieces that appeared in her papers. Her infraction bore evidence of the cheating, intertextual, and performance aspects of plagiarism: she had copied pieces, uncredited, from other sources; she was uncertain about how to denote even those sources she did cite; and she wished only to turn something in, complete her performance, and get some sleep and then go home for Christmas.

I asked what she thought the punishment should be. We agreed that she would rewrite the paper for a maximum of 50 percent credit and submit the revised version four days later. We wrote up a report of a "Violation of Academic Integrity," signed it, and sent a copy to the provost in charge of the honor code.

The second paper was a slightly revised version of the first. There was still strange, irrelevant detail; the paper still didn't really address the topic. And there were still strange words strung together. Back to Google: and again, I found several sentences that were lifted verbatim from another source. In one case she had included the author's name at the end of the paragraph but did not indicate that any words were quoted directly; the inference from her citation would be that she had paraphrased. In another case she quoted without citing an author at all, though the author was in the bibliography.

A second violation would likely lead to suspension or expulsion. (Ten or even five years earlier, I think, I would have gone all the way.) Meanwhile, she had left me two e-mail messages and two phone messages—this was over winter vacation—asking why her grade had not yet been changed. She was applying to graduate school and needed her transcript.

Over the telephone I explained the severity of the situation to her. She apologized and asked what I wanted her to do. I said that I really wanted her to *learn how* to do this work right. I gave her three assignments: to read a Web site devoted to teaching students how to avoid plagiarism;[2] to reread the assignment for this project; and then to start from scratch and redo the paper on a different topic.

The third version was unimpressive but clearly original. She did indeed learn from this experience, at least enough to have spent much more time on it than most students, and ended up producing something that coincided with my goals and the academy's.

I go into detail here because it demonstrates how hard a problem this presented. Here was a student at a highly selective university. She was a senior, planning to go to graduate school. We had already met to go over the penalties for plagiarism. And yet she did it again.

Perhaps I had not explained clearly enough. Perhaps I did not take the time needed to show exactly where her error lay. I am an anthropology professor, after all, and assumed that English teachers had taken care of this long ago. But I am an anthropology professor with a deep and long-standing interest in this issue; I had had this student in two classes, and she appeared to understand. But even in these circumstances, I failed to convey the needed information.

How can we expect a single sentence—"Avoid violations of academic integrity"—to suffice? This student cheated, then she failed to cite properly even when she tried. Although she was in a hurry, I certainly had her attention, and she was motivated to get it right. But she didn't.

Furthermore, the actual work of tracking down suspected violations is very hard and very time-consuming. I did not want to chase down the sources, confront the student, read several other versions of the same mediocre paper, and meet the student again, but I did it. I have a fairly light teaching load, compared to colleagues at many institutions, and I care about this issue.

And what about my colleagues at community colleges or four-year schools with four-course-a-semester teaching loads? High school teachers with hundreds of students? It is a lot of trouble to deal with a case of plagiarism, and we don't all have the skills to do it.

WE PROBABLY should admit, frankly, how hard this kind of enforcement is. We can also admit the artificiality and cultural specificity of our standards. We do that all the time. We don't let students write "I ain't gonna do it," though plenty of college students speak that way. We enforce rules at sporting events: no touching the ball with your hands in soccer; no batting with your feet in baseball. We regulate all kinds of things that happen only on campus. And in some ways enforcement of proper citation is like that. It is also paradoxical. We make students learn about the Heisenberg Uncertainty Principle. We could also teach the Citation Paradox Principle.

We all quote; we all use others' words. This is how we learn to speak. This is how we play with language and show our membership in a variety of groups. Academics do it too. We write of "discipline," and Michel Foucault comes to mind; people write of "governmentality," and Nikolas Rose is invoked. (If you don't know that, then you're not in the club.) Einstein need not be cited each time we write about relativity, but the technical terms must be used.

So our policing of inclusion, quotation, and so on is a very special kind of law. It is particularly unnatural. We do our students a disfavor if we claim that this law is eternal and obvious, because it is neither.

We must recognize the ways students incorporate texts in their daily lives and show them how the same practices can be channeled for the purposes of the academy.

There are a number of different approaches to the problem.

We might dismiss it as illusory, an artifact of our general uneasiness regarding intellectual property.

We might simply decide that we need to work harder to propagandize, to convince students and faculty that standards must be upheld.

We might give up entirely, throwing up our hands at the number of students who violate the rules, and conclude that ours are immoral times.

Or we might conclude that the pressures on the students are too great and all we can do is provide good counseling for them when they need it.

What I believe is that we must instead try to comprehend the revolutions that are occurring in technology, the self, education. Then solving the problem of plagiarism will have to be understood anew, as one of the many goals of higher education and of society as a whole.

Concretely, universities can take the following steps:

- Convene symposia and conferences with faculty and students. Put these issues out in public, spell them out so everyone knows what we are talking about. Students always detect hypocrisy, as in policies about consuming alcohol and downloading music. These issues are too complex for one-line credos. Only some aspects are moral; some are technical; some are philosophical (*What is an author?*). Allow students a voice in framing the issue. Admit that most faculty don't get it either.

- Foster broad, honest discussion of the value of higher education, and not only in education circles, and not only to lament the passing of a golden age. (But not only for cheerleading and fundraising either. I mean *honest* discussion.) Talk about what it means to be motivated by grades. Show that students with lower grades can nonetheless live happy and productive lives. Dissociate the extrinsic from intrinsic motives of education.
- Acknowledge students' abilities. They are very good at making presentations, working with others, being productive; the majority just don't like to read books or write like academics. What does that mean for faculty expectations of students?
- Admit that the rules are somewhat arbitrary. Intellectual property is not an eternal value, but we still have to abide by the values of our time and place.
- Demonstrate and admit the lack of agreement between students and faculty/administrators.
- Separate the intellectual from the legal from the bureaucratic dimensions of academic citation.
- Compare student quotation and intertextual practices with academic citation practices. Be explicit about the similarities and differences in citing and quoting, paraphrasing and borrowing. Show that there are different norms in different contexts—quoting from movies, on AIM, from books in papers—all legitimate in their own way. But make it clear that when the norms of one domain are applied in another, it demonstrates disrespect and may be treated severely.
- Raise the problem of intellectual property as a theoretical and historical issue. Discuss *openly* the recording industry's insistence on university enforcement of anti-copying laws and the many moral, economic, and philosophical questions involved.
- Sort out "cheating" and the various sorts of "plagiarism." Just as we distinguish between tasting a grape at the supermarket and stealing a car, we don't want to lump together all infractions of academic citation norms. There are big differences among imperfect mastery of citation norms, incorporating a sentence, omitting quotation marks, and turning in someone else's paper, even with permission, just as there are among sharing answers on homework, glancing at someone's test, stealing the answer key, and having someone take

your test for you. No wonder students throw up their hands in some cases.

- Don't panic!
- Really *educate* these young people. Empower them. Don't treat them as children to be disciplined "because I say so."
- A revolutionary approach would be to abolish college as the major adolescent challenge: separate the intellectual from other endeavors. Institutionalize a two-year service obligation prior to beginning higher education. Let students begin to grow up a little before they enter our classes.

That's all too hard, you might say. Well, yes. As I said, there's no simple answer.

I HAVE CHANGED my mind about almost this entire topic—sometimes going back and forth about a certain item several times in a single week—over the course of writing this book. But what is most clear to me is the mismatch between the academy's and students' expectations. This comes out in surveys of faculty and students, which show that they don't care about the same things. It comes out in the bewilderment faculty and administrators express about their nice students behaving so badly. It comes out in students' views of class work and play time. I have aimed in this book to fill in the context around the survey numbers.

I have learned that we are in a situation of both crisis and stasis. The crisis lies in a lack of understanding on the part of the elders of the changed world in which our young charges have been brought up. We do not entirely share their goals, and we certainly do not share their means of attaining those goals. The stasis lies in the fact that such mismatches are not new; in concentrating all of our most able youth into adult-free zones, we ensure that they will form identities at odds with those outside their social group. Although college faculty and administrators are hazily present during the daytime hours, at night the place is theirs alone, and that is when the writing happens—writing that gets them closer to the freedom to pursue their other interests. Whatever gets their papers completed is welcome.

Personally, I no longer see plagiarism as primarily a moral issue—for most students. But given academic norms of citation, there will always be occasions when, at least technically, we can find plagiarism. The least serious form of plagiarism is really a matter of simple ignorance and should be combated with more education. The most serious forms of plagiarism (and cheating in general) occur, and have long occurred, because students want to find the easiest way to complete their writing tasks. Since the 1990s, however, the pressures have mounted to the point of explosion.

I see plagiarism as a direct result of conflicting claims on students' diffuse attention, which have been compelled by those who love and cherish them most: the parents who got them to college and the teachers who want nothing but the best for them while they are there. In this misguided effort to pack more and more into a life already filled to the brim, the overflow valve is the shortcut into plagiarism, the rivulet that prevents the river from flooding and engulfing the delta.

The only genuine solution is to lower the water table and return the youth of our society to drier, calmer ground, where they can hop, skip, and jump rather than cut, paste, and graduate.

I began this book with a consideration of plagiarism and college culture. But I am ending with concerns, worries, grave doubts about the connection between our society's educational system and our ideas of childhood and success. To end intertextually, E. M. Forster did not, surely, have anthropology in mind when he wrote "Only connect," but if the shoe fits...

Notes

Introduction

1. Josephson Institute of Ethics 2002, CAI 2003, Hanna 2004, Hansen 2004, Newbart 2004, McGrath 2006a, 2006b.
2. McCormick 2003, Hanna 2004, Heuman 2005, from Stanford, Notre Dame, and Brown, respectively, to select a few articles.
3. Imperato 2000, Hoover 2002, McCabe and Treviño 2002.
4. Schemo 2001.
5. Duke University 1999, Josephson Institute of Ethics 2002.
6. Cole and Kiss 2000, Storch and Storch 2002, Vowell and Chen 2004.
7. All from Jordan 2001.
8. McCabe and colleagues (1997, 2001, 2002), like other researchers (Haines et al. 1986), distinguish "individual" and "contextual" influences on student behavior. Psychologists tend to focus on the former and sociologists on the latter. Anthropologists also are more interested in overall patterns than in predicting or explaining individual cases.
9. McCabe, Treviño, and Butterfield 2001, 223. See also Clegg and Flint 2006.
10. McCabe, Treviño, and Butterfield 2001, 223.
11. Ibid., 221.
12. Geertz 1986, 112.
13. As the anthropologists George and Louise Spindler note, an ethnographic approach requires that any information must be explained in its multiple contexts. Under such qualitative methods, especially semi-structured interviewing, as one's understanding deepens, one's questions change. In this research the questions changed as I felt we had gained a satisfactory understanding of one issue and as new issues were raised, either in the interviews or in the endless reading I was doing on the topic of higher education. Spindler and Spindler 1997 [1985]. See also Bernard 1995.
14. Most research on plagiarism and cheating relies on surveys and statistical profiles across a range of institutions. Donald McCabe, for instance, has surveyed approximately 120,000 students. See McCabe and Treviño 2002. Ethnographic research, by contrast, relies

on a closer look at a smaller sample. Anthropologists study relationships among various aspects of humankind, seeking patterns and explanation, connections and meaning. Many cultural anthropologists use data derived from their own face-to-face interaction with the people being studied, in an approach usually called "ethnographic." This approach yields a certain kind of data: local, detailed, particular, specific, deep. Much has been written about the virtues and limitations of ethnographic data. Similarly, the stance taken by many cultural anthropologists is known as "participant observation," as we simultaneously take part in and attempt to observe, record, and make sense of the events around us. This too has been scrutinized, its benefits and hazards well spelled out. Some ethnographic studies focus on a very small number of individuals followed for a period of time, such as Paul Willis's *Learning to Labour* (1981 [1977]), which focuses on twelve boys, or Vincent Crapanzano's *Tuhami: Portrait of a Moroccan* (1980) and Marcel Griaule's *Conversations with Ogotemmêli: An Introduction to Dogon Religious Ideas* (1965), in-depth analyses of single individuals that nonetheless reveal profound cultural meanings.

15. Carnevale and Rose 2003, 7–8.

16. Kuh and Pascarella 2004.

17. Josephson Institute of Ethics 2002. The university also has no fraternities or sororities, but I think my account can still explain the organized cheating said to characterize the Greek system, which essentially institutionalizes what in other places is done on an ad hoc basis by individual students.

1. A Question of Judgment

1. Thanks to Deborah Shamoon and Linda Shamoon, personal communication, June 28, 2007.

2. Tierney 2007.

3. Wilford 2007.

4. Magolda and Ebben 2007, 146.

5. Lerner, Rapoport, and Lomsky-Feder 2007, 170.

6. Julliard 1994.

7. Ibid.

8. Roig 2001.

9. Goodwin 1987.

10. History News Network 2005, Washington Speakers Bureau 2007.

11. See Lewis 1991, Carson 1993, Genovese 1995.

12. *New York Times* 2003.

13. Conan 2003.

14. Ibid., Rose 2003.

15. *Harvard Crimson* 2006.

16. Wilson 2006.

17. Gladwell 2006.

18. Andersen 2006.

19. Cowell 2006.

20. Reynolds 2006a, 2006b.

21. *Economist* 2002; see also Lewis 1991, Carson 1993, Genovese 1995.

22. Plotz 2002.

23. Posner 2007.
24. Byrne 2008, Guterman 2008.
25. Howard 1995.
26. Schneider 1999, Moore 2002.
27. Birchard 2006.
28. Callahan 2004.
29. England began to use such tests in 1870 to combat the monopoly of hereditary power, and the United States in 1883. Miyazaki 1981 [1963], 124.
30. Suen and Yu 2006, 50.
31. Miyazaki 1981 [1963], 19.
32. Elman 2000, 196.
33. Miyazaki 1981 [1963], 17, 21.
34. Suen and Yu 2006, 56–57.
35. Ibid., 57–58.
36. Miyazaki 1981, 121, 119–20.
37. Blum 2007, 68.
38. Mangan 2002, Wheeler 2002.
39. Walfish 2001.
40. *Beijing Review* 2002, Ding 2002.
41. In 2006 Sweden followed Finland, Iceland, and New Zealand (all tied for first, at 9.6 out of 10), Denmark (fourth at 9.5), and Singapore (fifth at 9.4) (Transparency International 2006). Sweden was ranked 9.2 out of 10. In contrast, the United States was ranked twentieth, at 7.3. China was ranked seventieth, along with India and Mexico, at 3.3. Russia was ranked 121, at 2.5, and last was Haiti, ranked 163, at 1.8.
42. Editorsweblog.org 2004.
43. Horowitz 1987, 23.
44. Summarized ibid., 33.
45. Howard 1999, xvii.
46. Ibid., 7.
47. Ibid., xviii.
48. McKillup and McKillup 2007, Posner 2007.

2. *Intertextuality, Authorship, and Plagiarism*

1. As occasionally happens in intellectual matters, the concept of "language ideology" named something that anthropologists, linguists, and other analysts of language had been aware of for some time: that different values are placed on various aspects of language at different times and in different places. We see it as early as in Malinowski, "The Problem of Meaning in Primitive Languages" (1923), in much work on the Ethnography of Speaking (e.g., Gumperz and Hymes 1986 [1972] and Bauman and Sherzer 1989 [1974]), including in Sherzer and Darnell 1986 [1972], "Outline Guide for the Ethnographic Study of Speech Use," especially the section titled "Attitudes toward the Use of Speech" (551–52), and in a good portion of the work of Michael Silverstein (1979, 1998). When Kathryn Woolard and Bambi Schieffelin gave a name to this approach to the understanding of language in 1994, they unleashed a new creative energy in this study (see also Schieffelin, Woolard, and Kroskrity 1998, Kroskrity 2000). One of the most exciting aspects of this approach, for me,

is the subtle analysis that we can achieve of how people regard the very nature of language. Elsewhere I have called this the ontology of language (Blum 2007), but I am willing to merge with the zeitgeist and use the prevailing term.

2. See, for example, Duke University 1999; see also *Chicago Manual of Style* 2003, Purdue University 2006, among others.

3. "Intertextuality" is a term coined by Julia Kristeva (1980 [1977]), inspired by Mikhail Bakhtin's notion of *heteroglossia*, a translation by Michael Holquist of Bakhtin's *raznorečie* (Bakhtin 1981 [1934–35], 263). Bakhtin points out in his often-cited work "Discourse and the Novel" that "language...lies on the borderline between oneself and the other. The word in language is half someone else's" (293). Bakhtin was concerned with language in general, as well as with language incorporated into verbal art, especially as capacious a genre as the novel.

4. At the heart of this topic is the fundamental question of what Erving Goffman (1983 [1979]) has called "participant roles," which in turn have a bearing on a speaker's degree of responsibility for action or words. In his brilliant analysis of what he termed "footing," Goffman differentiated the possible roles for "speaker" into Principal (the originator), Animator (the one who performs the message), and Figure (the persona being animated), among others; for "listener" there were the roles of "ratified participant" and "bystander"; the bystander could in turn be differentiated into "eavesdropper" or "overhearer." Similarly, Dell Hymes (1972) differentiated between at least two possible aspects of a "speaker": "animator" (the person giving voice to the words) and "author" (the originator of the words). Judith Irvine (1996) analyzed the insult poems (*xaxaar*) presented at engagement ceremonies among the Wolof of Senegal, which could be pinned down to no particular author. The words, uttered by griots (low-caste bards), were originally created by anonymous authors in secret at night, and sponsored by the bride's co-wives and other women in the community. The guests heard them and repeated them elsewhere, so that the insults became part of the common knowledge. The result was to produce speech that was nobody's responsibility yet got certain pejorative ideas into circulation. This is a clever way of permitting ambiguous speech—perhaps true, perhaps false, perhaps merely humorous—to become present as a potential threat to a new bride's reputation.

5. McDermott and Tylbor 1986.

6. Ochs, Schegloff, and Thompson 1996, Goodwin 2002, and others.

7. Gladwell 2004, Posner 2007.

8. Coulmas 1986; see also Cappelen and Lepore 2003.

9. Hill and Irvine 1992.

10. See Geurts and Maier 2003, Predelli 2003, Reimer 2003, Saka 2003.

11. Frege 1892, 58.

12. See Romaine and Lange 1991, Cukor-Avila 2002, Tagliamonte and D'Arcy 2005.

13. Klewitz and Couper-Kuhlen 1999.

14. See, e.g., Abbott 2003.

15. Hanks 2000, Bauman 2004. Some languages provide this kind of attribution through grammar. In English we *can* trace the sources of words and information but are not obligated to.

16. Pletsch 1991, Freedman 1994.

17. The study of oral epic poetry sidesteps the question of authorship altogether, since such oral genres relied on existing frameworks as a scaffold on which to build a performance at a particular moment. See Lord 1960, Thompson 1977, among others.

18. Rose 1993, 26.

19. Ibid., 25.

20. As I show in chapter 3, I believe that an ideology of authenticity/uniqueness is giving way to an ideology of performance.

21. The term first appeared in 1701. Rose 1993, 58n4.

22. Rose 1993.

23. Ibid., 18, 18n4.

24. Ibid., 32.

25. Ibid., 48–50, 56–65.

26. Patents, by contrast, protect ideas. Ibid., 65–74, 131, 89, 132.

27. Ibid., 109–12.

28. Ibid., 114.

29. Pletsch 1991, 1.

30. Bloom 1997 [1973], 27.

31. Pletsch 1991, 5.

32. Ibid., 177.

33. Rose 1993, 114–22, 125–28.

34. Ibid., 117.

35. Barthes 1977 [1968], Foucault 1979, Goffman 1983 [1979], Irvine 1996.

36. Barthes 1977 [1968], 142–43.

37. Ibid., 143.

38. Rose 1993, 142.

39. Ibid.

40. The legal definitions of property are convoluted and to some extent circular, sometimes applicable and sometimes not applicable to ideas and the expression of ideas. See Green 2002–3, 208–21.

41. Ibid., 218.

42. Ibid., 218–19.

43. Ibid., 224.

44. Ibid., 225. There are technicalities involving state versus federal laws as well.

45. Ibid., 234.

46. Ibid., 234–35.

47. In China the figure is over 90 percent. NationMaster.com. n.d.

48. Lessig 2004; see also Vaidhyanathan 2001, Free Culture 2007.

49. Lethem 2007a.

50. Lethem 2007b.

51. Grafton 1997.

52. Ibid., 22–23.

53. For writers on intertextuality, see Gladwell 2004, Delbanco 2005, Lethem 2007a.

54. Ede and Lunsford 1990, Howard 1999, Bawarshi 2003.

55. See atlyrics.com/quotes/, uselessmoviequotes.com.

56. Many societies foster such verbatim repetition—traditionally in so-called oral (non-literate) cultures. It is possible that this memory for observed performance is bringing students in the United States more into line with human practices elsewhere.

57. Blum et al. 2004, Blum 2005a.

58. I chose the word "gift" here prior to reading Lethem's article "The Ecstasy of Influence" (2007a), in which he describes the influences that go into one's writing—indeed,

into all art—as both gift and commodity. Did he influence me "pre-troactively"? Were we influenced by the same factors?

59. In Tannen 1989.

3. *Observing the Performance Self*

1. Salinger 1951, Kerouac 1957, Pirsig 1974.
2. Mauss 1938. See also Morris 1972, Lukes 1973, Taylor 1989.
3. Freud 1961 [1930].
4. Woodmansee 1984, Vaidhyanathan 2001.
5. Lowinsky 2003.
6. Woodmansee 1984, 427.
7. Ibid., 429.
8. Ibid., 445.
9. Cited ibid., 447.
10. Laing 1960.
11. Ibid., 39.
12. Authors Neil Howe and William Strauss present a portrait of what they term "the Millennials," the cohort of people born in the 1980s and arriving at universities around the turn of the millennium (Howe and Strauss 2000). In contrast to their immediate predecessors, "Gen X" (as portrayed in *Generation X Goes to College* [Sacks 1996]), the "Millennials" are conformist, hopeful, happy to work in groups, and so forth. Whereas "Gen Xers" needed constant affirmation of their worth, and "self-esteem" was their parents' and teachers' greatest concern, the Millennials are more other-oriented, and expect to make a difference in the world. This sort of generational analysis is provocative but also more superficial and headline-grabbing than what I am seeking to do. With its appeals to marketing and consumption, such analysis has become a kind of cottage industry; a new model is always going to be necessary, just as economists expect economic "growth" as the norm. See also McKibben 2007. The focus of Jean Twenge's research is what she calls "Generation Me," suggesting that they are narcissistic, entitled, and depressed, among other psychological characteristics (Twenge 2006).
13. Judith Butler has a different notion of "performance," which she contrasts with a prediscursive, given self prior to the expression of identity (Butler 1999).
14. Cited in Pascarella and Terenzini 2005, 22.
15. Christopher Lasch documents the simultaneous appeals to conformity and nonconformity, the "cult" and the "dogma of authenticity," evident in part in the collapse of authority, especially parents' authority (Lasch 1991, 166–68).
16. Gergen 1991, Turkle 2004, Sheppard 2007.
17. See Arens 1981 and Kottak and Kazaitis 1999, 26–27, for some discussion of the anthropology of football.
18. There is broad agreement that football culture increases the likelihood of rape. Anthropologist Peggy Reeves Sanday (1996, 2007) has studied the difference between "rape-prone" and "rape-free" campus cultures; prime factors include male dominance, gender segregation, the presence of fraternities, and an emphasis on athletics. Overall she cites estimates that one-fourth of all women and one-sixth of all men will experience unwanted sexual attention or rape during college. Alcohol is also a key factor.

19. Francis L. K. Hsu wrote in 1963 about the tendency of Americans, as individuals, to join groups such as clubs and voluntary associations. Robert Putnam, in *Bowling Alone* (2000), argues that Americans no longer participate in civic endeavors. At highly selective colleges, however, students are chosen in part because of their potential for contributing to the campus community, which they demonstrate through similar contributions during high school.

20. Wasik 2006.

21. Introversion is not the same thing as shyness. Shyness is defined as "a feeling of discomfort or inhibition in social or interpersonal situations that keeps you from pursuing your goals, either academic or personal" (Payne 2000, 4). Since the 1990s, after holding steady at 40 percent for a long time, Americans' self-reported rate of shyness has "escalated" to 50 percent, in contrast to 31 percent of Israelis and 57 percent of Japanese (Henderson, Zimbardo, and Carducci 2001). Henderson and Zimbardo attribute the increase in shyness to the increased use of computers and other electronic media, and to increased isolation stemming from social, technological, and economic processes (1998).

22. Horowitz 1987.

23. Michaelsen, Fink, and Knight 2006 [1997], CRLT 2006a.

24. McCorkle et al. 1999, Cockrell, Caplow, and Donaldson 2000.

25. CRLT 2006b.

26. Lenhart and Madden 2007.

27. Baker 2008.

28. Giles 2005.

29. Terdiman 2005.

30. Jaschik 2007.

31. Calore 2007, Fresh Air 2007.

32. Nunberg 2007.

33. Bluestein 2007, Conflict Research Consortium 2007, Martin 2007.

34. Erikson 1985 [1950].

35. Turkle 1984.

36. Turkle 2002, 5, 7.

37. The lines between this alternative world and RL are becoming less sharp; some people are willing to convert Second Life "Linden Dollars" into U.S. dollars. Companies and universities have set up SL campuses and recruit in them. Second Life 2007.

38. Suler 2007.

39. Turkle 1995, 178.

40. Ibid., 179.

41. Ibid., 180.

42. Ibid., 185–88, 192.

43. Merriam-Webster OnLine, 2006.

44. Palmer 2005.

45. Ede and Lunsford 1990, Rose 1993, Buranen and Roy 1999, Howard 1999.

4. Growing Up in the College Bubble

1. Liminal periods have always made people uncomfortable. Coming-of-age ceremonies occur during puberty in many societies, with sexuality the key feature; hence the common occurrence of circumcision at that age. Van Gennep 1960 [1909], Turner 1967 [1958].

2. Philippe Ariès is credited with pointing out the culturally constructed nature of childhood, which is to say that not all societies have a category of "childhood" set apart from other moments of human life in quite the same way. See, e.g., Ariès 1962, Postman 1994 [1982], Heywood 2001, Rogoff 2003, Stearns 2006. Scholars argue about the phases of childhood, about the universality of development, about the best fit between a given phase of childhood and a form of education. They wonder whether childhood is disappearing as children lose their innocence and know too much about the world, or whether adulthood is disappearing as adults attempt to retain their youthfulness and share tastes with their children. See also Gardiner and Kosmitzki 2008 and LeVine and New 2008.

3. Hall 1904, 615; see Schlegel and Barry 1991 for a different view.

4. For example, many try to link the attainment of "moral reasoning" with the development of brain synapses (Beckman 2004).

5. Chudacoff 1989.

6. Siegel and Scovill 2000, 779–80.

7. Arnett 2007.

8. Kenny and Rice 1995.

9. See, e.g., Willis 1981 [1977], Eckert 1989.

10. These figures come from Collegedata.com, except the acceptance rate for Indiana University South Bend, which came from the director of admissions, Jeff M. Johnston (July 2, 2008).

11. See, e.g., Lemann 1995a, 1995b, 1999, Frey and Detterman 2004, Grove, Wasserman, and Grodner 2006.

12. Goastellec 2003.

13. Harper 2002, Pelfrey 2003.

14. Vogel 2006, 33. Those who advertise the test-prep courses claim that scores can rise by 100 to 300 points (Harper 2002); Kaplan Test Prep promises only that scores will rise, and gives a money-back guarantee (Kaplan 2007).

15. Lemann 1995a, 1995b.

16. College Board 2006.

17. Bracey 2000, 27–28.

18. Vogel 2006.

19. But see Stumpf and Stanley 2002.

20. Fallows 2003, 108.

21. Dillon 2007, Finder 2008.

22. Bayot 2003.

23. See, e.g., Walter Benn Michaels, *The Trouble with Diversity: How We Learned to Love Identity and Ignore Inequality* (2006), and the furious reviews directed against it.

24. Attewell 2000, Bracey 2000.

25. Robbins 2006. See the fictional *Acceptance* for another account (Coll 2007).

26. Collegelab 2007.

27. *Business Week* 2006.

28. Admission is also much more selective for female applicants, who greatly outnumber their male classmates both in applications and in actual enrollment (Britz 2006).

29. Brooks wrote at the peak of the dot-com boom, when jobs were plentiful and the economy was showing a surplus, and before the Bush regime had entered Iraq—in fact before September 11. Students may have been relaxed then, but by 2007 experts were extremely concerned about students' mental health, writing of a cohort of fragile, damaged children

in need of medical and psychological care before they arrive on campus and continuing—indeed, intensifying—throughout their college years (Kadison and DiGeronimo 2004).

30. Meltz 2002.

31. Goffman 1961, iii.

32. Ibid., 5.

33. Heller and Eng 1996.

34. Ibid.

35. See also Seaman 2005. One study suggests that all this increased administration has not resulted in improved education but rather has had the reverse effect, with "administrative expenditures...negatively related to student engagement" (Ryan 2005, 235).

36. See Washburn 2005.

37. Bok 2003.

38. Astin et al. 2002.

39. Pryor et al. 2005, 8.

40. See Astin 1997, 396–437, Pascarella and Terenzini 2005.

41. Students nationwide report that they spend an average of 3.4 (first year) to 3.7 (seniors) hours per week per class in arts and humanities, and 4.0 or 4.1 for physical sciences, while faculty expect them to spend 5.7 to 6.2 hours per week per class in arts and humanities and 6.7 to 7.0 for physical sciences. With a five-course load, that means studying between 17 and 20.5 hours a week. FSSE 2005, 5.

42. Rojstaczer 2001.

43. Nathan 2005a, 18.

44. Arenson 2004.

45. Hartocollis 2002.

46. Johnson 2003, 237. At Duke, for instance, the chemistry department had the lowest average grades and the drama department the highest. Ibid., 210.

47. Johnson 2003, although Bain 2004 disputes this.

48. *Economist* 2001.

49. Felton and Koper 2005.

50. Johnson 2002.

51. Academics who study student engagement know that certain actions on the part of faculty can increase students' feeling of involvement (Light 2001). One faculty member I know was encouraged by consultants to have lunch with her students once a week; apparently students found her "remote," and she needed to find a way to relate to them. At Saint U. faculty are given some funds to invite students to their houses for meals. The funding offered is higher for events held earlier in the semester, when they are used as a way to foster involvement, than later in the semester, when they are seen simply as a reward.

52. Astin et al. 2002, 28–29.

53. Brandenberger and Trozzolo 2003.

54. Seaman 2005.

55. Hafner 2005.

56. Astin et al. 2002, 22.

57. Wechsler et al. 2002.

58. College Drinking Prevention 2005.

59. American Medical Association 2004.

60. In fall 2006, for instance, Stanford began to require all incoming freshmen to complete an on-line alcohol education/prevention program, which is used by more than

350 colleges and universities. It provides a student-friendly introduction to the risks of extreme drinking while attempting to be nonjudgmental about moderate alcohol use. AlcoholEDU 2006, Delgado 2006.

61. One prominent college administrator, John McCardell, former president of Middlebury College, has begun a campaign to lower the drinking age, arguing that this would take the wind out of the binge-drinking sails and keep students safer. Adults could teach young adults how to drink safely, and students could associate drinking with multi-age dinner parties rather than furtive under-age bouts of drunkenness. Needless to say, McCardell has encountered strong opposition from many parties. And it is probably no accident that he waited until he was no longer an administrator to make his views public. See Wasley 2007.

62. Much has been written about the "prohibitionistic" culture of the United States and its responsibility for the crisis in college drinking. Comparisons are often made with European cultures, in which children are taught to drink in moderation and in the context of social interaction and commensality. See, for instance, Douglas 1987, Seaman 2005.

63. Gusfield 1987, 74.

64. See Kadison and DiGeronimo 2004, 1, Levine 2006, and Twenge 2006, especially the chapter titled "The Age of Anxiety (and Depression, and Loneliness): Generation Stressed."

65. PR Newswire US 2007.

66. Draut 2007.

67. U.S. Department of Education 2007, 217.

68. Bombardieri 2006.

69. Millett 2003.

70. Baum and O'Malley 2003, MarksJarvis 2007.

71. U.S. Department of Education 2007, 214.

72. McCabe, Treviño, and Butterfield 2001, 223.

5. No Magic Bullet

1. McCabe and Treviño 2002.
2. Duke University 2006.
3. University of Virginia n.d.
4. USMA n.d.
5. Haverford College 2002.
6. College of William and Mary 2005.
7. Western Michigan University n.d.
8. Stanford University n.d. a.
9. Stanford University n.d. b.
10. CAI 2006b.
11. Ibid.
12. Moffatt 1989.
13. Carey 2006.
14. Turnitin.com 2006, Maruca 2006b.
15. Redden and Lederman 2006, Read 2006 and 2007, Bainwol and Sherman 2007, Green 2007, Redden 2007.

16. Linder 2007, Redden 2007.
17. Lessig 2004, 183.
18. Ibid., 48–52.
19. "Giving credit" has been analyzed as both a legal and a moral obligation. The word "credit" also has economic overtones; Shirley Rose even claims that it is a religious metaphor, linking *credit* and *credo* (Rose 1999, 242).
20. Whitaker 1993.
21. Crocker and Shaw 2002, 52, citing Swales and Feak 1994, 126; see also Swales and Feak, 2d ed., 2004, 172.
22. Swales and Feak 2004, 172–73, 251–54.
23. Lessig 2004.
24. Gladwell 2004.
25. Howard 1999, xvii. See also Foucault 1979, Woodmansee 1984, Whitaker 1993, Swearingen 1999.
26. Kelber 1983, Gerhardsson 1998 [1961].
27. Lord 1960.
28. Thomas 1989.
29. Duranti 1994.
30. LaFleur 1999.
31. Scollon 1995, 2001.
32. Bloom 1997 [1973], Buranen and Roy 1999, Howard 1999, Swales and Feak 2004 [1994], Delbanco 2005.
33. See, e.g., Rose 1993, Howard 1999, Delbanco 2005.
34. Hanks 2000, Bauman 2004.

Conclusion

1. Howard 1995.
2. Purdue 2006.

Bibliography

Abbott, Barbara. 2003. "Some Notes on Quotation." *Belgian Journal of Linguistics* 17:13–26.

Academy of American Poets. 2007. "Poetic Form: Cento." www.poets.org/viewmedia. php/prmMID/5771. Accessed February 1, 2007.

Adorno, Theodor W. 1973 [1964]. *The Jargon of Authenticity*. Translated by Knut Tarnowski and Frederic Will. Evanston: Northwestern University Press.

AlcoholEDU. 2006. "Outside the Classroom." AlcoholEdu for College. http://college.alcoholedu.com/. Accessed October 20, 2006.

American Medical Association. 2004. Minimum Legal Drinking Age. http://www.ama-assn.org/ama/pub/category/13246.html. Accessed May 25, 2006.

Andersen, Kurt. 2006. "Generation Xerox: Youth May Not Be an Excuse for Plagiarism. But It Is an Explanation." *New York Magazine*. May 15. http://www.nymag.com/news/imperialcity/16935. Accessed January 31, 2007.

Arens, William. 1981. "Professional Football: An American Symbol and Ritual." In *The American Dimension: Cultural Myths and Social Realities*. 2d ed., edited by William Arens and S. B. Montague, pp. 1–10. Sherman Oaks, Calif.: Alfred.

Arenson, Karen W. 2004. "Is It Grade Inflation, or Are Students Just Smarter?" *New York Times*. April 18. Sec. 4, p. 2.

Ariès, Philippe. 1962. *Centuries of Childhood: A Social History of Family Life*. Translated by Robert Baldick. New York: Knopf.

Arnett, Jeffrey Jensen. 2007. "Socialization in Emerging Adulthood: From the Family to the Wider World, from Socialization to Self-Socialization." In *Handbook of Socialization: Theory and Research*, edited by Joan E. Grusec and Paul D. Hastings, pp. 208–31. New York: Guilford Press.

Ashworth, Peter, and Philip Bannister. 1997. "Guilty in Whose Eyes? University Students' Perceptions of Cheating and Plagiarism in Academic Work and Assessment." *Studies in Higher Education* 22, no. 2:187–203.

Astin, Alexander W. 1997. *What Matters in College? Four Critical Years Revisited*. San Francisco: Jossey-Bass.

Astin, Alexander W., Leticia Oseguera, Linda J. Sax, and William S. Korn. 2002. *The American Freshman: Thirty-five Year Trends.* Los Angeles: Higher Education Research Institute, University of California, Los Angeles.

Atlyrics.com/quotes/. 2008. "Movie Quotes." http://www.atlyrics.com/quotes. Accessed June 26, 2008.

Attewell, Paul. 2000. "Mirage of Meritocracy." *American Prospect* 11, no. 16 (July 17): 12–14.

Austin, J. L. 1962. *How to Do Things with Words.* Cambridge: Harvard University Press.

Bain, Ken. 2004. *What the Best College Teachers Do.* Cambridge: Harvard University Press.

Bainwol, Mitch, and Cary Sherman. 2007. "Explaining the Crackdown on Student Downloading." *Inside Higher Education.* http://insidehighered.com/layout/set/print/views/2007/03/15/sherman. Accessed March 19, 2007.

Baker, Nicholson. 2008. "The Charms of Wikipedia." *New York Review of Books* 55, no. 4 (March 20): 6–10.

Bakhtin, M. M. 1981 [1934–35]. "Discourse in the Novel." In *The Dialogical Imagination: Four Essays,* edited by Michael Holquist, translated by Caryl Emerson and Michael Holquist, pp. 259–422. Austin: University of Texas Press.

Barthes, Roland. 1977 [1968]. "The Death of the Author." Translated by Stephen Heath. In *Image, Music Text,* pp. 142–48. New York: Noonday Press.

Bateson, Gregory. 1979. *Mind and Nature: A Necessary Unity.* Toronto: Bantam Books.

Baum, Sandy, and Marie O'Malley. 2003. "College on Credit: How Borrowers Perceive Their Education Debt." *NASFAA Journal of Student Financial Aid* 33, no. 3:7–19.

Bauman, Richard. 1983. *Let Your Words Be Few: Symbolism of Speaking and Silence among Seventeenth-Century Quakers.* Cambridge: Cambridge University Press.

———. 2004. *A World of Others' Words: Cross-Cultural Perspectives on Intertextuality.* Oxford: Blackwell.

Bauman, Richard, and Charles Briggs. 1990. "Poetics and Performance as Critical Perspectives on Language and Social Life." *Annual Review of Anthropology* 19:59–88.

Bauman, Richard, and Joel Sherzer, eds. 1989 [1974]. *Explorations in the Ethnography of Speaking.* 2d ed. Cambridge: Cambridge University Press.

Bawarshi, Anis. 2003. *Genre and the Invention of the Writer: Reconsidering the Place of Invention in Composition.* Logan: Utah State University Press.

Bayot, Jennifer. 2003. "Up for Auction at 92nd Street Y: Everything but a Nursery Spot." *New York Times.* January 19. Sec. 3, p. 2.

Becker, Alton L. 1984. "Biography of a Sentence: A Burmese Proverb." In *Text, Play, and Story: The Construction and Reconstruction of Self and Society,* edited by Edward M. Bruner, pp. 135–55. Washington, D.C.: American Ethnological Society.

Becker, Howard S., Blanche Geer, and Everett C. Hughes. 1968. *Making the Grade: The Academic Side of College Life.* New York: John Wiley and Sons.

Beckman, Mary. 2004. "Crime, Culpability, and the Adolescent Brain." *Science* (July 30): 596–99.

Beijing Review. 2002. "Academic Circles Buzz over Peking University Plagiarism Case." February 22. http://www.china.org.cn/english/2002/Feb/27368.htm. Accessed March 13, 2008.

Bellah, Robert N., Richard Madsen, William M. Sullivan, Ann Swidler, and Steven M. Tipton. 1985. *Habits of the Heart: Individualism and Commitment in American Life.* Berkeley: University of California Press.

Bernard, H. Russell. 1995. *Research Methods in Anthropology: Qualitative and Quantitative Approaches.* 2d ed. Walnut Creek, Calif.: Alta Mira.

Birchard, Karen. 2006. "Cheating Is Rampant at Canadian Colleges." *Chronicle of Higher Education.* October 13. P. A53.

Bloom, Harold. 1997 [1973]. *The Anxiety of Influence: A Theory of Poetry.* 2d ed. New York: Oxford University Press.

Bluestein, Jane. 2007. "What's Wrong with 'I-Messages'?" www.janebluestein.com/articles/whatswrong.html. Accessed April 19, 2007.

Blum, Susan D. 1997. "Naming Practices and the Power of Words in China." *Language in Society* 26, no. 3:357–59.

——. 2001. "Truth." In *Key Terms in Language and Culture,* edited by Alessandro Duranti, pp. 252–55. Malden, Mass.: Blackwell.

——. 2004. "La ruse et ses cousins de China" [Rusing and Its Cousins in China]. In *Les raisons de la ruse: une perspective anthropologique et psychanalytique,* edited by Serge Latouche, Pierre-Joseph Laurent, Olivier Servais, and Michael Singleton, pp. 265–81. Paris: Éditions la Découverte/M.A.U.S.S.

——. 2005a. "Buzzing and Writing the Day Away Instant Messaging: Studying a New Form of Communication." *Anthropology News* (February): 29–30.

——. 2005b. "Five Approaches to Explaining 'Truth' and 'Deception' in Human Communication." *Journal of Anthropological Research* 61, no. 3 (Autumn): 289–315.

——. 2005c. "Performance and Pastiche: The Norm of Non-originality." Paper presented at "Originality, Imitation, and Plagiarism: A Cross-disciplinary Conference on Writing," Sweetland Writing Center, University of Michigan, September 25.

——. 2007. *Lies That Bind: Chinese Truth, Other Truths.* Lanham, Md.: Rowman and Littlefield.

——. n.d. a. "Intention-less Sincerity in China: 'Script-Selection Metaphor' as Language Ideology." Unpublished article.

——. n.d. b. "Foreignness among Us: Meeting the Performance Self." Unpublished article.

Blum, Susan D., et al. 2004. "Instant Messaging: Functions of a New Communicative Tool." http://www.nd.edu/~sblum/InstantMessaging.pdf.

Boase, Jeffrey, John B. Horrigan, Barry Wellman, and Lee Rainie. 2006. "The Strength of Internet Ties." Pew Internet and American Life Project. January 25. http://www.pewinternet.org/.

Bogle, Kathleen A. 2008. *Hooking Up: Sex, Dating, and Relationships on Campus.* New York: New York University Press.

Bok, Derek. 2003. *Universities in the Marketplace: The Commercialization of Higher Education.* Princeton: Princeton University Press.

———. 2006. *Our Underachieving Colleges: A Candid Look at How Much Students Learn and Why They Should Be Learning More.* Princeton: Princeton University Press.

Bombardieri, Marcella. 2006. "N.E. College Students Facing a Growing Burden of Debt: Cost Called Prohibitive to Middle, Lower Class." *Boston Globe.* April 30. http://www.boston.com/news/local/articles/2006/04/30/ne_college_students_facing_a_growing_burden_of_debt/. Accessed May 18, 2007.

Bracey, Gerald W. 2000. *Thinking about Tests and Testing: A Short Primer in "Assessment Literacy."* Washington, D.C.: American Youth Policy Forum.

Bradley, David. 2001. "Language Policy for the Yi." In *Perspectives on the Yi of Southwest China,* edited by Stevan Harrell, pp. 195–213. Berkeley: University of California Press.

Brandenberger, Jay W., and Thomas A. Trozzolo. 2003. "An Ethic of Service and Learning: Student Participation in Service and Community-Based Learning Initiatives at Notre Dame." Studies in Social Responsibility, University of Notre Dame. Research Report: Report 5. April. Notre Dame, Ind.: Center for Social Concerns.

Britz, Jennifer Delahunty. 2006. "To All the Girls I've Rejected." *New York Times.* March 23. P. 25.

Brooks, David. 2001. "The Organization Kid." *Atlantic Monthly* (April): 40–54.

Brumann, Christoph. 1999. "Writing for Culture: Why a Successful Concept Should Not Be Discarded." *Current Anthropology* 40, Supplement (February): S1–13.

Buranen, Lise, and Alice M. Roy, eds. 1999. *Perspectives on Plagiarism and Intellectual Property in a Postmodern World.* Albany: SUNY Press.

Business Week. 2006. "What Price College Admission? Parents Are Spending Tens of Thousands on Advisers to Shape Their Kids' Game Plans." June 24. http://articles.moneycentral.msn.com/CollegeAndFamily/SavingForCollege/WhatPriceCollegeAdmission.aspx. Accessed January 17, 2007.

Butler, Judith. 1997. *Excitable Speech: A Politics of the Performative.* New York: Routledge.

———. 1999. *Gender Trouble.* New York: Routledge.

Byrne, Richard. 2008. "History-Journal Editors Grapple with the Perils of Plagiarism." *Chronicle of Higher Education.* January 18. P. A8.

Cahn, Steven M., and Christine Vitrano, eds. 2008. *Happiness: Classic and Contemporary Readings in Philosophy.* New York: Oxford University Press.

CAI. 2005. CAI Research. The Center for Academic Integrity, Duke University. http://www.academicintegrity.org/cai_research.asp. Accessed September 22, 2005.

———. 2006a. CAI Research. The Center for Academic Integrity, Duke University. http://www.academicintegrity.org/cai_research.asp. Accessed October 25, 2006.

———. 2006b. The Fundamental Values of Academic Integrity. Center for Academic Integrity, Duke University. http://www.academicintegrity.org/pdf/FVProject.pdf. Accessed October 16, 2006.

Callahan, David. 2004. *The Cheating Culture: Why More Americans Are Doing Wrong to Get Ahead.* Orlando: Harcourt.

Calore, Michael. 2007. "What Would Jesus Wiki?" *Wired*. February 28. http://www.wired.com/print/techbiz/it/news/2007/02/72818. Accessed June 7, 2007.

Cappelen, Herman, and Ernie Lepore. 2003. "Varieties of Quotation Revisited." *Belgian Journal of Linguistics* 17:51–76.

Carey, Benedict. 2006. "In the Execution Chamber, the Moral Compass Wavers." *New York Times*. February 7. P. F1.

Carnevale, Anthony P., and Stephen J. Rose. 2003. "Socioeconomic Status, Race/Ethnicity, and Selective College Admissions." New York: Century Foundation.

Carrithers, Michael, Steven Collins, and Stephen Lukes, eds. 1985. *The Category of the Person: Anthropology, Philosophy, History*. Cambridge: Cambridge University Press.

Carson, Clayborne. 1993. "Editing Martin Luther King, Jr.: Political and Scholarly Issues." In *Palimpsest: Editorial Theory in the Humanities,* edited by George Bornstein and Ralph G. Williams, pp. 305–16. Ann Arbor: University of Michigan Press.

Chicago Manual of Style. 2003. 15th ed. Chicago: University of Chicago Press.

Chomsky, Noam. 1986. *Knowledge of Language: Its Nature, Origin, and Use*. New York: Praeger.

Chronicle of Higher Education. 2002. "Corruption Plagues Academe Around the World." August 2. P. A32.

——. 2006. "The Nation" 53, no. 1 (August 25).

——. 2007. "How the New Generation of Well-Wired Multitaskers Is Changing Campus Culture." January 5. P. B10–15.

Chudacoff, H. P. 1989. *How Old Are You? Age Consciousness in American Culture*. Princeton: Princeton University Press.

Clegg, Sue, and Abbi Flint. 2006. "More Heat Than Light: Plagiarism in Its Appearing." *British Journal of Sociology of Education* 27, no. 3:373–87.

Cockrell, Karen Sunday, Julie A. Hughes Caplow, and Joe F. Donaldson. 2000. "A Context for Learning: Collaborative Groups in the Problem-Based Learning Environment." *Review of Higher Education* 23, no. 3:347–63.

Cohen, Anthony P. 1994. *Self Consciousness: An Alternative Anthropology of Identity*. London: Routledge.

Cohen, Stanley. 1980 [1972]. *Folk Devils and Moral Panics: The Creation of the Mods and Rockers*. New York: St. Martin's Press.

Cole, Sally, and Elizabeth Kiss. 2000. "What Can We Do About Student Cheating?" *About Campus* 5, no. 2:5–12.

Coll, Susan. 2007. *Acceptance*. New York: Farrar, Straus and Giroux.

College Board. 2006. "College Board Announces Scores for New SAT® with Writing Section." August 29. http://www.collegeboard.com/press/releases/150054.html. Accessed January 19, 2007.

College Drinking Prevention. 2005. "A Snapshot of Annual High-Risk College Drinking Consequences." September 23. http:www.collegedrinkingprevention.gov/StatsSummaries/snapshot.aspx. Accessed June 20, 2007.

Collegedata.com. 2007. "College 411: College Match." https://www.collegedata.com/cs/search/college/college_search_tmpl.jhtml. Accessed June 30, 2008.

Bibliography

CollegeLab. 2007. "Our College Admissions Quiz." http://www.collegelab.net/ 416609.html. Accessed January 17, 2007.

College of William and Mary. 2005. "The Honor Code." http://www.wm.edu/so/ honor-council/honorcode.htm. Accessed May 16, 2007.

Conan, Neal. 2003. "Analysis: Questions of Ethics and Integrity in Journalism." *Talk of the Nation*. National Public Radio. May 15.

Conflict Research Consortium. 2007. "'I' Statements Not 'You' Statements." International Online Training Program on Intractable Conflict. www.colorado.edu/ conflict/peace/treatment/istate.htm. Accessed April 19, 2007.

Coulmas, Florian, ed. 1986. *Direct and Indirect Speech*. Berlin: Mouton de Gruyter.

Cowell, Alan. 2006. "Eyebrows Are Raised over Passages in a Best Seller." *New York Times*. November 28. P. E1.

Crain, William. 2003. *Reclaiming Childhood: Letting Children Be Children in Our Achievement-Oriented Society*. New York: Times Books/Henry Holt and Company.

Crapanzano, Vincent. 1980. *Tuhami: Portrait of a Moroccan*. Chicago: University of Chicago Press.

Creative Commons. 2007. CreativeCommons.org. Accessed March 13, 2007.

CRLT (Center for Research on Learning and Teaching). 2006a. "Effectiveness of Cooperative Learning, Group Work, and Team Work." University of Michigan. http://www.crlt.umich.edu/crltext/clgt_effectivenesstext.html. Accessed May 4, 2007.

——. 2006b. "Resources on Cooperative Learning, Group Work, and Teamwork." University of Michigan. http://www.crlt.umich.edu/publinks/clgt.html. Accessed May 4, 2007.

Crocker, Jean, and Philip Shaw. 2002. "Research Student and Supervisor Evaluation of Intertextuality Practices." *Hermes: Journal of Linguistics* 28:39–58.

Crystal, David. 2004. *The Language Revolution*. Cambridge: Polity.

Cukor-Avila, Patricia. 2002. "*She Say, She Go, She Be Like:* Verbs of Quotation over Time in African American Vernacular English." *American Speech* 77, no. 1 (Spring): 3–31.

Danford, Natalie. 2002. "Scandal's Lessons." *Publishers Weekly* 249, no. 43:24.

Delbanco, Nicholas. 2005. "In Praise of Imitation." In *Anywhere Out of the World: Essays on Travel, Writing, Death*, pp. 1–16. New York: Columbia University Press.

Delgado, Ray. 2006. "New Online Alcohol Education Program Seeks to Reduce Risks for New Students." Stanford Report, Stanford University. http://news-service.stanford.edu/news/2006/september13/alcohol-091306.html. Accessed September 21, 2006.

Dillon, Sam. 2007. "A Great Year for Ivy League Colleges, but Not So Good for Applicants to Them." *New York Times*. April 4. P. B7.

Ding Yimin. 2002. "Scientific Misconduct: Beijing U. Issues First-Ever Rules." *Science* (April 19): 448.

Douglas, Mary, ed. 1987. *Constructive Drinking: Perspectives on Drink from Anthropology*. Cambridge: Cambridge University Press.

Douthat, Ross Gregory. 2005. *Privilege: Harvard and the Education of the Ruling Class*. New York: Hyperion.

Draut, Tamara. 2007. "College Costs and Debt." Hearing Testimony. Committee on Senate Health, Education, Labor and Pensions. *Congressional Quarterly.* February 16. Electronic Document. Accessed May 18, 2007.

Duke University. 1999. "The Fundamental Values of Academic Integrity." Center for Academic Integrity.

——. 2006. "The Duke Community Standard." http://www.duke.edu/web/Honor Council/communitystandard.html. Accessed May 16, 2007.

Duranti, Alessandro. 1992. "Language in Context and Language as Context: The Samoan Respect Vocabulary." In *Rethinking Context: Language as an Interactive Phenomenon,* edited by Alessandro Duranti and Charles Goodwin, pp. 77–99. Cambridge: Cambridge University Press.

——. 1994. *From Grammar to Politics: Linguistic Anthropology in a Western Samoan Village.* Berkeley: University of California Press.

Easterbrook, Gregg. 2004. "Who Needs Harvard?" *Atlantic Monthly* (October): 128–33.

Eckert, Penelope. 1989. *Jocks and Burnouts: Social Categories and Identity in the High School.* New York: Teachers College Press.

Eckert, Penelope, and Sally McConnell-Ginet. 1992. "Think Practically and Look Locally: Language and Gender as Community-Based Practice." *Annual Review of Anthropology* 21: 461–90.

Economist. 2001. "All Shall Have Prizes." April 14, 359, no. 8217:32.

——. 2002. "In Praise of Hucksters." March 16, 362, no. 8264:40.

Ede, Lisa, and Andrea Lunsford. 1990. *Singular Texts/Plural Authors: Perspectives on Collaborative Writing.* Carbondale: Southern Illinois University Press.

Editorsweblog.org. 2004. "Sweden: Accusations of Plagiarism at *Dagens Nyheter.*" July 2. http://wef.blogs.com/editors/2004/07/sweden_accusati.html. Accessed March 13, 2008.

Ehrenreich, Barbara. 2005. *Bait and Switch: The (Futile) Pursuit of the American Dream.* New York: Henry Holt.

Eisenstadt, S. N. 1990. "Functional Analysis in Anthropology and Sociology: An Interpretative Essay." *Annual Review of Anthropology* 19:243–260.

Elkind, David. 1981. *The Hurried Child: Growing Up Too Fast Too Soon.* Reading, Mass.: Addison-Wesley.

Elman, Benjamin A. 2000. *A Cultural History of Civil Examinations in Late Imperial China.* Berkeley: University of California Press.

Erikson, Erik H. 1985 [1950]. *Childhood and Society.* 35th anniversary ed. New York: Norton.

Fajans, Jane. 1985. "The Person in Social Context: The Social Character of Baining 'Psychology.'" In *Exploring Pacific Ethnopsychologies,* edited by Geoffrey M. White and John Kirkpatrick, pp. 367–97. Berkeley: University of California Press.

——. 1997. *They Make Themselves: Work and Play among the Baining of Papua New Guinea.* Chicago: University of Chicago Press.

Fallows, James. 2003. "The New College Chaos." *Atlantic Monthly* (November): 106–114.

Felton, James, and Peter T. Koper. 2005. "Nominal GPA and Real GPA: A Simple Adjustment That Compensates for Grade Inflation." *Assessment and Evaluation in Higher Education* 30, no. 6 (December): 561–69.

Finder, Alan. 2008. "Elite Colleges Reporting Record Lows in Admission." *New York Times*. April 1. P. 16.

Fingarette, Herbert. 1972. *Confucius: The Secular as Sacred*. New York: Harper & Row.

Fortes, Meyer. 1973. "On the Concept of the Person among the Tallensi." In *La notion de personne en Afrique Noire,* edited by Germaine Dieterlen. Paris: Éditions du Centre national de la recherche scientifique.

Foucault, Michel. 1979. "What Is an Author?" In *Textual Strategies: Perspectives in Post-structuralist Criticism,* edited and translated by Josué V. Harari, pp. 141–60. Ithaca: Cornell University Press.

Frank, Robert H., and Philip J. Cook. 1995. *The Winner-Take-All Society: Why the Few at the Top Get So Much More Than the Rest of Us*. New York: Penguin.

Free Culture. 2007. FreeCulture.org. Accessed March 13, 2007.

Freedman, Morris. 1994. "The Persistence of Plagiarism, the Riddle of Originality." *Virginia Quarterly Review* 70, no. 3: 507–17.

Frege, Gottlob. 1892. "On Sense and Meaning." In *Translations from the Philosophical Writings of Gottlob Frege*. 3d ed., edited by Peter Geach and Max Black, pp. 56–78. Oxford: Blackwell.

Fresh Air. 2007. "Jimmie Wales on the User-Generated Generation." National Public Radio. April 19. http://www.npr.org/templates/story/story.php?storyId=9683874. Accessed June 7, 2007.

Freud, Sigmund. 1961 [1930]. *Civilization and Its Discontents,* translated and edited by James Strachey. New York: W. W. Norton.

Frey, Meredith C., and Douglas K. Detterman. 2004. "Scholastic Assessment or *g*? The Relationship between the Scholastic Assessment Test and General Cognitive Ability." *Psychological Science* 15, no. 6: 373–78.

FSSE (Faculty Survey of Student Engagement). 2005. Indiana University, Bloomington. http://fsse.iub.edu/pdf/fsse2005_overview.pdf. Accessed March 16, 2008.

Gardiner, Harry W., and Corinne Kosmitzki. 2008. *Lives across Cultures: Cross-cultural Human Development*. 4th ed. Boston: Pearson.

Geertz, Clifford. 1966. "Person, Time, and Conduct in Bali." In *The Interpretation of Cultures,* pp. 360–411. New York: Basic Books.

———. 1983. "'From the Native's Point of View': On the Nature of Anthropological Understanding." In *Local Knowledge: Further Essays in Interpretive Anthropology,* pp. 55–70. New York: Basic Books.

———. 1986. "The Uses of Diversity." *Michigan Quarterly Review* (Winter): 105–23.

Genovese, Eugene D. 1995. "Martin Luther King, Jr.: Theology, Politics, Scholarship." *Reviews in American History* 23, no. 1:1–12.

Gergen, Kenneth J. 1991. *The Saturated Self: Dilemmas of Identity in Contemporary Life*. New York: Basic Books.

Gerhardsson, Birger. 1998 [1961]. *Memory and Manuscript: Oral Tradition and Written Transmission in Rabbinic Judaism and Early Christianity,* translated by Eric J. Sharpe. Grand Rapids, Mich.: William B. Eerdmans.

Gerth, H. H., and C. Wright Mills, trans., ed., intro. 1946. *From Max Weber: Essays in Sociology.* New York: Oxford University Press.

Geurts, Bart, and Emar Maier. 2003. "Quotation in Context." *Belgian Journal of Linguistics* 17:109–28.

Giles, Jim. 2005. "Internet Encyclopaedias Go Head to Head (Special Report)." *Nature* 438 (December 15): 900–901.

Gladwell, Malcolm. 2004. "Something Borrowed: Should a Charge of Plagiarism Ruin Your Life?" *New Yorker* (November 22): 40–48.

———. 2005. "Getting In." *New Yorker* (October 10): 80–86.

———. 2006. "Viswanathan-Gate." Gladwell.org. http://gladwell.typepad.com/glad wellcom/2006/04/viswanathangate.html. Accessed January 31, 2007.

Goastellec, Gaële. 2003. "Le SAT et l'accès aux études supérieures: le recrutement des élites américaines en question [SAT and Admissions to Higher Education: The Recruitment of American Elites under Question]." *Sociologie du Travail* 45, no. 4:473–90.

Goffman, Erving. 1961. *Asylums: Essays on the Social Situation of Mental Patients and Other Inmates.* Garden City, N.Y.: Anchor.

———. 1983 [1979]. "Footing." In *Forms of Talk,* pp. 124–59. Philadelphia: University of Pennsylvania Press.

Goode, Erich, and Nachman Ben-Yehuda. 1994a. "Moral Panics: Culture, Politics, and Social Construction." *Annual Review of Sociology* 20:149–71.

———. 1994b. *Moral Panics: The Social Construction of Deviance.* Oxford: Blackwell.

Goodwin, Charles. 2002. "Time in Action." *Current Anthropology* 43, Supplement (August–October): S19–35.

Goodwin, Doris Kearns. 1987. *The Fitzgeralds and the Kennedys.* New York: Simon and Schuster.

Grafton, Anthony. 1997. *The Footnote: A Curious History.* Cambridge: Harvard University Press.

Green, Kenneth C. 2007. "The Music Industry's 'Spring Offensive.'" *Inside Higher Education.* March 8. http://insidehighered.com/layout/set/print/views/2007/03/08/green. Accessed March 14, 2007.

Green, Stuart P. 2002–3. "Plagiarism, Norms, and the Limits of Theft Law: Some Observations on the Use of Criminal Sanctions in Enforcing Intellectual Property Rights." *Hastings Law Journal* 54:167–242.

Griaule, Marcel. 1965. *Conversations with Ogotemmêli: An Introduction to Dogon Religious Ideas.* London: International Africa Institute/Oxford University Press.

Grove, Wayne A., Tim Wasserman, and Andrew Grodner. 2006. "Choosing a Proxy for Academic Aptitude." *Journal of Economic Education* (Spring): 131–47.

Guess, Andy. 2008. "The Sociology of 'Hooking Up.'" *Inside Higher Education.* January 29. Insidehighereducation.com. Accessed January 29, 2008.

Gumperz, John J., and Dell Hymes, eds. 1986 [1972]. *Directions in Sociolinguistics: The Ethnography of Communication.* Oxford: Basil Blackwell.

Gusfield, Joseph R. 1987. "Passage to Play: Rituals of Drinking Time in American Society." In *Constructive Drinking: Perspectives on Drink from Anthropology,* edited by Mary Douglas, pp. 73–90. Cambridge: Cambridge University Press.

Guterman, Lila. 2008. "Plagiarism and Other Sins Seem Rife in Science Journals, a Digital Sleuth Finds." *Chronicle of Higher Education* (February 1): A9.

Hafner, Katie. 2005. "How Thursday Became the New Friday." *New York Times.* November 6. Sec. 4A, pp. 22–25.

Haines, V. J., G. M. Diekhoff, E. E. LaBeff, and R. E. Clark. 1986. "College Cheating: Immaturity, Lack of Commitment, and the Neutralizing Attitude." *Research in Higher Education* 25, no. 4:342–54.

Hall, G. Stanley. 1904. *Adolescence: Its Psychology and Its Relations to Physiology, Anthropology, Sociology, Sex, Crime, Religion, and Education.* Vol. 2. New York: D. Appleton.

Hall, Kira. 2001. "Performativity." In *Key Terms in Language and Culture,* edited by Alessandro Duranti, pp. 180–83. Malden, Mass.: Blackwell.

Handler, Richard. 1986. "Authenticity." *Anthropology Today* 2, no. 1:2–4.

Hanks, William F. 2000. *Intertexts: Writings on Language, Utterance, and Context.* Lanham, Md.: Rowman and Littlefield.

Hanna, Maddie. 2004. "Cheating the System." *The Observer* (Notre Dame) (November 5): 1.

Hannerz, Ulf. 1992. *Cultural Complexity: Studies in the Social Organization of Meaning.* New York: Columbia University Press.

Hansen, Suzy. 2004. "Dear Plagiarists: You Get What You Pay For." *New York Times.* August 22. Sec. 7, p. 11.

Harper, John W. 2002. "The New, Improved SAT: Surprisingly, the Revised College Admissions Test Is Better than the Old One." *Weekly Standard.* August 26–September 2. http://web.lexis-nexis.com.lib-proxy.nd.edu/universe/printdoc. Accessed January 16, 2007.

Hartocollis, Anemona. 2002. "Harvard Faculty Votes to Put the Excellence Back in the A." *New York Times.* May 22. Sec. 1, p. 20.

Harvard Crimson. 2006. "'Opal Mehta' Gone for Good; Contract Cancelled. Publisher Says that Sophomore's Novel Will Never Return to Shelves." May 2.

Harvey, David. 1989. *The Condition of Postmodernity: An Enquiry into the Origins of Cultural Change.* Oxford: Basil Blackwell.

Haverford College. 2002. "Haverford Honor Code." http://www.haverford.edu/hcweb/hchonor.html. Accessed May 16, 2007.

Heller, Karen, and Lily Eng. 1996. "Higher Education: How High the Price." *Philadelphia Inquirer.* March 31. P. A1.

Henderson, Lynne, and Philip Zimbardo. 1998. "Shyness." In *Encyclopedia of Mental Health,* vol. 3, pp. 497–509. San Diego: Academic Press.

Henderson, Lynne, Philip Zimbardo, and Bernardo J. Carducci. 2001. "Shyness." In *The Corsini Encyclopedia of Psychology and Behavioral Science,* 3d ed., edited by W. Edward Craighead and Charles B. Nemeroff. Vol. 4, pp. 1522–23. New York: John Wiley and Sons.

Hersh, Richard H., and John Merrow, eds. 2005. *Declining by Degrees: Higher Education at Risk.* New York: Palgrave Macmillan.

Herzfeld, Michael. 2001. *Anthropology: Theoretical Practice in Culture and Society.* Malden, Mass.: Blackwell.

Heuman, Linda. 2005. "Cheaters." *Brown Alumni Magazine Online.* May–June. Accessed May 25, 2005.

Heywood, Colin M. 2001. *A History of Childhood: Children and Childhood in the West from Medieval to Modern Times.* Cambridge: Polity.

Hill, Jane H. 1995. "The Voices of Don Gabriel: Responsibility and Self in a Modern Mexicano Narrative." In *The Dialogic Emergence of Culture,* edited by Dennis Tedlock and Bruce Mannheim, pp. 97–147. Urbana: University of Illinois Press.

Hill, Jane H., and Judith T. Irvine. 1992. Introduction to *Responsibility and Evidence in Oral Discourse,* edited by Jane H. Hill and Judith T. Irvine, pp. 1–23. Cambridge: Cambridge University Press.

History News Network. 2005. "How the Goodwin Story Developed." October 6. http://hnn.us/articles/590.html. Accessed January 31, 2007.

Hockett, Charles. 1960. "The Origin of Speech." *Scientific American* 203, no. 3 (September): 88–96.

Holland, Dorothy C., and Margaret A. Eisenhart. 1990. *Educated in Romance: Women, Achievement, and College Culture.* Chicago: University of Chicago Press.

Hoover, Eric. 2002. "Honor for Honor's Sake?" *Chronicle of Higher Education* 48, no. 34:A39.

Horowitz, Helen Lefkowitz. 1987. *Campus Life: Undergraduate Cultures from the End of the Eighteenth Century to the Present.* Chicago: University of Chicago Press.

Horton, Robin. 1983. "Social Psychologies: African and Western." In Meyer Fortes and Robin Horton, *Oedipus and Job in West African Religion,* pp. 41–82. Cambridge: Cambridge University Press.

Howard, Rebecca Moore. 1995. "Plagiarisms, Authorships, and the Academic Death Penalty." *College English* 57, no. 7 (November): 788–806.

——. 1999. *Standing in the Shadow of Giants: Plagiarists, Authors, Collaborators.* Stamford, Conn.: Ablex.

Howe, Neil, and William Strauss. 2000. *Millennials Rising: The Next Great Generation.* New York: Vintage.

Howell, Signe, ed. 1997. *The Ethnography of Moralities.* London: Routledge.

Hsu, Francis L. K. 1963. *Clan, Caste, and Club.* New York: Van Nostrand.

——. 1981 [1953]. *Americans and Chinese: Passage to Differences.* 3d ed. Honolulu: University of Hawaii Press.

Hymes, Dell. 1972. "Models of the Interaction of Language and Social Life." In *Directions in Sociolinguistics: The Ethnography of Speaking,* edited by John J. Gumperz and Dell Hymes, pp. 35–71. New York: Holt, Rinehart & Winston.

——. 1975. "Breakthrough into Performance." In *Folklore: Performance and Communication,* edited by Dan Ben-Amos and Kenneth S. Goldstein, pp. 11–74. The Hague: Mouton.

Imperato, Justin. 2000. "Trust Flourishes When Students Enforce Their Own Honor Code." *Christian Science Monitor.* November 7. P. 15.

Irvine, Judith T. 1996. "Shadow Conversations: The Indeterminacy of Participant Roles." In *Natural Histories of Discourse,* edited by Michael Silverstein and Greg Urban, pp. 131–59. Chicago: University of Chicago Press.

Jaschik, Scott. 2007. "A Stand against Wikipedia." *Inside Higher Education.* January 26. http://insidehighered.com/news/2007/01/26/wiki. Accessed April 20, 2007.

Johnson, Valen E. 2002. "An A Is an A Is an A...and That's the Problem." *New York Times.* April 14. Sec. 4A, p. 14.

——. 2003. *Grade Inflation: A Crisis in College Education.* New York: Springer.

Jordan, Augustus E. 2001. "College Student Cheating: The Role of Motivation, Perceived Norms, Attitudes, and Knowledge of Institutional Policy." *Ethics and Behavior* vol. 11, no. 3:233–47.

Josephson Institute of Ethics. 2002. "The Ethics of American Youth: Survey Documents Decade of Moral Deterioration; Kids Today Are More Likely to Cheat, Steal, and Lie Than Kids 10 Years Ago." http://www.josephsoninstitute.org/Survey2002/survey2002-pressrelease.htm. Accessed July 30, 2004.

——. 2004. "Report Card 2004: The Ethics of American Youth." http://www.josephsoninstitute.org/Survey2004/data-tables_2004_behavior.pdf. Accessed May 25, 2006.

Julliard, Kell. 1994. "Perceptions of Plagiarism in the Use of Other Authors' Language." *Family Medicine* 26, no. 6:356–60.

Kadison, Richard, and Theresa Foy DiGeronimo. 2004. *College of the Overwhelmed: The Campus Mental Health Crisis and What to Do about It.* San Francisco: Jossey-Bass.

Kaplan Test Prep and Admissions. 2007. "Higher Test Scores Guaranteed or Your Money Back." http://www.kaptest.com/hsg/index.jhtml. Accessed January 19, 2007.

Karabel, Jerome. 2005. *The Chosen: The Hidden History of Admission and Exclusion at Harvard, Yale, and Princeton.* Boston: Houghton Mifflin.

Kelber, Werner H. 1983. *The Oral and the Written Gospel: The Hermeneutics of Speaking and Writing in the Synoptic Tradition, Mark, Paul, and Q.* Philadelphia: Fortress Press.

Kenny, Maureen E., and Kenneth G. Rice. 1995. "Attachment to Parents and Adjustment in Late Adolescent College Students: Current Status, Applications, and Future Considerations." *The Counseling Psychologist* 23, no. 3 (July): 433–56.

Kerouac, Jack. 1957. *On the Road.* New York: Penguin.

Klewitz, Gabriele, and Elizabeth Couper-Kuhlen. 1999. "Quote—Unquote? The Role of Prosody in the Contextualization of Reported Speech Sequences." *Pragmatics* 9, no. 4:459–85.

Kottak, Conrad Phillip, and Kathryn A. Kozaitis. 1999. *On Being Different: Diversity and Multiculturalism in the North American Mainstream.* Boston: McGraw-Hill College.

Kristeva, Julia. 1980 [1977]. *Desire in Language: A Semiotic Approach to Literature and Art.* Edited by Leon S. Roudiez, translated by Thomas Gora, Alice Jardine, and Leon S. Roudiez. New York: Columbia University Press.

——. 1986. "Word, Dialogue, and Novel." Translated by Alice Jardine, Thomas Gora, and Leon S. Roudiez. In *The Kristeva Reader,* edited by Toril Moi, pp. 34–61. New York: Columbia University Press.

Kroskrity, Paul V., ed. 2000. *Regimes of Language: Ideologies, Polities, and Identities.* Santa Fe: School of American Research Press.

Kuh, George D., and Ernest T. Pascarella. 2004. "What Does Institutional Selectivity Tell Us about Educational Quality?" *Change* 36, no. 5:52–58.

LaFleur, Robert André. 1999. "Literary Borrowing and Historical Compilation in Medieval China." In *Perspectives on Plagiarism and Intellectual Property in a Postmodern World,* edited by Lise Buranen and Alice M. Roy, pp. 141–50. Albany: SUNY Press.

Lahr, John. 2006. "Citizen Penn: The Many Missions of Sean Penn." *New Yorker* (April 3): 48–59.

Laing, R. D. 1960. *The Divided Self: An Existential Study in Sanity and Madness.* Harmondsworth: Penguin.

Lasch, Christopher. 1991 [1979]. *The Culture of Narcissism: American Life in an Age of Diminishing Expectations.* New York: W. W. Norton.

Lemann, Nicholas. 1995a. "The Great Sorting." *Atlantic Monthly* (September): 84–100.

——. 1995b. "The Structure of Success in America." *Atlantic Monthly* (August): 41–60.

——. 1999. *The Big Test: The Secret History of the American Meritocracy.* New York: Farrar, Straus and Giroux.

——. 2006. "Amateur Hour: Journalism without Journalists." *New Yorker* (August 7): 44–49.

Lenhart, Amanda, and Mary Madden. 2007. "Social Networking Websites and Teens: An Overview." Pew Internet and American Life Project. January 7. http://www.pewinternet.org/.

Lerner, Julia, Tamar Rapoport, and Edna Lomsky-Feder. 2007. "The Ethnic Script in Action: The Regrounding of Russian Jewish Immigrants in Israel." *Ethos* 35, no. 2:168–95.

Lessig, Lawrence. 2004. *Free Culture: The Nature and Future of Creativity.* New York: Penguin.

Lethem, Jonathan. 2007a. "The Ecstasy of Influence." *Harper's Magazine* (February): 59–71.

——. 2007b. Promiscuous Materials Project. www.jonathanlethem.com/promiscuous_materials.html. Accessed March 13, 2007.

Levine, Madeline. 2006. *The Price of Privilege: How Parental Pressure and Material Advantage Are Creating a Generation of Disconnected and Unhappy Kids.* New York: HarperCollins.

LeVine, Robert A., and Rebecca S. New, eds. 2008. *Anthropology and Child Development: A Cross-cultural Reader.* Malden, Mass.: Blackwell.

Lewis, David Levering. 1991. "Failing to Know Martin Luther King, Jr." *Journal of American History* 78, no. 1 (June): 81–85.

Lewis, Mark. 2002. "More Controversy for Stephen Ambrose." Forbes.com. January 9. http://www.forbes.com/2002/01/09/0109ambrose.html. Accessed January 31, 2007.

Light, Richard J. 2001. *Making the Most of College.* Cambridge: Harvard University Press.

Linder, Sally. 2007. "Unauthorized P2P File Sharing Suppressed." Ohio University. http://www.ohio.edu/outlook/06–07/May/641n-067.cfm. Accessed May 16, 2007.

Bibliography

Lord, Albert B. 1960. *The Singer of Tales*. Cambridge: Harvard University Press.

Louv, Richard. 2005. *Last Child in the Woods: Saving Our Children from Nature-Deficit Disorder*. Chapel Hill: Algonquin Books of Chapel Hill.

Lowinsky, Edward E. 2003. "Musical Genius." *Dictionary of the History of Ideas*. http://etext.virginia.edu/cgi-local/DHI/dhi.cgi?id=dv2-37. Accessed June 13, 2006.

Lukes, Steven. 1973. *Individualism*. New York: Harper and Row.

Magolda, Peter, and Kelsey Ebben. 2007. "Students Serving Christ: Understanding the Role of Student Subcultures on a College Campus." *Anthropology and Education Quarterly* 38, no. 2:138–58.

Malinowski, Bronislaw. 1923. "The Problem of Meaning in Primitive Languages." In *The Meaning of Meaning*, edited by C. K. Ogden and I. A. Richards, pp. 296–336. New York: Harcourt, Brace.

Mallon, Thomas. 2001 [1989]. *Stolen Words: The Classic Book on Plagiarism*. San Diego: Harvest.

Mangan, Katherine S. 2002. "UCLA Heightens Scrutiny of Foreign Applicants." *Chronicle of Higher Education* 49, no. 5:A58.

MarksJarvis, Gail. 2007. "College Debt May Strangle Grads with Low-Pay Jobs." *Baltimore Sun*. April 29. http://www.baltimoresun.com/business/careers/bal-bz.ym.marksjarvis29apr29,0,5853770.story?coll=bal-careers-headlines. Accessed May 18, 2007.

Martin, Amy. 2007. "I-Messages and the Assertiveness Line." Teachable Moment. Morningside Center for Teaching Social Responsibility. www.teachablemoment.org/elementary/imessages.html. Accessed April 19, 2007.

Maruca, Lisa. 2003. "Plagiarism and Its (Disciplinary) Discontents: Towards an Interdisciplinary Theory and Pedagogy." *Issues in Integrative Studies* 21:74–97.

——. 2006a. "Plagiarism and Copyright: Connections in the Turnitin Culture." *Newsletter* (Gayle Morris Sweetland Writing Center, University of Michigan) (Winter): 8.

——. 2006b. "The Plagiarism Panic: Digital Policing in the New Intellectual Property Regime." In *New Directions in Copyright Law*, vol. 2, edited by Fiona Macmillan. Cheltenham, UK: Edward Elgar Publishing. Pp. 241–61.

Mauss, Marcel. 1938. "Une catégorie de l'esprit humain: la notion de personne, celle de 'moi.'" *Journal of the Royal Anthropological Institute of Great Britain and Ireland* 68: 263–81.

McCabe, Donald L., and Linda Klebe Treviño. 1997. "Individual and Contextual Influences on Academic Dishonesty: A Multicampus Investigation." *Research in Higher Education* 38, no. 3:379–96.

——. 2002. "Honesty and Honor Codes." *Academe* 88, no. 1:37–41.

McCabe, Donald L., Linda Klebe Treviño, and Kenneth D. Butterfield. 2001. "Cheating in Academic Institutions: A Decade of Research." *Ethics and Behavior* 11, no. 3:219–32.

McCorkle, Denny E., James Reardon, Joe F. Alexander, Nathan D. Kling, Robert C. Harris, and R. Vishwanathan Iyer. 1999. "Undergraduate Marketing Students, Group Projects, and Teamwork: The Good, the Bad, and the Ugly?" *Journal of Marketing Education* 21, no. 2:106–17.

McCormick, Ginny. 2003. "Whose Idea Was That?" *Stanford* (September–October): 66–71.

McDermott, R. P., and Henry Tylbor. 1986. "On the Necessity of Collusion in Conversation." In *Discourse and Institutional Authority,* edited by Sue Fisher and Alexandra Todd, pp. 123–39. Norwood, N.J.: Ablex.

McGrath, Charles. 2006a. "At $9.95 a Page, You Were Expecting Poetry?" *New York Times.* September 10. Week in Review. P. 1.

——. 2006b. "Term Paper Project, Part II." *New York Times.* September 17. Week in Review. P. 5.

McKibben, Bill. 2007. *Deep Economy: The Wealth of Communities and the Durable Future.* New York: Times Books.

McKillup, Steve, and Ruth McKillup. 2007. "An Assessment Strategy that Pre-empts Plagiarism." *International Journal for Educational Integrity* 3, no. 2 (December): 18–26.

Meltz, Barbara. 2002. "Child Caring: Is Your Child Spoiled? Maybe." *Boston Globe.* October 17. P. H1.

Merriam-Webster OnLine. 2006. http://www.m-w.com/.

Michaels, Walter Benn. 2006. *The Trouble with Diversity: How We Learned to Love Identity and Ignore Inequality.* New York: Metropolitan Books.

Michaelsen, Larry K., L. Dee Fink, and Arletta Knight. 2006 [1997]. "Ideas on Teaching: Designing Effective Group Activities: Lessons for Classroom Teaching and Faculty Development." University of Oklahoma Program for Instructional Innovation. http://www.ou.edu/pii/tips/ideas/groupact.html. Accessed May 4, 2007.

Millett, Catherine M. 2003. "How Undergraduate Loan Debt Affects Application and Enrollment in Graduate or First Professional School." *Journal of Higher Education* 74, no. 4:386–427.

Miyazaki, Ichisada. 1981 [1963]. *China's Examination Hell: The Civil Service Examinations of Imperial China.* Translated by Conrad Schirokauer. New Haven: Yale University Press.

Moffatt, Michael. 1989. *Coming of Age in New Jersey: College and American Culture.* New Brunswick, N.J.: Rutgers University Press.

Moore, Barbara J. 2002. "Truth or Consequences." *About Campus* (September–October): 25–28.

Morris, Colin. 1972. *The Discovery of the Individual, 1050–1200.* New York: Harper and Row.

Nathan, Rebekah [Cathy Small]. 2005a. *My Freshman Year: What a Professor Learned by Becoming a Student.* Ithaca: Cornell University Press.

——. 2005b. "Understanding Student Culture." *Anthropology News* (October): 17–18.

National Geographic. 2002. "Historian Steven [sic] Ambrose Dead at 66." http://news.nationalgeographic.com/news/2002/10/1015_021015_ambrose.html. Accessed January 31, 2007.

NationMaster.com. n.d. "Software Piracy Rate by Country." http://www.nationmaster.com/graph/cri_sof_pir_rat-crime-software-piracy-rate. Accessed July 2, 2007.

New York Times. 2003. "Correcting the Record: The Articles; Witnesses and Documents Unveil Deceptions in a Reporter's Work." May 11. Sec. 1, p. 26.

Newbart, Dave. 2004. "Cheating Soars, but 'It's All Right.'" *Chicago Sun-Times*. July 25. P. 16.

Nunberg, Geoff. 2007. "Wikipedia: Blessing or Curse?" *Fresh Air*. National Public Radio. June 5. http://www.npr.org/templates/story/story.php?storyId=10731811. Accessed June 7, 2007.

Ochs, Elinor. 1979. "Transcription as Theory." In *Developmental Pragmatics*, edited by Elinor Ochs and Bambi B. Schieffelin, pp. 43–72. New York: Academic Press.

Ochs, Elinor, Emanuel A. Schegloff, and Sandra Thompson, eds. 1996. *Interaction and Grammar*. Cambridge: Cambridge University Press.

Ochs, Elinor, and Bambi B. Schieffelin. 1984. "Language Acquisition and Socialization: Three Developmental Stories and Their Implications." In *Culture Theory: Essays on Mind, Self, and Emotion*, edited by Richard A. Shweder and Robert A. LeVine, pp. 276–320. Cambridge: Cambridge University Press.

Palmer, Parker. 2005. "A Life Lived Whole." *YES! Magazine*. Winter. http://www.yesmagazine.org/article.asp?ID=1166. Accessed April 17, 2007.

Pascarella, Ernest T., and Patrick T. Terenzini. 2005. *How College Affects Students*. Vol. 2. *A Third Decade of Research*. San Francisco: Jossey-Bass.

Payne, Karen. 2000. "Understanding and Overcoming Shyness." *GSC Newsletter* (Graduate Student Council, California Institute of Technology, Pasadena), 14, no. 4:4–5.

Pelfrey, Patricia A. 2003. "A Brief History of the Atkinson Presidency (1995–2003)." University of California, Office of the President. http://www.ucop.edu/pres/history.html. Accessed January 19, 2007.

Pirsig, Robert M. 1974. *Zen and the Art of Motorcycle Maintenance*. New York: William Morrow.

Pletsch, Carl. 1991. *Young Nietzsche: Becoming a Genius*. New York: Free Press.

Plotz, David. 2002. "The Plagiarist." Slate.com. http://www.slate.com/id/2060618/. Accessed January 31, 2007.

Posner, Richard A. 2007. *The Little Book of Plagiarism*. New York: Pantheon.

Postman, Neil. 1994 [1982]. *The Disappearance of Childhood*. New York: Vintage.

PR Newswire US. 2007. "National Poll Highlights Student Loan Crisis: AOL Coaches Survey Finds Half of College Grads More 'Stressed Out' by Student Loans Than Credit Card Debt, Half Owe More Than Their Annual Salary." April 30. http://www.prnewswire.com. Accessed May 18, 2007.

Predelli, Stefano. 2003. "'Subliminable' Messages, Scare Quotes, and the Use Hypothesis." *Belgian Journal of Linguistics* 17:153–66.

Pryor, John H., Sylvia Hurtado, Victor B. Saenz, Jennifer A. Lindholm, William S. Korn, and Kathryn M. Mahoney. 2005. *The American Freshman: National Norms for Fall 2005*. Los Angeles: Cooperative Institutional Research Program, Higher Education Research Institute, University of California, Los Angeles.

Purdue University. 2006. "Avoiding Plagiarism." http://owl.english.purdue.edu/owl/resource/589/01/. Accessed March 13, 2007.

Putnam, Robert D. 2000. *Bowling Alone: The Collapse and Revival of American Community.* New York: Touchstone.

Read, Brock. 2006. "Entertainment Officials Say Colleges Do Too Little to Fight Online Piracy." *Chronicle of Higher Education.* October 13. P. A45.

———. 2007. "Record Companies to Accused Pirates: Deal or No Deal? The Record Industry Asks Colleges to Help in Its New Strategy to Stop Music Sharing." *Chronicle of Higher Education.* March 16. P. A31.

Redden, Elizabeth. 2007. "Ohio U. Restricts File Sharing." *Inside Higher Education.* April 26. http://insidehighered.com/news/2007/04/26/ohio. Accessed May 2, 2007.

Redden, Elizabeth, and Doug Lederman. 2006. "In Congress's Crosshairs." *Inside Higher Education.* http://insidehighered.com/layout/set/print/news/2007/03/09/piracy. Accessed March 9, 2007.

Reimer, Marga. 2003. "Too Counter-intuitive to Believe? Pragmatic Accounts of Mixed Quotation." *Belgian Journal of Linguistics* 17:167–86.

Reynolds, Nigel. 2006a. "The Borrowers: 'Why McEwan Is No Plagiarist.'" *Telegraph* (U.K.). July 12. http://www.telegraph.co.uk/news/main.jhtml?xml=/news/2006/12/05/nwriters105.xml. Accessed April 10, 2007.

———. 2006b. "Recluse Speaks Out to Defend McEwan." *Telegraph* (U.K.). July 12. http://www.telegraph.co.uk/news/main.jhtml?xml=/news/2006/12/06/nwriter06.xml. Accessed April 10, 2007.

Richards, Simon. 2003. *Le Corbusier and the Concept of Self.* New Haven: Yale University Press.

Roach, Stephanie. 2005. "Panic as Policy: The 'Plagiarism Plague,' Copyright Confusion, and the.Com Cure." Paper presented at "Originality, Imitation, Plagiarism: A Cross-disciplinary Conference on Writing." Sweetland Writing Center, University of Michigan. September 24.

Robbins, Alexandra. 2006. *The Overachievers: The Secret Lives of Driven Kids.* New York: Hyperion.

Rogoff, Barbara. 2003. *The Cultural Nature of Human Development.* Oxford: Oxford University Press.

Rohsenow, John S. 1990. *A Chinese-English Dictionary of Enigmatic Folk Similes (Xiehouyu).* Tucson: University of Arizona Press.

Roig, Miguel. 2001. "Plagiarism and Paraphrasing Criteria of College and University Professors." *Ethics and Behavior* 11, no. 3:307–23.

Rojstaczer, Stuart. 1999. *Gone for Good: Tales of University Life after the Golden Age.* Oxford: Oxford University Press.

———. 2001. "When Intellectual Life Is Optional for Students." *Chronicle of Higher Education.* April 20. Electronic document. Accessed March 4, 2005.

Romaine, Suzanne, and Deborah Lange. 1991. "The Use of *Like* as a Marker of Reported Speech and Thought: A Case of Grammaticalization in Progress." *American Speech* 66:227–79.

Rosaldo, Michelle Z. 1980. *Knowledge and Passion: Ilongot Notions of Self and Social Life.* Cambridge: Cambridge University Press.

Rose, Mark. 1993. *Authors and Owners: The Invention of Copyright.* Cambridge: Harvard University Press.

Rose, Matthew. 2003. "New York Times Details Deceit by Its Reporter." *Wall Street Journal.* May 12. P. B1.

Rose, Shirley K. 1999. "The Role of Scholarly Citations in Disciplinary Economies." In *Perspectives on Plagiarism and Intellectual Property in a Postmodern World,* edited by Lise Buranen and Alice M. Roy, pp. 241–49. Albany: SUNY Press.

Ryan, John F. 2005. "Institutional Expenditures and Student Engagement: A Role for Financial Resources in Enhancing Student Learning and Development?" *Research in Higher Education* 46, no. 2:235–49.

Sacks, Peter. 1996. *Generation X Goes to College: An Eye-Opening Account of Teaching in Post-modern America.* Chicago: Open Court.

Saka, Paul. 2003. "Quotational Constructions." *Belgian Journal of Linguistics* 17:187–212.

Salinger, J. D. 1951. *The Catcher in the Rye.* Boston: Little, Brown.

Sanday, Peggy Reeves. 1996. *A Woman Scorned: Acquaintance Rape on Trial.* New York: Doubleday.

——. 2007. *Fraternity Gang Rape: Sex, Brotherhood, and Privilege on Campus.* 2d ed. New York: New York University Press.

Savage, Jon. 2007. *Teenage: The Creation of Youth Culture.* New York: Viking.

Schemo, Diana Jean. 2001. "U. of Virginia Hit by Scandal over Cheating." *New York Times.* May 10. Sec. A. p. 1.

Schieffelin, Bambi B., Kathryn A. Woolard, and Paul V. Kroskrity, eds. 1998. *Language Ideologies: Practice and Theory.* New York: Oxford University Press.

Schlegel, Alice, and Herbert Barry III. 1991. *Adolescence: An Anthropological Inquiry.* New York: Free Press.

Schneider, Alison. 1999. "Why Professors Don't Do More to Stop Students Who Cheat." *Chronicle of Higher Education* 45, no. 20:A8.

Schwartz, John. 2003. "Professors Vie with Web for Class's Attention." *New York Times.* January 2. Sec. A. p. 1.

Scollon, Ron. 1995. "Plagiarism and Ideology: Identity in Intercultural Discourse." *Language in Society* 24, no. 1:1–28.

——. 2001. "Plagiarism." In *Key Terms in Language and Culture,* edited by Alessandro Duranti, pp. 184–86. Oxford: Blackwell.

Seaman, Barrett. 2005. *Binge: Campus Life in an Age of Disconnection and Excess. What Your College Student Won't Tell You.* Hoboken, N.J.: John Wiley & Sons.

Second Life. 2007. "What Is Second Life?" http://secondlife.com/whatis/. Accessed April 18, 2007.

Seligman, Martin. 2006. "Authentic Happiness." http://www.authentichappiness.sas.upenn.edu/. Accessed July 3, 2007.

Shalala, Donna E. 1998. "Lessons as You Embark on Your Journeys." http://www.hhs.gov/news/speeches/estroud.html. Accessed June 24, 2007.

Sheppard, Kate. 2007. "What Adults Should Know about Kids' Online Networking." Alternet. January 24. http://www.alternet.org/module/printversion/46766. Accessed January 24, 2007.

Sherzer, Joel, and Regna Darnell. 1986 [1972]. "Outline Guide for the Ethnographic Study of Speech Use." In *Directions in Sociolinguistics: The Ethnography of*

Communication, edited by John J. Gumperz and Dell Hymes, pp. 548–54. Oxford: Basil Blackwell.

Siegel, Alexander W., and Lori C. Scovill. 2000. "Problem Behavior: The Double Symptom of Adolescence." *Development and Psychopathology* 12:763–93.

Silverstein, Michael. 1979. "Language Structure and Linguistic Ideology." In *The Elements: A Parasession on Linguistic Units and Levels,* edited by Paul R. Clyne, William F. Hanks, and Carol L. Hofbauer, pp. 193–247. Chicago: Chicago Linguistic Society.

———. 1998. "The Uses and Utility of Ideology: A Commentary." In *Language Ideologies: Practice and Theory,* edited by Bambi B. Schieffelin, Kathryn A. Woolard, and Paul V. Kroskrity, pp. 123–45. New York: Oxford University Press.

Silverstein, Michael, and Greg Urban, eds. 1996. *Natural Histories of Discourse.* Chicago: University of Chicago Press.

Sontag, Susan. 1978. *Illness as Metaphor.* New York: Farrar, Straus and Giroux.

Spindler, George, and Louise Spindler. 1997 [1985]. "Ethnography: An Anthropological View." In *Educational and Cultural Process: Anthropological Approaches,* edited by George D. Spindler, pp. 50–55. 3d ed. Long Grove, Ill.: Waveland.

Stanford University. n.d. a. "The Fundamental Standard." http://www.stanford.edu/dept/vpsa/judicialaffairs/guiding/fundamental.htm. Accessed May 16, 2007.

———. n.d. b. "Honor Code." http://www.stanford.edu/dept/vpsa/judicialaffairs/guiding/honorcode.htm. Accessed May 16, 2007.

Stearns, Peter N. 2006. *Childhood in World History.* New York: Routledge.

Storch, Eric A., and Jason B. Storch. 2002. "Fraternities, Sororities, and Academic Dishonesty." *College Student Journal* 36, no. 2:247–52.

Stossel, Sage. 2004. "Crying in the Kitchen over Princeton." *Atlantic Monthly* (September). http://www.theatlantic.com/doc/print/200409u/int2004-09-07. Accessed January 22, 2007.

Strauss, William, and Neil Howe. 1991. *Generations: The History of America's Future, 1584–2069.* New York: Morrow.

Stumpf, Heinrich, and Julian C. Stanley. 2002. "Group Data on High School Grade Point Averages and Scores on Academic Aptitude Tests as Predictors of Institution Graduation Rates." *Educational and Psychological Measurement* 26: 1042–52.

Suen, Hoi K., and Lan Yu. 2006. "Chronic Consequences of High-Stakes Testing? Lessons from the Chinese Civil Service Exam." *Comparative Education Review* 50, no. 1:46–65.

Suler, Janet, and Roger Openshaw. 1992. "When Is a Moral Panic Not a Moral Panic? Some Difficulties in Utilising the Theory of Moral Panic in Educational History." *History of Education Review* 21, no. 1:19–28.

Suler, John. 2007. "The Psychology of Avatars and Graphical Space in Multimedia Chat Communities." *The Psychology of Cyberspace.* January. http://www.rider.edu/~suler/psycyber/psyav.html. Accessed June 7, 2007.

Sun-Sentinel (Fort Lauderdale). 2003. "Hall of Shame." Editorial. June 22. http://www.accessmylibrary.com/coms2/summary_0286-6947343_ITM. Accessed July 1, 2008.

Swales, John M., and Christine B. Feak. 2004 [1994]. *Academic Writing for Graduate Students: Essential Tasks and Skills.* 2d ed. Ann Arbor: University of Michigan Press.

Swearingen, C. Jan. 1999. "Originality, Authenticity, Imitation, and Plagiarism: Augustine's Chinese Cousins." In *Perspectives on Plagiarism and Intellectual Property in a Postmodern World,* edited by Lise Buranen and Alice M. Roy, pp. 19–30. Albany: SUNY Press.

Tagliamonte, Sali, and Alex D'Arcy. 2005. "When People Say '*I Was Like...*': The Quotative System in Canadian Youth." *University of Pennsylvania Working Papers in Linguistics* 10, no. 2:257–72.

Tannen, Deborah. 1989. *Talking Voices: Repetition, Dialogue, and Imagery in Conversational Discourse.* Cambridge: Cambridge University Press.

Tannen, Deborah, and Piyale C. Öztek. 1981. "Health to Our Mouths: Formulaic Expressions in Turkish and Greek." In *Conversational Routine: Explorations in Standardized Communication Situations and Prepatterned Speech,* edited by Florian Coulmas, pp. 37–54. Rasmus Rask Studies in Pragmatic Linguistics. Vol. 2. The Hague: Mouton.

Taylor, Charles. 1989. *Sources of the Self: The Making of the Modern Identity.* Cambridge: Harvard University Press.

Tedlock, Dennis. 1983. *The Spoken Word and the Work of Interpretation.* Philadelphia: University of Pennsylvania Press.

Terdiman, Daniel. 2005. "Wikipedia Faces Growing Pains." *Wired.* January 10. http://www.wired.com/print/culture/lifestyle/news/2005/01/66210. Accessed June 7, 2007.

Thielfoldt, Diane, and Devon Scheef. 2004. "Generation X and the Millennials: What You Need to Know about Mentoring the New Generations." Law Practice Today. http://www.abanet.org/lpm/lpt/articles/nosearch/mgt08044_print.html. Accessed June 28, 2007.

Thomas, Rosalind. 1989. *Literacy and Orality in Ancient Greece.* Cambridge: Cambridge University Press.

Thompson, Stith. 1977 [1946]. *The Folktale.* Berkeley: University of California Press.

Tierney, John. 2007. "A Renowned Bachelor, and a Search for a Mate." *New York Times.* May 8. Sec. F, p. 1.

Transparency International. 2006. http://www.transparency.org/policy_research/surveys_indices/cpi/2006/regional_highlights_factsheets. Accessed April 9, 2007.

Trilling, Lionel. 1972. *Sincerity and Authenticity.* Cambridge: Harvard University Press.

Turkle, Sherry. 1984. *The Second Self: Computers and the Human Spirit.* New York: Simon and Schuster.

———. 1995. *Life on the Screen: Identity in the Age of the Internet.* New York: Simon and Schuster.

———. 2002. "Our Split Screens." *Etnofoor* 15, nos. 1–2:5–19.

———. 2004. "Collaborative Selves, Collaborative Worlds: Identity in the Information Age." In *Electronic Collaboration in the Humanities: Issues and Options,* edited by James A. Inman, Cheryl Reed, and Peter Sands, pp. 3–12. Mahwah, N.J.: Lawrence Erlbaum Associates.

Turner, Victor. 1967 [1958]. "Symbols in Ndembu Ritual." In *The Forest of Symbols: Aspects of Ndembu Ritual*, pp. 19–47. Ithaca: Cornell University Press.

Turnitin.com. 2006. "Plagiarism Prevention." http://turnitin.com/static/plagiarism. html. Accessed October 25, 2006.

Twenge, Jean M. 2006. *Generation Me: Why Today's Young Americans Are More Confident, Assertive, Entitled—and More Miserable Than Ever Before*. New York: Free Press.

Ungar, Sheldon. 2001. "Moral Panic Versus the Risk Society: The Implications of the Changing Sites of Social Anxiety." *British Journal of Sociology* 52, no. 2:271–91.

University of Richmond. 2005. "What Do You Think?" http://law.richmond.edu/ ipi/whatdoyouthink.htm. Accessed May 16, 2007.

———. 2006. "One in Three College Students Illegally Downloads Music, National Survey Finds." National CyberEducation Project, Intellectual Property Institute, University of Richmond School of Law. Electronic document. Accessed May 16, 2007.

University of Virginia. n.d. "The Pledge" (The Honor Committee). http://www. virginia.edu/honor/pledge.html. Accessed May 16, 2007.

U.S. Department of Education. 2004. "Total Expenditure for Education in U.S." http://www.ed.gov/about/overview/budget/budget05/summary/edlite-appendix3. html. Accessed June 24, 2007.

———. 2007. *The Condition of Education, 2007*. National Center for Education Statistics, Institute of Education Sciences. http://nces.ed.gov/pubs2007/2007064.pdf. Accessed June 28, 2007.

U.S. Department of Labor. 2007. Bureau of Labor Statistics, National Longitudinal Surveys. http://www.bls.gov/nls/nlsfaqs.htm#anch41. Accessed June 24, 2007.

Uselessmoviequotes.com. 2008. "Useless Movie Quotes." http://uselessmoviequotes. com. Accessed June 26, 2008.

USMA (United States Military Academy). n.d. "The Cadet Honor Code." http:// www.usma.edu/Committees/Honor/Info/main.htm. Accessed May 16, 2007.

Vaidhyanathan, Siva. 2001. *Copyrights and Copywrongs: The Rise of Intellectual Property and How It Threatens Creativity*. New York: New York University Press.

Van Gennep, Arnold. 1960 [1909]. *The Rites of Passage*, translated by Monika B. Vizedom and Gabrielle L. Caffee. Chicago: University of Chicago Press.

Vega, Suzanne. 2006. "The Ballad of Henry Timrod." *New York Times*. September 17. Sec. 4, p. 15.

Vogel, Carl. 2006. "SAT Trends: This Year's SAT Scores Dropped More Than They Have in a Generation; Is the New Test to Blame?" *District Administration* (November): 33–34.

Vowell, Paul R., and Jieming Chen. 2004. "Predicting Academic Misconduct: A Comparative Test of Four Sociological Explanations." *Sociological Inquiry* 74, no. 2:226–49.

Walfish, Daniel. 2001. "Chinese Applicants to U.S. Universities Often Resort to Shortcuts or Dishonesty: Students Can Buy Essays, Stand-ins for Exams, and Improper Access to Standardized Tests." *Chronicle of Higher Education* (January 5): A52.

Washburn, Jennifer. 2005. *University, Inc.: The Corporate Corruption of American Higher Education.* New York: Basic Books.

Washington Speakers Bureau. 2007. http://www.washingtonspeakers.com/speakers/speaker.cfm?SpeakerId=1613. Accessed April 11, 2007.

Wasik, Bill. 2006. "My Crowd; Or, Phase 5: A Report from the Inventor of the Flash Mob." *Harper's Magazine* (March): 56–66.

Wasley, Paula. 2007. "Taking on 21: A Former College President Starts a National Campaign to Lower the Drinking Age." *Chronicle of Higher Education* (April 6): A35–36.

Weber, Max. 1930. *The Protestant Ethic and the Spirit of Capitalism,* translated by Talcott Parsons. New York: Scribner's.

Wechsler, Henry, Jae Eun Lee, Meichun Kuo, Mark Seibring, Toben F. Nelson, and Hang Lee. 2002. "Trends in College Binge Drinking During a Period of Increased Prevention Efforts: Findings from 4 Harvard School of Public Health College Alcohol Study Surveys, 1993–2001." *Journal of American College Health* 50, no. 5:203–17.

Western Michigan University. n.d. "Integrity and Plagiarism at WMU." http://atis.wmich.edu/integrity.php. Accessed July 1, 2008.

Wheeler, David L. 2002. "Testing Service Says GRE Scores from China, South Korea, and Taiwan Are Suspect." *Chronicle of Higher Education.* August 16. P. A41.

Whitaker, Elaine E. 1993. "A Pedagogy to Address Plagiarism." *College Composition and Communication* 44, no. 4:509–14.

Whitfield, Stephen J. 1997. "Cherished and Cursed: Toward a Social History of *The Catcher in the Rye.*" *New England Quarterly* 70, no. 4:567–600.

Whitley, Bernard E., Jr., and Patricia Keith-Spiegel. 2002. *Academic Dishonesty: An Educator's Guide.* Mahwah, N.J.: Lawrence Erlbaum Associates.

Whyte, William H., Jr. 1956. *The Organization Man.* New York: Simon and Schuster.

Wilford, John Noble. 2007. "How the Inca Leapt Canyons." *New York Times.* May 8. Sec. F, p. 1.

Willimon, William H., and Thomas H. Naylor. 1995. *The Abandoned Generation: Rethinking Higher Education.* Grand Rapids, Mich.: Wm. B. Eerdmans Publishing Co.

Willing, Linda F. 2007. Letter to the Editor. *New York Times Magazine* (May 20): 20.

Willis, Paul E. 1981 [1977]. *Learning to Labour: How Working Class Kids Get Working Class Jobs.* New York: Columbia University Press.

Wilson, Shane. 2006. "Did Opal Author Plagiarize—or Was It Her Handlers? Harvard-Novelist Scandal Throws Spotlight on Chicklit 'Book Packager.'" *Harvard Independent.* April 27. http://www.HarvardIndependent.com/ViewArticle.aspx?ArticleID=9906. Accessed January 31, 2007.

Wolf, Margery. 1968. *The House of Lim: A Study of a Chinese Farm Family.* New York: Appleton-Century-Crofts.

Wolfe, Tom. 2004. *I Am Charlotte Simmons.* New York: Farrar, Straus and Giroux.

Woodmansee, Martha. 1984. "The Genius and the Copyright: Economic and Legal Conditions of the Emergence of the 'Author.'" *Eighteenth-Century Studies* 17:425–48.

Woolard, Kathryn A., and Bambi B. Schieffelin. 1994. "Language Ideology." *Annual Review of Anthropology* 23:55–82.

Wrong, Dennis H. 1961. "The Oversocialized Conception of Man in Modern Sociology." *American Sociological Review* 26:183–93.

Acknowledgments

This research could not have taken place without the devotion, energy, and insight of my fantastic student researchers Theresa Davey, Katherine Kennedy Johnson, Rupa Jose, and Jacob Weiler. Our weekly meetings were the highlight of each semester of research. My only complaint is that they all graduate and leave! The consistent (or sometimes inconsistent) transcription provided by Hillary Brass, Mary Corrigan, Megan Healy, Kaitlin Ramsey, Justin Smith, and Emily Weisbecker has proved invaluable, as these students attempted to extricate me from the mountains of cassettes inundating my office. Hillary especially stuck with the project, even after she went on to graduate school in linguistic anthropology. The funding for this project came from a Pilot Fund for Faculty-Student Research Teams in the Social Sciences through the Institute for Scholarship in the Liberal Arts, the College of Arts and Letters, and a Faculty Research Grant, Office of Research and the Graduate School, both at the University of Notre Dame. I am grateful for the generous support of my home institution.

I also thank the administration and students at the University of Notre Dame for opening up their walls to an inquisitive anthropologist. Many universities regard the high rates of plagiarism as their shameful secret; I hope this book in part lays that shame to rest. (There *are* significant challenges in higher education, but I don't think they lie in the prevalence of plagiarism.)

Strange things happen when we're writing, something I'd noticed before but this time have a theory about: I came up with the same ideas as other people working on this topic, independently, but only discovered that fact later. Even one of the potential titles I invented for the book, "Whose Words These Are," a variant of Robert Frost's line "Whose woods these are," was used by Alice M. Roy in her article "Whose Words These Are I Think I Know" in a collection I had in my office but had only half read. I moved from topic to topic on my own, only to find that Rebecca Moore Howard had covered many of them in her book *Standing on the Shoulders of Giants*. This serendipitous convergence makes sense when we regard our words and ideas as only partly our own, when we recognize the powerful cultural and intellectual currents that direct our individual thoughts. Thus the artificiality of claiming ownership is borne out even by a single person's self-conscious tracing of influence in one work.

I have benefited *consciously* from conversations about this and related topics with colleagues at several institutions, including Joyce Block, Lizzie Fagen, Teresa Ghilarducci, Dennis Jacobs, Debra McDougall, Mary McIntosh, Tami Moore, M. J. Murray Vachon, Darcia Narvaez, Carolyn Nordstrom, Ava Preacher, Linda Shamoon, Andrea Rusnock Turbow, and Henry Weinfeld. (Please forgive omissions.) Don McCabe visited Notre Dame and encouraged this project. His valiant efforts on behalf of academic integrity must be recognized by all who labor in this area. The conference "Originality Imitation, and Plagiarism: A Cross-disciplinary Conference on Writing" held at the Sweetland Writing Center at the University of Michigan under the direction of Martha Vicinus, was inspirational. She later invited me to participate in a seminar for graduate students in the Sweetland Writing Program, and I spent a thrilling morning and afternoon in Ann Arbor talking to Martha and others about this work. William O'Rourke spent a precious weekend reading the final draft of the manuscript, taking his well-worn red pen to my text, and encouraging me by saying he learned a lot. He is an ideal reader and colleague—and friend.

Three very different and very careful readers helped in guiding me to find the voice for this potentially controversial topic. Cathy Small bolstered me by identifying herself to me and conveying her enthusiasm for the book's publication. Mary-Anne Gilbert at Cornell University Press has been an effective facilitator of the birth of the book; Amanda Heller and Ange Romeo-Hall greatly improved the book's readability and succinctness. Frances Benson has been the utterly ideal editor, speaking to

Acknowledgments

me about my project even before I finished the research, providing suggestions and criticism and prodding me to revise, as I saw it, to discern the sculpture in the stone, to carve away the excess and find the real figure at the center.

My daughters, Hannah Neora Blum Jensen and Elena Oriana Blum Jensen, are my window into the future. They are teenagers, Hannah on the threshold of college and Elena just having entered high school as I finish this final draft. Their interactions with educational institutions of various sorts (especially the Montessori Academy at Edison Lakes and John Adams High School), their hours on-screen, their friends and friends' parents, their classmates and teachers—and our family discussions about all of it—have provided me with much to contemplate as I move from an image of college and high school left shimmering from my own days to the vivid reality of college and high school in theirs.

My dearest partner, Lionel Jensen—with roles as spouse, parent, teacher, coach, friend, and social critic—urged me to stride courageously from my quiet China studies to rather more public studies of American education. In his quest for truth and justice, those around him are not permitted fear or qualms. We spent many hours pondering the meaning of my research for me, whether as an anthropologist, teacher, or mother. We share our hopes for all our children, and in this spirit I offer the book from one generation to another...and another?

April 15, 2008

Notre Dame, Indiana

Index

Index

BAC (blood alcohol content), 134–35
Bach, Johann Sebastian, 167
bad faith, 63
Bagg, Lyman, 25
Bakhtin, Mikhail, 184n3
Band of Brothers (Ambrose), 18
Barthes, Roland, 34–35
Bartlett's, 30
Bauman, Richard, 183–84n1
Becker, Howard, 105
Beijing University, 24
Bentham, Jeremy, 22
Bible, the, 32
Big Brothers/Big Sisters, 132
*Binge: Campus Life in an Age of Discon-
nection and Excess* (Seaman), 105
binge drinking, 135, 138
Blair, Jayson, 17
blogs, 70, 167
Bloom, Harold, 33, 38, 53, 58
Boas, Franz, 93
Bok, Derek, 109
Boston University, 16
Bourdieu, Pierre, 45
Bowling Alone (Putnam), 187n19
Brooks, David, 104, 138
Brown, Dan, 168
Brown University, SAT scores, 96
"bubble," 106
Business Week, 101
Butler, Judith, 186n13
Butterfield, Kenneth, 2

Campus Life (Horowitz), 25
Canada, lack of plagiarism penalty
enforcement, 21
Canterbury Tales, 32
careers, as motives for college, 114–17
Carleton College, 68
caste, 149
Catcher in the Rye (Salinger), 62
Catholic social teaching, 131
cell phones, 64, 67, 89
Center for Academic Integrity, 150, 153
cento, 32
cheating. *See* plagiarism and cheating
chengyu (Chinese four-character fixed
phrases), 30
Chickering, Arthur, 65
Childers, Thomas, 18

childhood, 3, 91, 103–4, 105, 180, 188n2
China, cheating and plagiarism in, 21–24;
pirated software in, 185n47; transparency ranking of, 183n41
China's Examination Hell (Miyazaki),
23–24
Chinese, oral transmission of traditional
texts, 168
Cho, Seung-hui, 67
Chosen, The (Karabel), 95
Christian scripture, oral transmission
of, 168
Chronicle of Higher Education, 1, 19,
117, 125
Circle K, 12
citation index, 168
Citation Paradox Principle, 177
citation practices, 2, 13–15, 154; academic,
14, 39–41, 51–54, 57–58, 61, 168–70,
176–78; apprenticeship in, 13, 26–27,
40, 165–71; contentious nature of, 15;
in journalism, 13–14; variations among,
13–15, 71, 79, 165, 171
civil service examination. *See* keju
Civilization and Its Discontents (Freud),
62
class rank, high school, as predictor of
college success, 98
class work. *See* school work
co-curricular activities, 109, 131–33
collaboration, 42, 55–58, 68–71, 88–89,
144, 170
collective authorship, 70–71
college application counselors, 99–101
College Board, 97–98
colleges and universities: administration
and staff, 108–9, 189n35; as businesses,
109; coeducation, 95; costs of, 4, 108,
139–40; facilities, 108–9; integration of,
94–95; as liminal periods, 92; reasons
for attending, 7–8, 105–6, 112–17
colleges and universities, selective, 9,
98–99; acceptance rates, 5, 96, 99;
admissions process, 98–104, 105,
188n28; definition of, 96, 99; and
wealth of students, 99
College of William and Mary, 151
comfort, as goal, 72–75, 77
Coming of Age in New Jersey (Moffatt),
9, 105, 156

Index

Index

methods, research, 7–10, 181n13; qualitative, 181–82nn13–14
Mexico, 143; transparency ranking of, 183n41
Middlebury College, 71
Milgram, Stanley, 67
Millar v. Taylor, 34
Millennials, the, 186n12
MIT (Massachusetts Institute of Technology): acceptance rates at, 96; SAT scores, 96
Miyazaki, Ichisada, 23–24
Moffatt, Michael, 9, 105, 156
moral reasoning and brain development, 188n4
morality and ethics, 3, 6, 149–57, 162–63, 177–79
motivations, 2, 125, 127–31, 140–47, 178
movie quotes, 42–44, 50–51
movies, watching, 66
MUD (multi-user domain), 78–79
multiplicity of self, 64, 71–79, 89–90
music downloading, 2, 8, 37–38, 161–63
My Freshman Year (Small/Nathan), 9, 105, 122
MySpace, 46–47

names, screen. *See* screen names
names, views of, 64
Napoleon Dynamite, 44
Nathan, Rebekah. *See* Small, Cathy
National Public Radio, 1
Nature, 19, 71
Naylor, Thomas H., 105
Nazi era, 149
need, as justification for cheating and plagiarizing, 81, 88
new media, 4
New York (magazine), 18
New York Times, 1, 13, 17, 25, 98, 102, 125, 133
New Yorker, 151, 167
New Zealand, transparency ranking of, 183n41
nineteenth century, 62
Ninety-second Street Y, 99
norms, literary, 36
norms, scholarly, 39–41, 57–58
norms, student, 41–47, 50–58
Nunberg, Geoffrey, 71

Ohio University, 162
Old School, 42–44
"Ole Miss." *See* University of Mississippi
On the Road (Kerouac), 62
online fantasy games, 78. *See also* Dungeons and Dragons
Open Access, 38
Open Source, 38
open source software, 70, 167
oral epic poetry, 184n17
oral transmission, 168, 185n56
"organization kid" (Brooks), 104, 138
originality, 2, 5, 30, 32–35, 42, 46, 47–59, 63, 89–90, 154, 160, 164, 166–67, 170–71
outcomes, as motives for cheating and plagiarizing, 82
Overachievers, The (Robbins), 101
Ownership. *See* ideas, ownership of; text, ownership of
Oxford English Dictionary (OED), 12

Palmer, Parker, 82
parents' involvement, 103, 104, 105, 142
participant observation, 181–82n14
participant roles, 184n4
parties, partying, 106, 134–35. *See also* drinking
pastiche, 42, 54–55, 58
patchwriting, 26–27, 167
peer-to-peer file sharing, 161–63. *See also* music downloading
penalties. *See* plagiarism, penalties for
perfectionism, 104, 138–39
performance, 4, 5, 61, 63–64, 171, 186n13
performance self, 61, 63–66, 71, 77–79, 83, 89
performativity, 64
personal development as outcome of college, 114–16
Philadelphia Inquirer, 108
phoniness, 62
Pirsig, Robert M., 62
plagiarism: contrasted with cheating, 12; contrasted with copyright infringement, 19, 36–37; cross-cultural cases, 21–26, 168; definitions of, 2, 6, 11–13, 48, 49, 165–67; as desirable, 167; detection and prevention instruments, 2, 25,

Index

screen names, 64, 89
Seaman, Barrett, 105
Second Life, 78, 187n37
second self, 78
Seigel, Alexander, 93
selection versus creation, 55, 89
selective colleges. *See* colleges and universities, selective
self: authentic (*see* authentic self); changing notions of, 10; self-concept, 8; self-consciousness, 70, 75; divided, 63, 82, 89; self-esteem, 105, 186n12; finding the, 78, 114; performance (*see* performance self); presentation of, 79, 85–87; self-plagiarism, 19; representing the, 78–79; and words (text) (relationship between), 60–61, 63, 65, 70–71, 79–82, 89–90, 171
Senegal, 184n4
separation-individuation, 94
sexual assault, 134, 138
Shakespeare, William, 32, 34, 48
Shaw, Philip, 165–66
Sherzer, Joel, 183–84n1
shyness, 187n21
Silverstein, Michael, 183–84n1
Sim games, 79
SimCity, 78
Sincerity and Authenticity (Trilling), 62
Singapore, transparency ranking of, 183n41
Singularity. *See* individual, individualism, individuality
Sixties (1960s), 62, 116
Small, Cathy, 9, 105, 122
social networking sites, 46–47, 66, 70. *See also* Facebook
socializing, 118–19, 121–22, 129
socioeconomic status, social class, students', 25, 97, 141
sociology, and approaches to plagiarism, 181n8
software, pirated, 37
solitary, solitude, 62, 65, 67, 90
sororities, 182n17 (Introduction)
speech, effect of, 61
Spindler, George, 181n13
Spindler, Louise, 181n13
split personalities, 78
spontaneity, 62

Standing in the Shadow of Giants (Howard), 26
Stanford University, 102, 111, 151–52, 189–90n60; selectivity of, 98
Statute of Anne, 33
Strauss, William, 186n12
student effort. *See* school work
student engagement, 189n51
student solidarity, 156–57
substance abuse, 104
success, 4, 5, 8, 62, 65, 90, 112, 139, 156, 164, 180
Suen, Hoi K., 23
suicidal tendencies, suicide, 104, 138
Swales, John, 166
Swarthmore College, 38
Sweden, plagiarism in, 25; transparency ranking of, 183n41

Tannen, Deborah, 58
teaching evaluations, 126
teamwork, 69
technology, 4, 38, 61, 64, 66
test preparation courses, 97, 188n14
testing, 3, 70. *See also* ACT, AP, GRE, SAT, SAT-II TOEFL
testing, high-stakes, 21–24
texts, 3, 4, 6, 10; ownership of, 32–37, 38, 55, 89
Tillich, Paul, 16
time management, 123–24, 138
Times Literary Supplement, 1
TOEFL (Test of English as a Foreign Language), 24
total institutions, colleges as, 105–7
transcripts, conversational, 41
Treviño, Linda Klebe, 2
Trilling, Lionel, 62
truth, 76–77, 85–87
Tuhami: Portrait of a Moroccan (Crapanzano): 181–82n14
tuition, 108, 139–40. *See also* colleges and universities, costs of
Turkle, Sherry, 78
Turnitin.com, 1, 48–49, 158
Twenge, Jean, 186n12
Twenty-twenty (TV show), 1

Undaunted Courage (Ambrose), 18
unitary self, 65